The Welfare State Nobody Knows

The Welfare State Nobody Knows

DEBUNKING MYTHS ABOUT U.S. SOCIAL POLICY

Christopher Howard

PRINCETON UNIVERSITY PRESS

PRINCETON AND OXFORD

Third printing, and first paperback printing, 2008
Paperback ISBN: 978-0-691-13833-6

The Library of Congress has cataloged the cloth edition of this book as follows

Howard, Christopher, 1961–
The welfare state nobody knows : debunking myths about U.S. social policy /
Christopher Howard.
  p.   cm.
Includes bibliographical references and index.
ISBN-13: 978-0-691-12180-2 (hardcover : alk. paper)
ISBN-10: 0-691-12180-X (hardcover : alk. paper)
1. United States—Social policy. 2. United States—Social conditions.
3. Public welfare—United States. I. Title
HN57.H68 2007
361.6′10973—dc22   2006011959

British Library Cataloging-in-Publication Data is available

This book has been composed in Sabon

Printed on acid-free paper. ∞

press.princeton.edu

Printed in the United States of America

10 9 8 7 6

Contents

Boxes, Figures, and Tables

Acknowledgments

SOME PEOPLE'S MINDS FUNCTION LIKE WOKS. They operate at high temperatures and quickly produce a complete meal that looks good and tastes good. I envy those people because my mind works more like a Crock-Pot. It operates on low heat and takes a long time before anything is fully cooked. This is one reason that I have so many people and organizations to thank for their help in writing this book.

My debts go back at least as far as my undergraduate years at Duke, when William Chafe and Sydney Nathans demonstrated different ways of bringing their own research into the classroom. They also showed me that scholars can write about subjects that interest the general public. I'm not sure that my previous book about tax expenditures lived up to that standard; I hope this book does. In graduate school, Ellen Immergut, Michael Lipsky, Jill Quadagno, and Theda Skocpol taught me much about social policy and encouraged me to think broadly about the subject. They sparked my interest in challenging the conventional wisdom, and sometimes that meant their wisdom as well.

Working at a liberal-arts college has many rewards, but there are drawbacks. The biggest one is finding time to think and write. I am very grateful for financial support from the American Council of Learned Societies and the National Endowment for the Humanities, which enabled me to spend a year wrestling with some of the themes of this book. I thought at the time that I was going to write an entire book about federalism and social policy. Although that did not happen, chapters 8 and 9 analyze the impact of federalism on several different social programs. I am also thankful for a faculty research assignment from the College of William and Mary, which allowed me to start expanding the focus beyond federalism. Another drawback of college teaching can be the lack of research assistants. At William and Mary, however, I have been helped by graduate students from our public policy program and by an occasional undergraduate. Elisabeth Moss and Klaus Schultz deserve special mention for their efforts. Finally, William and Mary has worked very hard to ensure that Swem Library's print and electronic resources rival those of much larger universities.

For a couple of years, I presented my research at the Georgetown Public Policy Institute, Harvard's Kennedy School of Government, the University of California–Berkeley, the University of Virginia, the University of Wisconsin–Madison, and Yale University, as well as William and Mary. While I always benefited from these visits, some of my presentations were much better thought-out than others. Some people who heard me talk then may now be surprised by the publication of this book. For helping me to figure out when I was dull or misguided and when I had something interesting to say, I thank Brian Balogh, Leonard Burman, David Canon, John Coleman, Judith Feder, Charles Franklin, Daniel Gitterman, William Gormley, Kristin Goss, Michael Graetz, Jacob Hacker, Michael Lipsky, Theodore Marmor, Jerry Mashaw, Sidney Milkis, Mark Nadel, Herman Schwartz, Kent Weaver, and many others whose names I cannot remember.

With a few chapters in good shape and some plans for the rest of the book, I approached Princeton University Press about publishing it. Everything since that point has gone as well as I could have hoped. The expert reviewers (who, I learned later, were Martha Derthick and Judith Feder) offered me pages of constructive criticism. Their detailed knowledge of social policy proved invaluable, and both reviewers made me think carefully about my general arguments. The earlier version of this book moved in many different directions, and the reviewers were instrumental in helping me move several different ideas in the same general direction. Terri O'Prey managed the production process efficiently, and William Hively copyedited the manuscript with a remarkable eye for detail, clarity, and consistency. My editor, Chuck Myers, did not hesitate to offer his own comments, and they were always helpful. Best of all, he gave me enough time to figure out what I was doing.

As I approached the finish line, several kind souls read all or large parts of the book. My friend and former teacher, Rick Valelly, pushed me to rethink the introduction and thus the overall argument. Rick helped me understand that a central puzzle running through the book is how a dynamic welfare state can accomplish so little. He and Chuck Myers share credit for the book's title. Ed Berkowitz noted several places where my history was incomplete or inaccurate, and he prompted me to reorganize the chapters and find other ways of increasing the overall coherence of the book. Paul Manna enlivened my prose and suggested several ways to help readers see the larger themes without getting lost in the details. I managed to convince Dee Holmes that reading my manuscript was implicitly covered by our wedding vows, and she repeatedly offered words of encouragement. After a steady diet of critical comments, a little unqualified praise is awfully sweet. My father read more drafts than anyone else, in large part because I knew that he could help me on everything from word choice and tone to logical consistency and an understanding of my audience. One of the best parts of this whole process was discussing chapters with my ninety-eight-year-old grandfather, who is as lucid as I hope to be at the age of fifty.

Other people had little choice but to read my work. I assigned several chapters to students in my American Welfare State class in 2003, and the whole manuscript in 2005. Frankly, I was worried that students either would take every word as gospel, not wanting to offend their teacher, or would not be convinced at all by my arguments. Instead, they gave me several ideas for improving the substance and presentation of my arguments, and most of them walked away thinking that I had written something worthwhile. That's about as good as it gets.

Many people helped me without reading a word, either by influencing the kinds of questions I asked or by giving me a little more energy to complete the book. Conversations over the years with Jacob Hacker and Paul Pierson persuaded me that I needed to pay more attention to the distributive consequences of social policy. They kept reminding me that one of the central questions in politics is who gets what from government. While their influence is most evident in the concluding chapter, it touches many parts of the book. My colleagues and students at William and Mary have made it enjoyable to come to work each day for more than a decade. Williamsburg, Virginia, is a little off the beaten path, and it really helps to be surrounded by bright, lively, and often funny people. My mother and stepmother asked often about the book but always with interest, never impatience. My kids, Julia and Stephen, are at the wonderful age where they are too old for diapers but too young to drive. I get to watch them do all sorts of wonderful things on the ball field and the stage, and they're not embarrassed by my presence. I can't finish without thanking the makers of A&W root beer and peanut M&Ms, who helped me overcome writer's block more often than I care to admit. Their impact will probably stay with me for a long time.

Acronyms

AARP	American Association of Retired Persons
ADA	Americans with Disabilities Act
ADC	Aid to Dependent Children
AFDC	Aid to Families with Dependent Children
AMA	American Medical Association
BOB	Bureau of the Budget
CBO	Congressional Budget Office
CEA	Council of Economic Advisers
CES	Committee on Economic Security
COBRA	Consolidated Omnibus Budget Reconciliation Act
CTC	Child Tax Credit
DHHS	Department of Health and Human Services
DI	disability insurance
EC	European Community
EITC	Earned Income Tax Credit
ERISA	Employee Retirement Income Security Act
FDR	Franklin Delano Roosevelt
FHA	Federal Housing Administration
FMLA	Family and Medical Leave Act
FPL	federal poverty line
GDP	gross domestic product
GOP	Republican Party (Grand Old Party)
GSS	General Social Survey
HIPAA	Health Insurance Portability and Accountability Act
IRS	Internal Revenue Service
ISSP	International Social Survey Program
LBJ	Lyndon Baines Johnson
LIS	Luxembourg Income Study
MCCA	Medicare Catastrophic Coverage Act
NCSC	National Council of Senior Citizens
NES	National Election Studies
OAA	Old Age Assistance
OAI	Old Age Insurance
OASI	Old Age and Survivors Insurance
OECD	Organization for Economic Cooperation and Development
OMB	Office of Management and Budget
OSHA	Occupational Safety and Health Act

PBGC   Pension Benefit Guaranty Corporation
SCHIP   State Children's Health Insurance Program
SSI   Supplemental Security Income
TANF   Temporary Assistance for Needy Families
UI   unemployment insurance
UMW   United Mine Workers
VA   Veterans Administration
VISTA   Volunteers in Service to America

The Welfare State Nobody Knows

THE AMERICAN WELFARE STATE is known far and wide as a chronic under-achiever. Historically, the United States created social programs later than many nations. Currently, essential pieces of the American welfare state are poorly developed or completely missing. Eligibility rules and benefits can vary widely from state to state. The United States spends less on social programs than most affluent democracies, and its rates of poverty and inequality are substantially higher. Analysts have cataloged these short-comings for years and asked variants of the same basic question: *How could a nation that has been so wealthy for so long fail to develop a real welfare state?* Some have then attributed the failure to national values, saying that Americans have never really wanted to have much of a welfare state. Others have pointed to the fragmentation of public authority, within and among institutions, that makes any significant policy change hard to enact. Alternatively, the weakness of organized labor or the ab-sence of strong left-wing political parties may have been the main culprits. The list goes on.

This book takes issue with the thinking behind the question and many of the stock answers to it. In the process, it offers a much different portrait of U.S. social policy. Although the American welfare state did not turn out just like its relatives in Europe and Canada, it did become large and far-reaching. The general public has called for more government involve-ment, and elected representatives from both parties have responded. U.S. officials have created a variety of social programs throughout the twenti-eth century. In recent decades, they have managed to expand some pro-grams for the poor and near poor. There has actually been a remarkable amount of activity in the American welfare state—but you need to know where to look. And if you do know where, then all sorts of stories about failure and obstruction in social policy become suspect.

On the other hand, all this activity has not had much impact on the core problems of poverty and inequality. If traditional accounts of the American welfare state boil down to "little effort, little progress," my account highlights the paradox of lots of effort and little progress. No matter how successful advocates have been in creating and expanding social programs, certain features of American politics have limited the benefits of many official changes in policy. Some of their accomplishments have even made it harder to reduce poverty and inequality. The American welfare state contains greater possibilities and tighter constraints than commonly believed. Recognizing these possibilities and constraints is essential for anyone who wants to understand the American welfare state or change it.

This book challenges a number of myths, misunderstandings, and half-truths about the American welfare state. Some pieces of conventional wisdom are based on questionable assumptions, or just plain wrong. In other places, analysts have the facts right but the explanations or implications wrong. These errors are not random; they spring from at least four sources. The first is that many analysts use European welfare states as their reference point when investigating the American welfare state. Historically, European welfare states (and Canada) have relied heavily on social insurance programs. Because the United States does not meet this standard, it seems to lag behind. While this approach may lead to a number of interesting and important comparisons, it misses alternative ways of addressing social needs. The American welfare state happens to rely less on social insurance and more on tax expenditures, loan guarantees, and social regulation than welfare states elsewhere. Once we include these other tools of government, our understanding of the size, shape, and historical development of the American welfare state changes substantially.[1] Social insurance is one way to build a welfare state but not the only way. The significance of this error is introduced in chapter 1.

A second source of error has been overreliance on a few social programs, particularly Social Security and welfare, to support more general claims.* Social Security is supposed to represent everything that is right with U.S. social policy and welfare everything that is wrong. From these two programs we are supposed to make all sorts of inferences about social policy, many of which turn out to be faulty because many social programs do not work like Social Security or welfare. It's like visiting California and Louisiana and assuming that you now understand the entire United States. This error is first discussed in chapter 2.

Third, while many economists and policy analysts examine the recent performance of social programs, scholars interested in the politics of social policy have concentrated primarily on developments between the late nineteenth century and the early 1970s.[2] Scholars who have ventured into the latter decades of the twentieth century usually focus on a single program, legislative milestone, or group of beneficiaries.[3] Few scholars have tried to generalize broadly about recent developments in the American

---

* Throughout the book, Social Security means Old Age and Survivors Insurance (OASI) and not disability insurance. The two programs have such distinct functions, sizes, and clienteles that they should be treated separately. "Welfare" refers to Aid to Families with Dependent Children (AFDC) and its successor, Temporary Assistance for Needy Families (TANF). These programs will be described more fully in chapter 2.

welfare state.[4] Chapter 3 begins to make the case for looking more closely at recent decades. What was true about social policy in the middle of the twentieth century was not necessarily true at the end.

Am I arguing that the conventional wisdom has always been wrong? No. In a number of instances, the old truths worked well for a time. Unified Democratic control of government was essential to passage of new social programs in the 1930s and 1960s. Many of the means-tested programs emerging from the New Deal and the Great Society were politically vulnerable. Public support for the welfare state was lower in the United States than in Canada and Europe in the 1970s. But none of these "old truths" does a very good job of capturing the world we live in now. The American welfare state has changed in recent decades, and our understanding must change with it.

All three of these errors contribute to faulty inferences based on limited evidence. The final source of error is methodological. Unlike other parts of the social sciences, the study of social policies has seldom devolved into battles over the One Right Way to acquire useful knowledge.[5] Scholars have certainly disagreed about the relative influence of social movements, public opinion, political elites, and other factors. But seldom have they faulted each other for choosing a fundamentally flawed research design or relying on qualitative versus quantitative evidence. Some scholars are quite good at admitting the limitations of their own research methods and encouraging readers to consult work by scholars from alternative research traditions. The prevailing attitude is "live and let live."

One problem with this attitude is that it can lead to peaceful segregation rather than genuine integration. True research communities, with scholars working on similar problems using different but complementary research strategies, are rare. We have many qualitative case studies analyzing developments in the first two-thirds of the twentieth century and many large-N quantitative studies aimed at the last third of the century.* We have fairly distinct groups of people working at the cross-national, national, and state levels. What emerges from the literature is a long list of important insights, affecting any number of social policies and historical eras, that never quite add up to a coherent whole. So much has been written by scholars marching happily, and often productively, in very different directions.

This book is unusual in pulling different research traditions together in a single study of U.S. social policy. It draws on three of the most important traditions—the policy analytic, the behavioral, and the historical—each of which has something valuable to offer. Scholars working in these traditions hail from political science, history, economics, sociology, and law.

---

* N is shorthand for the number of cases in a study.

In some chapters, one tradition is featured; in other chapters, two or three traditions work together. If these traditions remain separate, then myths and misunderstandings about the American welfare state will likely persist. At a minimum, integrating these approaches will enable us to ask better questions about the politics of U.S. social policy.

THE PLAN OF THE BOOK

This book grew out of my experiences teaching a course called The American Welfare State to college students. I originally designed the course to convey general patterns of social policy making. Over the years the course evolved into a list of the many exceptions to these patterns, and recent editions of the course could fairly be titled (How Not to Think About) The American Welfare State. This book is my way of trying to state those objections more clearly and connect them in interesting ways. Each chapter typically opens with some piece of conventional wisdom, followed by evidence that it is wrong or seriously incomplete. Wherever possible, I have tried to offer some new generalizations about social policy to replace the old ones. Essentially, this book is a recurring process of demolition and reconstruction.

My attacks on the conventional wisdom cut across ideological lines. I challenge claims that liberals make about the size and shape of the American welfare state, and about the vulnerability of means-tested social programs. By the same token, the chapters concerning the impact of public opinion, of federalism, and of race on social policy will probably not sit well with conservatives. Such evenhandedness could signify a relentless pursuit of truth, or it might simply reflect a perverse desire to pick a fight with as many people as possible (personally, I prefer relentless).

Because I want this book to be used in classrooms, I presume little in the way of prior knowledge. Social science jargon is kept to a minimum, and most of the quantitative analysis is displayed in simple tables. These steps should have the added benefit of making the book accessible to a more general audience interested in social policy. In doing so, I run some risk of losing my audience of scholars and specialists, but I hope that a wide-ranging attack on the conventional wisdom might hold their interest. Some of the chapters end with ideas for future research, and I hope that some readers will be intrigued enough to investigate. The book is intended to spur debate over what is and is not possible in U.S. social policy, and I do not expect to have the last word.

Part 1 surveys the size, shape, and historical development of the American welfare state. The underlying premise of this "Basic Tour" is that we need to know what the American welfare state looks like and how it began before we can start analyzing its politics. Rather than cite a long list of numbers and dates, I organize the most important facts around a few key debates. Chapter 1, "She's So Unusual," challenges the notion that the American welfare state is considerably smaller than its European counterparts. For one thing, different measures of size yield very different results. Moreover, the closer you look at the full range of policy tools, the bigger the American welfare state appears. The key question to ask is not why the United States does less than other welfare states but why the United States does things differently.

Chapter 2, "Tracks of My Tiers," analyzes the overall shape of the American welfare state. We have been told repeatedly that the American welfare state has two distinct tiers. The upper tier of social insurance programs is supposed to enjoy numerous advantages, politically and programmatically, over the lower tier of public assistance programs. One has only to contrast Social Security with welfare to appreciate the gulf separating these two tiers. And yet, the more we learn about other social programs, the more suspect the two-tiered model becomes. Important programs such as Medicaid, the Earned Income Tax Credit (EITC), unemployment insurance, and workers' compensation do not fit very well in their designated tiers. Tax expenditures, social regulation, and other tools of social policy further compound the problems of the two-tiered model. It may make more sense to think about how different tools of social policy are used to help people at different stages of their lives.

Chapter 3, "Twice in a Lifetime," lays out a basic chronology of the American welfare state with emphasis on the origins of social programs. Everybody knows, for example, that the American welfare state emerged dramatically during two "big bangs" of activity in the mid-1930s and mid-1960s. Social Security, welfare, unemployment insurance, Medicare, Medicaid, and a number of other programs originated during these two brief moments in time. Political scientists, historians, and sociologists have long debated what made these moments possible—extraordinary presidents, social movements, policy experts, struggles between business and labor, or something else. That debate is less compelling if a number of social programs were created at other points in U.S. history, which they were. They may not have been the kinds of social programs found in Europe, but they addressed many of the same problems and groups. This revised history leads to a greater sense of political possibilities, particularly with respect to political parties.

The emphasis in Part 1 is on breadth: comparing the size of welfare states in many countries, comparing important features of many U.S. social programs, and finding patterns in the enactment of many social programs across the entire twentieth century. Part 2 of the book offers more analytic depth. Chapters 4–7 focus on interesting anomalies and causal relationships that can lead us to a richer understanding of the American welfare state. This part is titled "New Horizons" because one common theme is how scholars have overestimated the constraints on social policy. Chapter 4, "Ogres, Onions, and Layers," picks up where chapter 3 left off by comparing three recent cases of social programs enacted under divided government—the Employee Retirement Income Security Act, the Americans with Disabilities Act, and the Child Tax Credit. The most surprising finding is that Republican officials were pivotal actors in each case. The party usually known for bashing the welfare state has been instrumental in creating new social programs.

Problems with the two-tiered model of the American welfare state are analyzed more fully in chapter 5. After all that we have read and learned about the vulnerability of means-tested programs, how in the world did the EITC grow faster than any other major U.S. social program between 1980 and 2000? Why were so many politicians, liberals and conservatives, singing its praises? Did its success have anything in common with the equally remarkable expansion of Medicaid during the same period? These questions are not asked very often. Many scholars believe in the old saying "Programs for the poor are poor programs," meaning that they are doomed to fail politically. Inclusive programs like Social Security are supposed to offer the only blueprint for sustainable social policy. By comparing the recent history of Medicaid and the EITC with that of other means-tested programs, I will demonstrate that some programs for the poor are much less vulnerable than others, and I will offer reasons why this is so.

In chapter 6, I return to the cross-national comparisons introduced earlier in the book. National values have often been cited as the main reason why the American welfare state is relatively small, but if analysts have been wrong about its size then they may be wrong about the impact of values as well. This chapter opens by comparing public support for the welfare state in a handful of affluent democracies. While support in the United States may lag behind the support in other countries, it is strong in a number of areas. The rest of the chapter shows how durable and broad this support has been. Contrary to reports of a "right turn" in American politics, public support for the American welfare state has not waned in recent decades. Even people who call themselves Republican want to spend more on some social policies. Public opinion data help explain the size and distinctive shape of the American welfare state, as well as some of the curious behaviors described in chapters 4 and 5.

Despite recent efforts to help the disabled, the poor, and families with children, the fact remains that the largest U.S. social programs benefit the elderly. These older individuals just happen to belong to one of the largest and most feared interest groups in the country, AARP, and just happen to be very involved in elections. Much less public money is spent on younger families with children, who are less organized than senior citizens and either cannot vote or do not vote as often. Therefore, older Americans, through sheer political muscle, must be controlling the direction of social policy—unless, of course, lots of people who are not elderly agree with these spending priorities. Then AARP would not look so imposing, and claims about generational war would be highly exaggerated. Chapter 7, "The World According to AARP," raises doubts about the political clout of senior citizens by looking carefully at the history of AARP and comparing the policy preferences of older and younger Americans.

Part 3 of the book, "Checkpoints and Roadblocks," helps explain how a welfare state that is larger, more diverse, and more popular than commonly believed can nevertheless fall short in addressing social problems. These chapters indicate how federalism, race, public opinion, and existing social programs may be larger barriers than commonly believed. Many policy makers think of the American states as "laboratories of democracy" where different experiments in social policy can be conducted and evaluated, which ultimately leads to better outcomes. The history of workers' compensation offers clear evidence to the contrary. In chapter 8, I explain how the American states have retained control of workers' compensation despite several efforts to remedy its flaws by increasing the role of the national government. The main message of this chapter is how political power trumps problem solving.

Many scholars believe that the negative influence of race on social policy has been eliminated or confined to welfare. I find in chapter 9 that race continues to affect a number of social programs. Its impact even extends beyond programs for the poor. The main evidence comes from comparing benefits across the American states. That race still matters seems clear; exactly how it matters is explored but not settled.

In the final chapter, I start to explain how a welfare state that is large and dynamic can nevertheless do relatively little to reduce poverty and inequality. A number of observers believe that these problems persist because the have-nots in the United States lack political power. Most of the poor and near poor, however, do not want the government to redistribute income. In fact, the public may be more sensitive to the gap between the rich and the middle class than between rich and poor. And social policy may reflect those concerns. Chapter 10 ends on a rather pessimistic note, finding that many of recent achievements in social policy benefit middle- and upper-middle-class individuals more than the poor and near poor. We seem to have trouble making progress against inequality because large parts of the American welfare state are not designed to do so. There is a large gap between creating social policies and programs and actually improving the lives of needy citizens.

Had I been trained as a historian, these chapters would have been arranged chronologically. As a political scientist, I am inclined to organize my thoughts based on specific questions or debates. Each chapter is therefore devoted to a single question such as "Is the American welfare state unusually small?" or "Why are some programs for the poor quite large and popular, while others are politically vulnerable?" The organization of my arguments is not so much linear as layered. We will move back and forth across the twentieth century, depending on the question at hand. Doing so will help us understand how the American welfare state is itself layered.

Had I approached this book like most political scientists, I would have narrowed the focus and explored one or two questions in depth. Readers who want to learn a lot about Social Security, poverty, the rise and fall of the Clinton health plan, or any number of topics might want to read the studies cited earlier in this introduction. It is in large part because we have so many good studies of specific programs and policies that the time is right to draw general lessons from them. What I offer instead is breadth of coverage and some synthesis—a trip past well-known and lesser-known trees, and a sense of the whole forest. My story is not simple: it includes many social programs and a variety of policy tools; it highlights decisive moments and long-term trends; it moves between different levels of government; and it tries to account for the influence of prominent officials, political parties, interest groups, public opinion, federalism, race, and policy design. But the American welfare state is not simple, either, and trying to grapple with its complexity is essential to understanding its politics.

METHODS AND DATA

One of the distinguishing features of this study is that it draws on three separate research traditions, using the strengths of one to compensate for the weaknesses of another. The first of these traditions is policy analysis. Policy analysts are adept at describing and evaluating programs, policies, and government agencies. They possess considerable factual knowledge about the American welfare state: they understand the ins and outs of eligibility, financing, and benefits. This wealth of specific knowledge enables policy analysts to challenge facile generalizations. Another distinguishing feature of this tradition is the attention paid to the real-world impact of social policies. Policy analysts want to know if governments are using scarce resources effectively and efficiently to address social problems. They want to know whether a particular government action reduces poverty, and at what cost. Their research is filled with surprising results and practical wisdom, and many of my students have enjoyed learning "what works and what doesn't" from these authors.[6] The influence of policy analysis on this book is most obvious in my analysis of the size and shape of the American welfare state, the remarkable growth of some means-tested programs, and poverty and inequality (chapters 1, 2, 5, and 10).

What you will not usually learn from these scholars is who or what influences the direction of social policy. Behavioralists offer a number of important insights into the influence of public opinion and interest groups on social policy.[7] I will explore the often surprising contours of public opinion in chapters 2, 6, 7, and 10, using evidence from national and international surveys; interest group behavior will be analyzed in chapter 7 as well. Behavioralists gravitate toward statistical analysis of numerical evidence and therefore gather information about lots of cases in order to be confident of their findings. In the literature cited above, the individual citizen is the main unit of analysis. Other scholars working within this tradition take advantage of the federal structure of American politics and compare the behavior of individual states, such as their spending patterns.[8] My analysis of race and social policy in chapter 9 adopts this latter approach.

The behavioral approach has its limits. These studies tend to focus on a fairly narrow slice of time and on recent decades, and thereby have trouble supporting broad generalizations.[9] Further, the influence of elected officials, policy experts, political parties, and institutional design—no matter what the era—is harder to quantify than the results of opinion polls. Scholars investigating these factors need to rely more on textual evidence from government documents, periodicals, biographies, and secondary sources, and this is exactly the point where more historically oriented scholars can add value. A large number of historians, political scientists, and political sociologists have analyzed processes of development and change in the American welfare state.[10] For these scholars, history offers a storehouse of evidence for testing theories about social policy making, an approach I use in chapters 3, 4, 5, 7, and 10. History also offers a way of understanding how choices made in the past, even small ones, can shape politics for decades (i.e., path dependence). Chapter 8, concerning the history of workers' compensation, provides a vivid illustration of this process.

I use history in conventional and unconventional ways. The usual way is to analyze long-run processes or events that happened long ago, and I do that in chapters 3 and 8. This approach can also illuminate important developments in recent decades, and I use history to identify patterns in the enactment, the expansion, and the retrenchment of social policies since the 1970s (chapters 4, 5, 7, and 10). Like Paul Pierson, I reject the

"Faustian bargain" in political science whereby historically oriented scholars are valued as long as they stick to subjects that seem to have little contemporary relevance.[11] Some of the most interesting trends in U.S. social policy are relatively recent.

The historical approach also has its limits. Sometimes the urge to generalize is so great that scholars overlook or downplay exceptions. On these occasions, it helps to think like a policy analyst and investigate social programs in more detail. As we will see in chapters 2 and 3, sweeping claims about the existence of a two-tiered welfare state and about two "big bangs" of welfare state formation do not hold up well under close scrutiny.

Drawing on these three traditions has implications for my research design. Some chapters entail quantitative analysis of many cases (though my use of statistics is never complicated). This design is good for detecting general patterns and identifying associations among different variables. Other chapters are more intensive investigations of one, two, or three cases, using mainly qualitative data. Careful comparisons over time or across a small number of cases can help identify interactions among important factors and the causal mechanisms at work in a given relationship. When drawing on the work of policy analysts and behavioralists, I tend to use numerical evidence from government documents and public opinion polls. The historical approach leads me to consult books and periodicals. The unit of analysis in each chapter may be nations, U.S. states, demographic groups, individuals, policy tools, or social programs. It all depends on the question. Staying firmly rooted in just one of these research traditions limits the kinds of questions we can ask as well as the quality of the answers we can offer.[12]

PART I

Basic Tour

CHAPTER 1

She's So Unusual

MAKING COMPARISONS IS ONE of the most important ways we make sense of the world, and our tour of the American welfare state begins with some cross-national comparisons. Forty years ago, the distinguished social scientist Harold Wilensky declared the United States a "reluctant welfare state."[1] In the decades since, many observers have reached essentially the same conclusion: the United States has been called a semi–welfare state, a welfare state laggard, a residual welfare state, an incomplete welfare state, and similar terms denoting inadequacy. Implicitly or explicitly, the American welfare state seems to fall short of European welfare states. For their part, contemporary studies of American exceptionalism routinely note the shortcomings of the American welfare state when highlighting the limited reach of American government. Introductory textbooks about American government often convey the same message. Consensus on this point has become so complete that few people have stopped to question its accuracy. The more common pattern has been to assert the existence of an underdeveloped welfare state and then move on quickly to explain why the United States is so different, or to call for a more generous welfare state.[2]

In this chapter, I challenge the most common claim about the exceptional nature of the American welfare state—that it is unusually small.[3] This judgment, in my view, is misleading. It is based on an overstatement of the social benefits received in other nations and an underestimate of the social benefits distributed by the United States. The latter results from a narrow focus on just two tools of government action, social insurance and grants, and from a misleading measure of size. The American welfare state is actually bigger than most people think.

The prevailing wisdom is easy to summarize. Researchers typically measure the size of welfare states by the share of gross domestic product (GDP) devoted to public social spending, which is sometimes called a nation's welfare state effort. This figure includes spending by all levels of government on retirement and survivors' pensions, disability, sickness, occupational injury and disease, public health, family allowances,[4] a wide range of social services, housing, unemployment, job training, and aid

An earlier and somewhat briefer version of this chapter appeared as "Is the American Welfare State Unusually Small?" *PS: Political Science & Politics* 36, 3 (July 2003): 411–16.

to the poor. It reflects primarily the use of social insurance and grants. According to this measure, the United States devoted 15.8 percent of its GDP to public social expenditure in 1997. While that may seem like a lot of effort, Denmark, Sweden, and Finland devoted 33 percent or more of their GDP to public social spending. Several other European nations spent 25 to 30 percent. The obvious conclusion, and the one conveyed in much of the cross-national literature, is that many affluent democracies are putting almost twice as much effort into their welfare states as the United States. Even when compared to Canada (20.7%) and the United Kingdom (23.8%), nations that analysts often categorize as low spenders, it seems clear that the American welfare state is unusually small.[5]

Money Spent, Benefits Received

The source of these figures is the Organization for Economic Cooperation and Development (OECD), whose professional staff collects statistical data from member countries and publishes a steady stream of useful cross-national comparisons. In recent years, the OECD has started to modify its social expenditure figures—though you would be hard-pressed to find the new calculations in studies of the American welfare state.[6] One important change has been to recognize that social benefits can be taxed, often at quite high rates. Suppose country X gives the average retiree a pension of $1,000 each month but counts the pension as income and taxes it at a rate of 25 percent. The net benefit received is $750. In contrast, country Y gives out a smaller pension, say $800 each month, but does not subject any of it to income taxation. Which country has the larger retirement program? (Hint: it's not X.) Similarly, many countries impose consumption taxes that vary in size and scope; in Europe they might be called value-added taxes, in the United States sales taxes. These indirect taxes also reduce the amount of money that retirees actually have available to spend; the same logic applies to beneficiaries of other social programs. Normatively, it makes more sense to compare how much money stays with citizens than how much money governments initially distribute.

The extent of direct and indirect taxation varies quite a bit among the OECD nations. Table 1.1 shows that taxation of benefits alters our perception of welfare state laggards and leaders. Column A of the table lists the standard measure of welfare state effort, discussed previously, while column B adjusts that figure for direct and indirect taxation. We now see that social benefits received do not exceed 30 percent of GDP in any of these countries. Spending in Denmark drops from 35.9 to 26.7 percent of GDP, and in Sweden from 35.7 to 28.5 percent. In effect, Scandinavian governments tell their citizens, "I'll spend a dollar on your social welfare as long

TABLE 1.1
The Relative Size of the American Welfare State (1997)

Country	A Public social spending/GDP	B Column A minus taxes	C Column B plus tax expenditures
Denmark	35.9%	26.7%	26.7%
Sweden	35.7	28.5	28.5
Finland	33.3	24.8	24.8
Belgium	30.4	25.8	26.3
Norway	30.2	24.4	24.4
Italy	29.4	24.1	24.1
Germany	29.2	25.5	25.5
Austria	28.5	23.0	23.4
Netherlands	27.1	20.2	20.3
United Kingdom	23.8	21.1	21.6
Czech Republic	21.7	19.3	19.3
Canada	20.7	17.8	18.7
New Zealand	20.7	17.0	17.0
Ireland	19.6	16.7	17.1
Australia	18.7	17.6	17.9
United States	**15.8**	**15.0**	**16.4**
Japan	15.1	14.4	14.8
Average	25.6%	21.3%	21.6%

Source: Willem Adema, *Net Social Expenditure*, 2nd ed. (Paris: OECD, 2001), table 7.
Note: Some tax expenditures have been captured in column B (see text). The OECD refers to the figures in column C as net social spending.

as you give me 25 cents right back." The big spenders in column B would rank as average spenders in column A. The seventeen-country average drops to 21 percent, and countries tend to converge toward the mean.[7]

Because we know that taxes in the United States tend to be lower than in Europe, an adjustment for taxation of social benefits should make the American welfare state seem less exceptional. With taxes factored in, the American welfare state shrinks a little, from about 16 to 15 percent of GDP. The United States still ranks at the bottom of the list but is not quite so far from the average nation. Whereas the American welfare state once appeared to be about 60 percent as large as the average OECD welfare state (column A), it now appears to be 70 percent as large. The gap between the United States and the other low-spending countries is also narrower.

OTHER POLICY TOOLS

A second change in the OECD figures has been prompted by a broader, and I think more accurate, perspective on how governments spend money. The normal method has been to count only direct social spending, such as benefits paid on a weekly or monthly basis to retirees, the unemployed, the poor, and the like. Such spending comes either from social insurance programs like Social Security and Medicare or from public assistance programs like TANF and Food Stamps.[8] One problem with this method is that it misses the ways in which governments spend money indirectly, through special provisions in the tax code. The technical name for this tool is tax expenditures, which are departures from the normal tax system that are designed to promote some socially desirable objective.[9] The United States, for example, uses tax deductions to promote home ownership and tax credits to subsidize child care expenses. To enhance retirement income, the United States excludes most Social Security benefits from income taxation, which is another kind of tax expenditure.

In some quarters, tax expenditures are not equated with direct spending. They are viewed simply as a way to let taxpayers keep more of their own money. Since the 1970s, however, the U.S. government has formally recognized tax expenditures as a form of spending in its major budget documents, and other OECD governments have followed suit. The tax expenditure concept is widely accepted among public finance experts as well. The rationale is that with tax expenditures, the government is essentially collecting what taxpayers would owe under a "pure" tax system and simultaneously cutting some taxpayers a check for behaving in certain desired ways, such as buying a home. In a pure system, everyone with the same income would pay the same amount of income tax. In the real world, people with the same income often do not pay the same tax, because some are able to take advantage of tax expenditures while others are not.

Although the U.S. tax code has many tax expenditures aimed at specific industries and business in general, most of this spending goes to tax expenditures with social welfare objectives. The big-ticket items are tax subsidies to employers who offer retirement pensions and health insurance to their employees, and a handful of sizable tax breaks for home owners. These tax expenditures serve the same social welfare functions mentioned earlier in the chapter (e.g., retirement income, medical care, housing). In a previous book, I summed up spending on tax expenditures with social welfare objectives and found that they cost roughly $400 billion in 1995. Adding them to more direct forms of social spending increased the size of social spending at the national level by almost 50 percent. Suddenly, the American welfare state did not look so small anymore.[10]

At the time, I knew that other welfare states used tax expenditures as well, but I had no fair or accurate way to compare them. Some evidence suggested that the United States relied more heavily on tax expenditures than other nations, which would have made the true size of its welfare state seem less exceptional, but there was no way to know for sure. I am happy to report that comparable figures are now available, care of the OECD.[11] Unfortunately, the OECD does not display those figures in one place when calculating net social spending. Some tax expenditures, such as the exclusion of most Social Security benefits from income taxation, have been accounted for in column B (table 1.1). The remaining tax expenditures, such as the Earned Income Tax Credit and, more important, tax expenditures that encourage employers to offer benefits such as retirement pensions and health insurance to their workers, are accounted for in column C. As a result, the figures in column C understate the true impact of tax expenditures. But our main concern here is in developing a more accurate measure of a nation's welfare state effort, and the net social spending figures in column C are better than the traditional spending figures in column A.

The OECD countries vary in their use of tax expenditures to promote social welfare objectives. In several countries the figures in columns B and C are identical. Most of the increase between columns B and C is due to change at the bottom of the list, which in turn means more convergence among nations. In column C, spending figures in Canada and especially the United States are up. Now it appears that 16.4 percent of GDP in the United States consists of social benefits that are paid directly or indirectly by government and that stay in recipients' pockets. The overall average in column C increases slightly. The American welfare state is now three-fourths as large as the average for all seventeen nations. Another way to appreciate the change is to compare the United States to the classic big-spending welfare state, Sweden. If you look only at pretax direct spending (column A), you will say that the Swedish welfare state is 2.3 times the size of the American welfare state. If you look instead at net social spending (column C), you will say that the Swedish welfare state is 1.7 times larger.[12]

The evidence so far suggests that we should tone down but not abandon claims about the small size of the American welfare state. Welfare states are actually more alike than they first appear, but as a general rule no matter which column you examine in table 1.1, the big spenders are in Scandinavia, the average spenders are in continental Europe, and the low spenders are the former British colonies (Australia, Canada, Ireland, United States). Except for Japan, the United States always ranks at the bottom.

Nevertheless, once we realize that governments spend money both directly and indirectly, we start to think about other tools of government. Regulation is one of the most important. Governments in several European countries mandate that employers create retirement pensions for their employees. While the money for such pensions does not flow through government accounts, these pensions are the direct result of government action. In the United States, the vast majority of employers are required to pay into a workers' compensation fund, and private insurance companies or employers (via self-insurance) run most of those funds.[13] Estimating the cost of such publicly mandated, private social expenditures is admittedly difficult, and any figures must be taken with a grain of salt. In the nations listed in table 1.1, the addition of such spending, net of taxes, would raise the welfare state effort figures of individual countries by up to 1 percent of GDP. The basic portrait would remain unchanged. Such spending would increase the overall average of welfare state effort to 22 percent of GDP and the U.S. figure to 17 percent, which would still be more than three-quarters of the average. The United States would be ahead of Japan and more or less tied with Ireland and New Zealand.[14]

The revised OECD figures undoubtedly understate the importance of regulatory approaches to social welfare. They capture only those forms of regulation that can be translated readily into spending figures. Missing, for example, are minimum wage laws, which many countries use to raise the incomes of the poor and near poor. In the United States, these laws affect millions of workers and are routinely linked in policy debates to welfare reform and poverty. The current U.S. minimum wage of $5.15 per hour is higher than in central or southern Europe but lower than in France, the Netherlands, or the United Kingdom. Germany and Sweden have no such laws, relying instead on collective bargaining agreements between workers and employers.[15]

Arguably one of the most important pieces of U.S. social legislation passed in the last twenty years is the 1990 Americans with Disabilities Act (ADA). The basic intent of ADA is to make it easier for the disabled to enter the labor force and become self-sufficient. The scope of the law is potentially very broad, affecting tens of millions of disabled people, millions of public accommodations, hundreds of thousands of employers, and tens of thousands of state and local governments.[16] Historically, many European governments have given employers direct subsidies to hire the disabled and make necessary changes in the work environment. Those subsidies show up in international comparisons of welfare state effort, whereas U.S. regulations do not.

Loan guarantees are an essential component of U.S. housing policy. Through this tool, the U.S. government enables individuals with little income, few assets, or a poor credit history to qualify for mortgage loans from private lenders. As of 2003, the Federal Housing Administration (FHA) had more than $400 billion worth of home loans outstanding, and the Veterans Administration (VA) had over $300 billion. FHA and VA guarantees backed over 7 million mortgages that year; black or Hispanic families held about 2 million of those mortgages. These loan guarantees affected more households than the two major forms of direct spending, public housing and Section 8 vouchers.[17] In the European Union, such government guarantees appear to be in violation of the European Community (EC) Treaty because they privilege lenders in one country over those in another and thus impede the creation of a single, unified credit market.[18]

Finally, consider tort law. In European welfare states, those who are injured can look to the government for medical care and replacement income. They can tap into some public fund. In the United States, those who are injured may, depending on their circumstances, be able to tap into a publicly funded program such as Medicare or Medicaid, a publicly mandated but privately financed program such as workers' compensation, a disability policy offered voluntarily by their employer—or they can "sue the bastards" who caused their injury. This last option is quite popular. In their cross-national study, Kagan and Axelrad have noted that the United States "relies on lawsuits rather than social insurance . . . for injury compensation" much more than countries in Europe.[19] By one estimate, the combination of legal costs, claims administration, and monies that injured persons have won in court consumes at least twice as large a share of GDP in the United States as in other OECD countries.

In short, the American welfare state may be unusual, but less for its small size than for its reliance on a wide variety of policy tools to achieve what many European welfare states do primarily through social insurance. While it is hard to say this with certainty, given the difficulties of comparing policy tools such as regulations and loan guarantees across nations, the evidence certainly suggests that we should be highly suspicious of anyone who declares that the United States has a small welfare state (see box 1.1 for a detailed comparison of housing policies that reinforces this point).

Do These Other Tools Really Belong?

In making the case that we ought to include a wide variety of policy tools, and not just social insurance and grants, I risk stretching the concept of

BOX 1.1

The Multiple Tools of U.S. Housing Policy

The case of housing policy shows clearly how the American welfare state looks more or less different in cross-national perspective, depending on which policy tools are included. The best-known forms of housing assistance in the United States target the poor and are administered as grants from the national government to states and localities. The two most significant programs are Section 8 rental vouchers and public housing. In the late 1990s, these housing programs helped about 11 million people, fewer than the 15 million recipients of subsidized school lunches and far fewer than the 37 million recipients of Social Security. Low-income housing programs did not come close to serving half of the poor (at the time, about 35 million).

One way to compare the importance of housing assistance across countries is to calculate the fraction of all occupied units that are subsidized by government. The low-income housing programs mentioned above total approximately 5 million units, or less than 5 percent of all residential dwellings in the United States. Government-subsidized rental units account for about 15 percent of all dwellings in France and Germany, 25 percent in the United Kingdom and Denmark, and 40 percent in the Netherlands. Clearly, the United States lags behind.

That is, unless we consider other tools of government. As mentioned previously, the U.S. government offers loan guarantees to promote home ownership, particularly among the less affluent. Over 5 million home owners had FHA-backed home mortgages in 1999, and another 2 million had mortgages backed by the Veterans Administration and Farmers Home Administration. The combination accounted for over 10 percent of all owner-occupied homes and a little over 7 percent of all dwellings. In other words, loan guarantees more than double our previous estimate of the number of publicly subsidized residences in the United States.

The numbers really shoot up after we include tax expenditures. The home mortgage interest deduction was claimed on an estimated 30 million income tax returns in 1999. The total revenue lost to the national treasury from this one provision was estimated to be $53 billion. The tax deduction for property taxes paid on homes benefited 32 million home owners to the tune of $18 billion. The exclusion of capital gains on home sales cost an additional $12 billion. Together, these and related tax expenditures cost almost three times what the United States spends on traditional grants for low-income rental housing. These tax expenditures benefit about one-half of all home owners in the United States (those who do not benefit are primarily those who have paid off their mortgages completely). They affect about one-third of all residences. If we conservatively assume substantial overlap between home owners who benefit from loan guarantees and tax expenditures, then total U.S. government assistance to housing would be in the range of 35 to 40 percent of all residences. That is a far cry from the initial figure of 5 percent.

(boxed text continued on following page)

In addition, it seems safe to assume that many home owners who had their mortgages paid off by 1999 benefited from housing tax expenditures in previous years. If the same fraction of home owners benefited in the past as in 1999, then we can count another 15 to 20 percent of residences as government subsidized. In short, a reasonable estimate is that 50 to 60 percent of all residences in the United States currently have or once had financial assistance from the government. That, in my book, is a fairly substantial public presence.

These revised estimates do not mean that the United States is more involved in housing than France, Germany, or other European nations. The latter also offer favorable tax treatment for home mortgage interest and for any capital gains from the sale of a home. Some governments also offer tax relief to those who rent in the private sector. Some offer grants to help the elderly and disabled remodel their homes. Regulatory tools are used as well: rent control, though declining in importance, is still more common in Europe than the United States.

I know of no study aggregating these various forms of government intervention in housing and attaching either a number or a rank to various countries. For my purposes, what matters is that the U.S. government is much more involved in housing policy than a simple look at public housing and Section 8 vouchers would indicate. The public role in housing might trail that in Europe, but it is considerable. Our initial estimate, however—that European governments subsidized three to eight times as large a fraction of their housing units as the U.S. government—is simply mathematically impossible with the revised U.S. figures. The gap cannot be that wide.

Sources: Paul Burke, *A Picture of Subsidized Households in 1998: United States Summaries* (Washington, DC: U.S. Department of Housing and Urban Development, 1998); Directorate General for Research, Social Affairs, *Housing Policy in the EU Member States*, Working Document W14 (Brussels: European Parliament, 1996); Hugo Priemus and Frans Dieleman, "Social Housing Policy in the European Union: Past, Present and Perspectives," *Urban Studies* 39, 2 (2002): 191–200; U.S. Census Bureau, *Statistical Abstract of the United States, 2001* (Washington, DC: Government Printing Office, 2001); U.S. Congress, Joint Committee on Taxation, *Estimates of Federal Tax Expenditures for Fiscal Years 2000–2004* (Washington, DC: Government Printing Office, 1999).

"welfare state" so far that it loses its shape and falls limply to the floor. I certainly don't want that to happen, so let me make a brief case for including these other tools. The prevailing view is that welfare states emerged in many affluent democracies during the late nineteenth and early twentieth centuries. The defining feature was not government aid to the needy. Poor laws in Europe had existed for centuries. The local poorhouse was already a fixture in the United States. Rather, the defining feature was the introduction of social insurance: public programs that pooled risks among a large number of workers and their families, and linked benefits to earnings. Thus, the modern welfare state is commonly understood to be the old layer of programs targeted at the poor combined with this new layer of social insurance programs for a larger group of citizens.[20]

While the introduction of social insurance was unquestionably a milestone, the more fundamental change was the involvement of national governments. No longer would assistance depend so heavily on which town or province one resided in. Increasingly, social benefits were distributed nationally. It became legitimate to speak of *a* German or *a* British or *an* American welfare state. Historically, the rise of social insurance and national involvement coincided, so it is easy to see why scholars might see the two as inseparable. My reading of this history is that individuals living in the nineteenth and twentieth centuries did not go around demanding social insurance per se. They wanted their national government to do something, anything, to help them cope with insecurity and misfortune. They wanted their national government to step in and compensate for the many shortcomings of local poor relief. When President Roosevelt established the Committee on Economic Security in 1934, he did not tell its members to devise a package of social insurance and grant programs. He issued a broad charge to "determine the best way to safeguard Americans 'against misfortunes which cannot be wholly eliminated in this manmade world of ours.' "[21]

It is true that national officials turned early and often to social insurance. Sometimes they created new grant programs for the poor. And sometimes they reached for other kinds of policy tools that promoted the same kinds of policy objectives and helped the same groups of people. By the end of the twentieth century, multiple tools were the norm and not the exception. The U.S. government currently provides retirement income via social insurance, grants, tax expenditures, social regulation, and insurance. U.S. housing policy is based on grants, vouchers, loan guarantees and, most of all, tax expenditures. For the disabled, the key tools are social insurance, grants, and social regulation. To my mind, limiting the welfare state to social insurance and grants makes about as much sense as limiting national defense to the army and navy. Those branches of the military have long been central to national defense, but shouldn't we say a few words about the air force?[22]

Readers might take comfort in knowing that I am not alone in defining the welfare state to include a broad range of policy tools. Charles Noble's political history of the American welfare state is based on the premise that "in capitalist societies, welfare states exist to protect the public from unregulated market forces." This leads him to analyze not only Social Security but also minimum wage laws, a classic example of social regulation. Theda Skocpol has pointed to the GI Bill, which used a combination of grants and loan guarantees, as a model of politically sustainable social policy. Michael Katz, a leading historian of the American welfare state, argues that its three key components are social insurance, public assistance, and tax expenditures.[23] Between these scholars and the OECD, there are definitely precedents for defining the concept of welfare state to include a greater number of policy tools.

COMPARED TO WHAT?

My final reservation about the supposedly small size of the American welfare state does not depend so much on the range of policy tools considered. It is more a question of whether one agrees that social spending should be understood solely in the context of national GDP. To illustrate my point, I present Bill and Melinda, a couple who live in the suburbs of a major city. Bill works full-time, and Melinda splits her time between caring for their three children and doing charitable work. As part of a study of household consumption patterns, we discover that less than 2 percent of Bill and Melinda's annual expenses goes for food. This includes all food purchased at grocery stores or restaurants. Nationwide, food accounts for 14 percent of the average family's expenses. The conclusion seems obvious: Bill, Melinda, and the kids are malnourished, perhaps even starving. Someone from social services ought to take the children into protective custody.

In this case, however, the family in question is headed by Bill and Melinda Gates, the wealthiest couple in the world. Two percent of their annual expenses can still buy a lot of nice meals. They are definitely not starving. With people as rich as the Gates family, it might make more sense to calculate spending per person. The same is true when comparing the size of welfare states. Of all the nations discussed so far, the U.S. has the largest GDP and the highest GDP per capita. While the gap is definitely not as large as that separating the Gates family from the rest of us, it is significant. The United States government can devote a relatively smaller share of its GDP to social welfare and still spend more per person than nations devoting a higher share of GDP. Continuing with the food metaphor, it may be that two slices of a large pizza (in the United States) are as big as three slices of a medium pizza (in Europe).

Table 1.2 contrasts net social spending as a fraction of GDP to net social spending per person. Based on the former measure, the United States has a relatively small welfare state that ranks sixteenth out of seventeen nations. Based on the latter measure, the American welfare state ($4,809 per person) is the largest among the English-speaking OECD nations. It

TABLE 1.2
Smaller Slice, Bigger Pie

Rank	Net social spending as % GDP	Net social spending per person
1	Sweden (28.5%)	Denmark ($6,812)
2	Denmark (26.7)	Norway (6,532)
3	Belgium (26.3)	Belgium (6,113)
4	Germany (25.5)	Sweden (5,784)
5	Finland (24.8)	Germany (5,622)
6	Norway (24.4)	Austria (5,400)
7	Italy (24.1)	Italy (5,125)
8	Austria (23.4)	Finland (5,081)
9	United Kingdom (21.6)	**United States (4,809)**
10	Netherlands (20.3)	Netherlands (4,495)
11	Czech Republic (19.3)	Canada (4,443)
12	Canada (18.7)	United Kingdom (4,424)
13	Australia (17.9)	Australia (3,929)
14	Ireland (17.1)	Japan (3,637)
15	New Zealand (17.0)	Ireland (3,528)
16	**United States (16.4)**	New Zealand (3,034)
17	Japan (14.8)	Czech Republic (2,526)
Average	21.6%	$4,782

Sources: Adema, Net Social Expenditure, table 7; U.S. Census Bureau, Statistical Abstract of the United States 1999, table 1363, available at http://www.census.gov/prod/www/statistical-abstract-1995_2000.html.

Note: The figures for net social spending are identical to those in column C of table 1.1, and date from 1997. The per capita spending figures have been adjusted for purchasing power parity among the nations.

is larger than the Dutch welfare state ($4,495). It even compares favorably with the Finnish ($5,081) and Italian ($5,125) welfare states. The per capita figure for the United States is slightly above the seventeen-nation average of $4,782. By this measure the size of the American welfare state is average, not small.[24]

Because these figures reflect only social insurance, grants, and tax expenditures—and not publicly mandated but privately financed social spending, regulations, loan guarantees, or tort law—they actually understate the true size of the American welfare state and its placement relative to other welfare states. Based on social benefits per capita, the United States probably belongs in the top third of affluent welfare states.

CONCLUSION

The answer to the original question is no: the American welfare state is not unusually small. It compares favorably with some of the largest welfare states in the world. Its size has been measured incorrectly by many people and organizations for a long time. Those analysts who spend a lot of time and energy explaining why the American welfare state is so small should reconsider their initial premise. I cannot be certain that the American welfare state has always been larger than the literature suggests. My data come from the 1990s, and it is possible that the American welfare state used to be relatively small but no longer is. In that case, we may be seeing some convergence among modern welfare states. Nevertheless, the various policy tools discussed in this chapter are not recent creations. Tax expenditures in the United States have existed for much of the twentieth century. National minimum wage laws and loan guarantees originated in the 1930s at the same time as key social insurance and grant programs. Tort law has been around forever. It is an open question just when and for how long the American welfare state has been exceptional—a question I think worth pursuing. What seems clear is that its size is not now exceptional.[25]

These findings also have implications for our understanding of American exceptionalism more generally. If the American welfare state is not unusually small, and social welfare functions are a large component of government activities, then the overall size of American government may not be that small, either. The question for future researchers may not be why the U.S. government does relatively little compared to European governments. Rather, the question is why governments of similar size devote comparable resources to pursuing similar policy objectives through such a diverse mix of policy tools.

It is quite possible that the answer to this new question will be quite similar to past explanations for American exceptionalism. Compared to other affluent democracies, the United States may rely less on direct forms of government assistance (social insurance, grants) and more on indirect forms (tax expenditures, loan guarantees, regulations) because of the long-standing tension Americans feel between their humanitarian and individualistic impulses.[26] By offering tax incentives to people who behave in socially desirable ways, by helping individuals secure credit from private lenders, and by telling employers how they must treat their workers, Americans can help those in need without seeming to expand public bureaucracies or government budgets. Even with many grant programs in the United States, third-party providers in the for-profit and nonprofit sectors frequently deliver the actual service, such as medical care and job training. The importance of core American values like individualism and limited government may appear more in the techniques used to assist needy groups of people than in the amount of aid these people receive.

Alternatively, an institutional explanation may account for these patterns. The American political system has long been noted for its fragmentation. Perhaps the combination of many access points and many veto points makes it difficult to construct a single towering edifice of social insurance, overseen by a small number of legislators and bureaucrats. That is the classic European model. Instead, the United States has built several moderate structures—Tax Expenditures, Social Insurance, Grants, Loan Guarantees, Regulations, Tort Law—administered by a large number and wide range of public authorities.

Of course, size is not the only feature of welfare states worth discussing. The American welfare state may still be exceptional for its limited scope (e.g., family policy, health insurance), heavy reliance on means-tested benefits, historically late start, weak levels of public support, or failure to reduce inequality and poverty. Which groups benefit from social spending may be just as important as how much money governments spend. Such features are important and deserve careful consideration, and some will be discussed in later chapters. My hope is that readers will view the size of the American welfare state as a good example of why we need to describe something accurately before trying to explain it.

CHAPTER 2

Tracks of My Tiers

The United States actually has a two-tiered welfare state. The bottom tier, welfare for the poor and children, has been under attack, but the upper tier, welfare for the elderly and the middle class, is thriving. The popular Social Security and Medicare programs, which return more to recipients than they paid in to the system, have grown enormously.[1]

—*U.S. government textbook*

The Social Security Act created the contemporary meaning of "welfare" by setting up a stratified system of provision in which the social insurance programs were superior both in payments and in reputation, while public assistance was inferior—not just comparatively second-rate but deeply stigmatized. Public assistance is what Americans today call "welfare"; recipients of the good programs are never said to be "on welfare." And while most people hate "welfare," they pay the utmost respect to Old-Age Insurance.[2]

—*Linda Gordon*

Compared to European welfare states, the United States combines comprehensive, universalistic social policies for the elderly with an assortment of means-tested transfers, social services, and private benefits for the nonelderly. . . . In a society characterized by pervasive racial discrimination in labor and housing markets, this outcome has led to a racially stratified welfare state: blacks have been disproportionately excluded from mainstream programs and have received lower benefits than whites. In addition, they have been made to depend on putative racially neutral means-tested programs, such as Aid to Families with Dependent Children (AFDC), that have become racially stigmatized.[3]

—*Michael K. Brown*

In the United States especially, scholars speak of a "two-tier" or "two-track" welfare state in which programs targeted on men and labor market problems tend to be contributory social insurance while those primarily for women and family-related are means-tested social assistance; they emphasize the disadvantages of relying on second-tier programs in terms of

benefit generosity, the restrictiveness of eligibility regulations
and the extent of concomitant supervision and intrusion.[4]

—*Ann Orloff*

Americans make a sharp conceptual and evaluative distinction between "social security" and "welfare." *Social
Security* refers to old-age insurance and the associated
programs of survivors', disability, and medical coverage
for the elderly; and these programs are seen as sacred
governmental obligations to deserving workers who have
paid for them through "contributions" over their working
lifetimes. *Welfare*, by contrast, is often discussed as a set of
governmental "handouts" to barely deserving poor people
who may be trying to avoid honest employment—trying to
get something for nothing.[5]

—*Theda Skocpol*

WHEN COMPARING WELFARE STATES, analysts think about more than their
size. They think about crucial questions such as who benefits, how benefits are financed, and which levels of government are involved. When they
ask these questions, they often look to Europe and see social programs
that treat citizens equitably and generously. Virtually everyone is brought
into the same public retirement program, covered by national health insurance, and entitled to a family allowance. In some of these countries,
social benefits are considered a right of citizenship. Over the course of
the twentieth century, European nations gradually adopted a coherent
network of inclusive social insurance programs to replace the patchwork
of nineteenth-century public assistance programs. These social insurance
programs define the modern welfare state.

When analysts look at the United States, they see something different.
The American welfare state consists of a few broad-based programs and
many smaller programs targeted at the poor. Some of these programs are
generous and some are not. Some programs offer uniform benefits across
the nation, and some vary widely by state. Some are popular and others
are vilified. The result is a distinctively two-tiered welfare state. On every
count, the upper tier is superior to the lower tier—larger, more generous,
more uniform, more popular, and less vulnerable to cutbacks. In short, new
social insurance programs have been layered on top of public assistance
programs and have not replaced them. The quotations at the start of this
chapter give you some idea of how often historians, political scientists, and
sociologists describe U.S. social policy in these terms. While scholars may
argue over whether race, gender, class, or age divides the tiers, they all
agree that two tiers define the shape of the American welfare state.

The clear policy implication, at least for those on the political left, is that the United States should create more upper-tier programs.[6] Policy makers should design new programs to guarantee everyone health insurance, paid parental leave, subsidized child care, and greater access to educational and training opportunities. Individuals currently benefiting from means-tested programs such as Medicaid could then shift over to more inclusive social programs. Likewise, policy makers should resist calls to means-test or privatize existing programs like Social Security, which would weaken them politically.[7] Over time, the upper tier should expand and the lower tier contract, allowing the American welfare state to resemble its European counterparts.

This vision of the future rests on two sets of arguments, one normative and the other empirical. Putting aside the question of whether we should want to live in a world of large, inclusive social programs, I will focus on the empirical question of whether a two-tiered American welfare state exists. The main message of this chapter is that we should be skeptical of such claims. The prevailing approach to categorizing social programs suffers from serious flaws. This is no small problem; the idea of separate tiers is arguably the single most important characterization of the American welfare state, and it underlies a lot of received wisdom about what can and should be done in social policy.

Too many arguments about separate tiers are based on a comparison between Social Security and welfare.* Social Security is supposed to represent the upper tier of European-style social insurance programs, and AFDC/TANF the lower tier of public assistance programs. It is hard to imagine a starker contrast. These two programs constitute polar opposites on almost every dimension imaginable. In fact, the differences are so numerous that it is hard to know which ones are truly decisive. It is not surprising that Social Security and welfare have been used to support a wide range of arguments about age, class, race, and gender.

These two programs certainly belong in any portrait of the American welfare state. Nevertheless, we should not assume that everything in the upper tier looks just like Social Security or that everything in the lower tier looks just like AFDC/TANF. We need to test our inferences by examining a larger number of social programs. Doing this will enhance our ability to make accurate generalizations about U.S. social policy. It will give us some crucial factual knowledge about the American welfare state that will make the rest of this book easier to comprehend. And it will reveal puzzling anomalies that will be analyzed in more depth in later chapters.

---

* As mentioned in the introduction, Social Security refers to Old Age and Survivors Insurance (OASI), while welfare refers to Aid to Families with Dependent Children (AFDC) and its successor, Temporary Assistance for Needy Families (TANF).

As we shall see, Social Security is not typical of the upper tier. The other core programs —Medicare, disability insurance (DI), and especially unemployment insurance (UI) and workers' compensation (workers' comp)—diverge from Social Security in a variety of ways. Likewise, key programs in the lower tier deviate from welfare. The most problematic cases are Medicaid and the Earned Income Tax Credit (EITC), which is significant considering that they are two of the largest programs in the lower tier. There is too much variation within each tier and too much overlap between them for this typology to work. We should reject the two-tiered model and search for a better alternative.

In theory, one could compare social programs along any number of dimensions. I will focus on the most important features of social programs and try not to overwhelm readers with factual details. Many of these features have been cited in past studies of the two-tiered welfare state. The bottom line for most analysts is how much help the government offers in each tier, and to whom. Eligibility and benefits are supposed to be more uniform and more generous in the upper tier than in the lower tier. Is this true? Are men, whites, the elderly, and the more affluent really the main beneficiaries of the upper tier, while women, racial minorities, the nonelderly, and the less affluent are relegated to the lower tier? Over time, does spending on programs in the lower tier grow more slowly than spending in the upper tier? Answers to these questions are important indicators of advantage and disadvantage, and they affect individuals directly.

I turn next to features of social programs that are commonly believed to explain differences in benefits, eligibility, and spending. Upper-tier programs are supposed to be favored because they serve a larger number of politically powerful individuals. These people are highly motivated because they expect to receive benefits at some point in their life. Means-tested programs in the lower tier have a much smaller and politically weaker constituency. Upper-tier programs are also supposed to be favored because they are financed by payroll taxes and classified as budgetary entitlements, which protect them from competition with other spending priorities. Because this is a lot of ground to cover, I will focus on identifying general patterns and then major exceptions to those patterns. Most of the analysis will be limited to traditional social insurance and public assistance programs. Near the end of the chapter, I will suggest how less traditional tools such as tax expenditures and social regulation challenge our understanding of tracks and tiers.

Who Gets What from Government

Before the Social Security Act of 1935, all states had some form of poor relief, and most states had workers' compensation and mothers' pensions

TABLE 2.1
Major Programs of the American Welfare State

Common Name	Formal name/acronym	Basic purpose
UPPER TIER		
Social Security	Old Age and Survivors Insurance (OASI)	Income support for retirees, their survivors, and their children
Medicare	Part A: Health Insurance (HI) Part B: Supplementary Medical Insurance (SMI) Part C: Medicare Advantage (formerly Medicare + Choice; managed care rather than fee-for-service medicine) Part D: Prescription drug benefit	Medical care for the elderly, as well as some nonelderly disabled and people with end-stage renal disease
Disability insurance	DI; also known as Social Security Disability Insurance (SSDI)	Income support for disabled adults and their families
Workers' comp	Workers' compensation	Income support and medical care for those who are injured on the job or have work-related illness
Unemployment insurance	UI	Income support for the unemployed
LOWER TIER		
Medicaid	Medicaid	Medical care for poor elderly, disabled, pregnant women, and children
Earned Income Tax Credit	EITC; also known as Earned Income Credit (EIC)	Income support for poor and near-poor wage earners
Supplemental Security Income	SSI	Income support for poor disabled, blind, and elderly
Welfare	Temporary Assistance for Needy Families (TANF), which replaced Aid to Families with Dependent Children (AFDC)	Income support and services (e.g., child care) for poor families with children
Food Stamps	Food Stamps	Vouchers for the poor and near poor to buy food
Subsidized/low-income housing	Public housing	Public rental housing for the poor
	Section 8	Vouchers for private rental housing for the poor

Note: The lower tier also includes a number of smaller programs such as Head Start, job training, subsidized school meals, and Title XX social services.

(the forerunner of welfare). Some states had pensions for the elderly poor, and one state, Wisconsin, had approved but not yet implemented an unemployment insurance program. Huge disparities across the country were the norm. Depending on the state or the region within the state, public aid might be modest, minimal, or nonexistent.[8] The Social Security Act was designed in part to reduce these disparities and create a genuinely national program. That was one of the novel features of Old Age Insurance, now called Social Security. Another objective of the Act was to reduce human suffering by increasing the level of government aid. Because benefits are more uniform and generous, the upper tier of social programs is supposed to accomplish these objectives far better than the lower tier.

Uniformity

Social Security is a truly national retirement program. State and local governments have no role in determining eligibility or setting benefit levels. Every person in every state plays by the same rules. In practice, the average Social Security recipient in New York receives a larger monthly check than his counterpart in New Mexico, but that is because the average New Yorker earns more during his or her working years. If one person in New York and another in New Mexico both have the same earnings history, they receive the same amount. The pattern is much different under the old AFDC and current TANF programs, where authority is shared between national and state governments. States help decide how many families will receive welfare, and how much. Someone who is eligible for TANF in one state might be "too rich" for TANF in another, especially if that state happens to be in the South. Benefits show similar variation. In 2002 the maximum monthly TANF cash benefit for a family of three was a princely $201 in Texas. The same family in Connecticut could receive up to $636 each month. It definitely does not cost three times as much to live in Hartford, Connecticut, as it does in Dallas, Houston, or San Antonio, Texas. This is not an isolated example. The disparity in TANF benefits is just as large between Montana and Mississippi, or Kansas and Alabama.[9]

Clearly, welfare does not treat people as equally as does Social Security. What about other social programs? Medicare, which offers health insurance for the elderly, is like Social Security, with uniform eligibility and benefits nationwide.[10] So far, the two tiers are distinct. The contrast between them diminishes once we move beyond Social Security and Medicare, partly because the influence of the American states extends into the upper tier. In disability insurance, for example, state agencies determine eligibility, and the rate of rejecting applicants and denying appeals varies a fair amount around the country.[11] Unemployment benefits are set by the states, and in 2001 they ranged from less than $175 per week in Alabama, Arizona, and California to more than $300 per week in Massachusetts, Minnesota, and Washington. These differences do not simply reflect the cost of living in different parts of the country. As a fraction of average pay in each state, unemployment benefits were just as variable. In California, the average UI benefit replaced 22 percent of the average worker's pay. Better to get laid off in Iowa, where the average UI check was 45 percent of average pay.[12] We can also compare benefits available to hypothetical workers in similar states. Someone who worked full-time at minimum wage in 2000 would have been entitled to a weekly unemployment check of $128 in Massachusetts and $216 in neighboring Connecticut.[13]

State governments have near-total control of workers' compensation, and some of the variations are mind-boggling. Consider a few comparisons of neighboring states. In 2001 the maximum weekly benefit for a permanent, total disability was $531 in Alabama and $316 in Mississippi. Benefits in Alabama were paid for the duration of the disability, whereas in Mississippi they expired after nine years. Lose a hand on the job in Indiana, and you could be compensated up to $53,500. Next door in Illinois, that same hand could fetch $181,700. (Perhaps this is why Allstate Insurance, the "good hands people," is headquartered in Illinois.) If you were killed on the job in Minnesota, your family could receive up to $15,000 for your burial expenses. In Iowa, where presumably the ground is softer and easier to dig, burial expenses were capped at one-third that amount.[14] Clearly, individuals with similar needs can be treated very differently in the upper tier of the American welfare state. It is hard to imagine any program in the lower tier exhibiting more geographic variation than workers' compensation.

In the lower tier, Medicaid is a large and complicated program, making it hard to render a simple verdict about coverage or benefits. For one thing, Medicaid covers poor people with very different medical needs. While poor children represent the single largest group of recipients, most of the money goes to care for the poor disabled and the poor elderly. Another complicating factor is that Medicaid is run jointly by national and state governments. "Variability across State Medicaid programs is the rule, not the exception. . . . Income eligibility levels, services covered, and the method for and amount of reimbursement for services differ from State to State."[15] Benefits averaged about $4,000 per patient in 2001, with some states spending over $6,000 and some less than $3,000. Yet these figures obscure variations in the mix of Medicaid recipients from state to state. A state with an unusually large number of disabled and elderly Medicaid recipients will naturally spend more. The elderly and disabled have more chronic health problems, a higher rate of hospitalization, and greater need of expensive nursing-home care. Benefits for each elderly and disabled patient were approximately $10,600. Poor children cost about $1,300 each. Even small changes in the proportion of elderly and disabled recipients will have a large impact on total Medicaid spending in a given state.

The more telling comparisons involve Medicaid spending for distinct groups. There, huge differences remain. States spent anywhere from $5,000 to $21,000 on each elderly Medicaid patient in 2001. Even after controlling for variations in cost of living across the nation, wide differences remain. Cost of living cannot explain why spending per elderly Medicaid patient was over 50 percent higher in Maryland than in Virginia, or twice as much in North Dakota compared to Vermont. The story for Medicaid children is quite similar, ranging from $900 to $3,100 per child. The figures for the disabled range from under $5,000 to over $20,000 per person.[16]

Some analysts believe that since government officials have more control over which groups are covered and what services are offered under Medicaid, it makes more sense to compare these features than spending.[17] While all states must cover certain populations (e.g., all pregnant women with income less than 133 percent of the poverty line, all children age six and under who live below the poverty line, and all elderly and disabled SSI recipients with income less than 75% of the poverty line), they can choose to cover a number of optional populations. States can offer Medicaid to the same groups mentioned above at higher income levels. In other cases, states may cover "medically needy" groups with high recurring medical expenses, such as HIV/AIDS patients. A recent report by the Kaiser Family Foundation concluded that "Medicaid eligibility above the federal requirement varies widely from state to state."[18] Similarly, all state Medicaid programs must cover certain medical services, including hospital care and physicians' services, and can opt to cover additional services. As of 2003 most states covered dental services, prosthetic devices, and podiatrist services, but some did not. Every state Medicaid program covered prescription drugs, but they differed significantly over the size of co-payments and the maximum number of prescriptions covered per year.[19] While differences among the states have diminished in recent decades, for reasons that will be discussed in chapter 5, they are still substantial.[20] In short, whether we examine dollars spent, groups covered, or services provided, Medicaid differs considerably from state to state and thus belongs in the lower tier.

If eligibility and benefits in the rest of the lower tier vary as much as they do for welfare and Medicaid, then we might concede some exceptions in the upper tier and conclude that separate tiers really do exist. However, several means-tested programs are more uniform than welfare or Medicaid. As Paul Pierson has noted, the trend in recent decades has been "the gradual if incomplete nationalization of income transfer programs."[21]

While a large part of this trend has been driven by the growth of Social Security, another important part involves programs for the poor. Creation of Supplemental Security Income (SSI) in 1972 effectively nationalized means-tested cash assistance to the blind and the disabled.[22] Eligibility criteria related to recipients' income and assets are now uniform across the states. The maximum monthly SSI benefit is the same in every state.[23] As a result, SSI benefits are more uniform than AFDC/TANF or even unemployment benefits.[24]

The Food Stamps program, created in the early 1960s, is comparable to SSI. The national government provides almost all the funding, sets eligibility criteria, and establishes a uniform benefit. States can choose whether to pay for individuals who are ineligible under the national guidelines, whether to spend money to boost public awareness of and participation in the program, and whether to modify a few other administrative details. By and large, the Food Stamps program operates remarkably similarly around the country.[25]

Nationalization of income transfers has also occurred through the addition of new programs. The Earned Income Tax Credit, established in 1975, is every bit as national a program as Social Security. States have nothing to do with the EITC. Implementation is handled through tax forms prepared and reviewed by the U.S. Internal Revenue Service.[26]

Based on equal treatment of individuals around the country, there is a clear difference between Social Security and Medicare on the one hand and Medicaid and welfare on the other.[27] A number of medium-size programs, however, do not fit this pattern. Given their collective weight (over $200 billion per year), the failure of disability insurance, unemployment insurance, workers' comp, the EITC, Food Stamps, and SSI to respect the boundary separating the upper and lower tiers spells trouble for theories of the two-tiered welfare state.

Generosity

Perhaps I have put too much emphasis on geographic differences. One might concede that benefits are not consistently uniform in the upper tier or variable in the lower tier, yet contend that benefits in the upper tier are still more generous. If you were laid off from work, you would fare better collecting unemployment benefits in Iowa than in California. But no matter where you lived, you would be better off on unemployment benefits than if you were a single-mother family on welfare. By this logic, we should compare benefit levels between programs in the two tiers.[28]

Social Security benefits are definitely larger than TANF benefits. The average welfare *family of three* received a smaller monthly check in 2000 than the average Social Security *retiree*. Add in the cash value of Food

Stamps and child care, and the welfare family was still worse off. Social Security benefits are also more generous than means-tested SSI benefits for the elderly. The gap is not as wide, because SSI benefits are bigger than TANF benefits, but it is large nonetheless.[29]

If we move beyond Social Security and look at other programs in the upper tier, the picture becomes fuzzier. One good comparison pairs unemployment insurance and TANF, because both are designed to provide temporary income support for individuals and families in their working years. In 2000 UI benefits averaged $221 a week, which works out to over $900 per month. That was well beyond what TANF families were receiving. Even in Alabama and Mississippi, states with the lowest unemployment benefits in the country, welfare benefits were even lower. This is an important piece of evidence in favor of the traditional two-tiered model.[30]

Yet, in some ways unemployment benefits look more generous than they really are. Benefit levels are based on past earnings and are not adjusted for family size, as is the case in TANF. A low-wage worker who is laid off and has a large family might not be much better off than a welfare family of similar size. A more important problem is that unemployment benefits typically expire after six months, while TANF benefits last for up to two years.[31] Finally, we need to keep in mind that most of the unemployed do not collect unemployment benefits. Fewer than 40 percent did so in 2000, and fewer than half have done so since the mid-1970s. This represents a big drop from the late 1940s, when 80 percent of the unemployed collected UI benefits. Graetz and Mashaw argue that changes in the economy, such as the growth of service industry jobs and part-time work, have reduced the number of unemployed people who can meet states' requirements for employment and earnings. A decline in unionization has not helped, either.[32] In contrast, 70 to 80 percent of those families eligible for welfare received benefits in the 1980s and early 1990s. Although the participation rate dropped sharply after the 1996 welfare reforms, the rate has remained higher than UI's, and the average over the last few decades was much higher. Compared to welfare, unemployment benefits are higher—but only for those who can get them.[33]

Suppose we want to compare the generosity of medical benefits in the two tiers. We know that the patient mix is different; Medicaid includes children and Medicare does not. It is better to compare the benefits to the elderly in Medicare and Medicaid. That way, we can eliminate the impact that Medicaid children have in lowering the cash value of the average Medicaid benefit. As noted, the average elderly person covered by Medicaid cost over $10,000 in 2001. That person's counterpart in Medicare, combining parts A and B, cost about $6,000. The conclusion seems inescapable: Medicaid is more generous than Medicare.

"But wait," you say, "Medicaid for the elderly means expensive nursing homes. It means caring for people who could not afford to see a doctor when they were younger. The Medicaid elderly may have more chronic medical problems than the Medicare elderly. Of course Medicaid costs are higher." I agree. Medicaid and Medicare are designed to address different medical problems for overlapping but distinct clienteles. That is why it is difficult to make definitive comparisons.

We might be better off comparing disabled recipients in each program. All these individuals are certified by the same state agencies. Medicaid spent over $10,000 per disabled client in 2001, compared to $6,000 in Medicare.[34] This is the same gap we observed among the elderly. These results do not constitute clear proof that Medicaid is more generous than Medicare. Some of the differences might reflect the higher administrative costs in Medicaid. There may be objective differences in the medical needs of each group of disabled people. The apparently large gap in benefits does, however, raise doubts about the greater generosity of the upper tier. (In fact, until 2004 Medicaid paid for prescription drugs and Medicare did not. These drugs cost $20 billion in 2000, which averaged out to a little under $500 per Medicaid recipient.)[35]

Alternatively, one might compare benefits within individual programs. As a number of analysts have noted, benefits in the upper tier are tied to individuals' past history of earnings. Someone who was a highly paid lawyer will receive a larger Social Security check than someone who was a poorly paid secretary. In 2002 the average monthly benefit for retirees was $1,008 for men and $774 for women. It was $912 for whites and $775 for blacks.[36] The same pattern holds for unemployment and disability benefits. Thus, social insurance programs are supposed to reproduce gender and racial inequalities in the labor market. Because the upper tier is such a large component of the American welfare state, these effects are profound.

This is one of the more persuasive arguments for separate tiers, but even it has limitations. Although the dollar value of Social Security benefits is greater for the affluent, the benefit formula is designed to narrow the gap between rich and poor. The best measure of this is the replacement rate. If past earnings average $2,000 per month and the Social Security check equals $700 per month, the replacement rate is 35 percent (700/2,000). The replacement rate for a hypothetical high earner was 33 percent in 2002, compared to 40 percent for an average earner and 54 percent for a low earner. The high earner still, in absolute dollars, receives a larger check than the low earner, but the income gap separating high and low is smaller than before they retired. This practice works to the advantage of women and racial minorities. The replacement rate was 36.5 percent for men compared to 50.8 percent for women that year. Comparable figures for racial minorities are harder to find. Given the sizable gaps in income between whites on the one hand and blacks and Hispanics on the other, we can safely assume that racial minorities have a higher replacement rate than whites.[37]

Does the benefit formula help to compensate for the regressive nature of the Social Security payroll tax? Yes. Economist C. Eugene Steuerle and two colleagues have calculated the average returns on payroll taxes for individuals born between 1931 and 1940 (essentially the most recent group of retirees). In other words, they have measured the net benefit of Social Security and disability insurance to individuals. Their figures show that every major demographic group will receive more in benefits than it paid in taxes. Comparing across groups, they found that Social Security has been a significantly better deal for women than for men and a slightly better deal for blacks and Hispanics than for whites. Their figures for disability insurance show a small bias in favor of men and blacks. When the retirement and disability programs are combined, women and racial minorities remain ahead. The authors estimate that those patterns will be sustained for the cohort born at the end of the baby boom and retiring in the coming decades.[38] From this angle, one could just as easily commend upper-tier programs for reducing gender and racial inequalities. The fundamental problem is inequality generated by the labor market, not social insurance.

At the extremes, benefits in the upper tier of the American welfare state are more generous than those in the lower tier. It is far better to receive Social Security than welfare. Once we move beyond these programs, the line between the two tiers starts to blur and at times simply evaporates. Readers should therefore be skeptical of any blanket statement about the generosity of upper-tier programs and demand to see carefully designed comparisons.

Beneficiaries

Scholars have identified the upper tier as the home of the middle class, men, the elderly, and whites. The lower tier is the exact opposite—the refuge of the poor, women, children, and racial minorities. These lines are not absolute; there are certainly whites in the lower tier and women in the upper tier. Certain groups are supposed to appear disproportionately in one tier or the other. A quick look at the numbers raises questions about these divisions.

Programs in the lower tier are designed to serve people with limited income and few assets. Recipients usually live below the federal poverty line. Programs such as welfare, public housing, and SSI serve only the poor. The Earned Income Tax Credit, however, extends to families with incomes almost twice the poverty line. Medicaid covers pregnant women and young children up to 133 percent of the poverty line. Many of the elderly who rely on Medicaid for their nursing-home care spent their working years firmly in the middle class.[39] Consequently, the lower tier serves the poor as well as the near poor and the newly poor. Many of these same people also reside in the upper tier. Social Security and disability benefits, for instance, are distributed fairly evenly across income groups. Thirty-five percent of benefits went to the poorest 40 percent of adults in 2000. Twenty-four percent of benefits went to the most affluent 20 percent. The pattern in Medicare is even starker, with 70 percent of benefits going to individuals with less than $25,000 in annual income.[40] The less fortunate are not exactly shut out of the upper tier.

The classic face of welfare is a single mother with children. Although legislation enacted in 1996 changed many aspects of welfare, that picture remains accurate. Women represent 90 percent of the adults on TANF. The gender profile in other means-tested programs is similar, if not quite as pronounced. Women comprise 70 percent of the adults on Food Stamps and 60 percent of Medicaid recipients. The problem, and it is a big one, is in the upper tier. Women also account for 60 percent of recipients in Social Security and Medicare. The main reason is simple: any program targeted at the elderly will have a bias in favor of women, given their longer life expectancy. Women are thus the majority in both tiers of the American welfare state.[41]

Most of the people who receive Social Security checks are elderly. The same goes for Medicare benefits. In the lower tier, most TANF recipients are children, as are half of Medicaid and Food Stamps recipients. In some smaller programs, for example Head Start and subsidized school lunches, children are the exclusive target. It is easy to see why age seems to divide the American welfare state. The main exceptions are the smaller programs in the upper tier. Disability insurance, unemployment insurance, and workers' compensation all target people in their working years, before they retire. The age profiles of their beneficiaries bear no resemblance to those of Social Security or Medicare.

Racial divisions in the American welfare state are more obvious than gender divisions. Blacks and Hispanics reside disproportionately in the lower tier. Despite being one-quarter of the nation's population, these two groups constitute over half of all TANF, Food Stamps, and Head Start recipients, and almost half of Medicaid recipients. All these facts reflect the lower incomes and higher poverty rates that racial minorities experience. In contrast, blacks and Hispanics account for only 12 percent of Medicare recipients. Only 8 percent of the people receiving Social Security retirement benefits are black, and an even smaller percentage are Hispanic. The chief culprit is life expectancy. Any program targeted at the elderly will have a bias against most racial minorities, much as it will favor women. If we compare the fraction of Medicare and Social Security recipients who are black to the fraction of individuals age sixty-five and over who are black (8%), we find parity. Programs for the elderly are unusually white because the elderly themselves are unusually white.

Not all social insurance programs fit this pattern. The same factors depressing the number of minority recipients of retirement pensions should boost the number of minorities receiving survivors insurance, and they do (13% were black in 2001). The biggest exception is disability insurance. Blacks represent 18 percent of DI recipients, which is more than their share of the general population or their share of working-age adults.[42] Granted, this is not entirely good news, for it suggests that blacks are suffering debilitating injuries or illnesses more often than whites. Racial profiles of unemployment insurance and workers' comp beneficiaries are unavailable.[43] Thus, racial lines are easier to discern among the young and the old than among working-age adults.

Trends in Spending

The simplest and most common way of distinguishing between the two tiers is to compare spending over time. Programs in the upper tier are supposed to grow faster and resist cutbacks better than programs in the lower tier. Greater spending makes it possible for more people to enjoy higher benefits. There is good evidence for this view. Between 1950 and 1980, spending on social insurance did increase more rapidly than spending on public assistance in the United States.[44] The creation of disability insurance and Medicare and the repeated expansion of Social Security translated into far more dollars than everything spent on the so-called War on Poverty. However, recent trends in social spending have followed a much different trajectory.

Between 1980 and 2000, real (i.e., inflation-adjusted) spending on Social Security grew almost four times faster than welfare. That is exactly what we would expect in the two-tiered model. Spending in the entire upper tier, including Social Security, grew at an average annual rate of 4.0 percent. Coming at a time when large deficits and divided government were the norm, this is a fairly impressive record. Growth in the lower tier averaged. . . . 5.2 percent.[45] That is definitely unexpected. Despite reductions to several means-tested programs in the early 1980s, casualties of the "Reagan revolution," spending increased faster in the lower tier. Despite large cuts to SSI and Food Stamps as part of welfare reform in 1996, spending increased faster in the lower tier.

The source of this surprising growth is easy to identify—Medicaid. It expanded at the remarkable rate of 14 percent every year. In 1980 Medic-

aid accounted for one-quarter of all means-tested spending. By 2000 it
was almost one-half. Without Medicaid, annual spending growth in the
lower tier drops from 5.2 to 2.2 percent. The other key source of growth
was the Earned Income Tax Credit, which expanded an astounding 25
percent each year. Without Medicaid and the EITC, the lower tier grew
by only 1.5 percent each year. There may be a temptation to dismiss these
exceptions and insist that, for the most part, lower-tier programs do not
grow as fast as upper-tier programs. That would be a serious mistake. We
cannot ignore two programs that comprise over half of all spending in
the lower tier.

Even if we discount these outliers, the variations within each tier are
considerable. The fastest-growing parts of the upper tier, parts A and B
of Medicare, averaged 7 and 15 percent annual growth, respectively. Disability benefits, in contrast, grew only 1 percent. In the lower tier, besides
Medicaid and the EITC, Section 8 housing vouchers experienced double-
digit growth. Other means-tested programs such as Food Stamps and
subsidized school lunches barely grew at all. It is very difficult to see
any difference between the upper and lower tiers with respect to recent growth.

Table 2.2 summarizes the evidence so far for the two-tiered welfare
state. Within the upper tier, some social programs are truly national while
others operate quite differently from state to state. Some programs benefit
more women than men, and some serve a disproportionately large share
of African-Americans. Some upper-tier programs grow much faster than
others. Within the lower tier, some programs look like welfare while others are as uniform or as fast-growing as anything in the upper tier. In
short, the classic distinctions between the two tiers are repeatedly violated. Although these distinctions were more evident in the 1960s and
1970s, they no longer capture important differences in how government
treats recipients of social programs.

WHY THE TWO TIERS DIFFER

Scholars have offered a variety of explanations for why one tier of social
programs is advantaged over the other. The inclusive nature of upper-tier
programs, for instance, is supposed to give them a larger base of support
than means-tested programs in the lower tier. Programs in the upper tier
are supposed to benefit because they are financed out of payroll taxes
and trust funds rather than general revenues. Policy makers have given
programs like Social Security and Medicare added protection by designat-
ing them as entitlements, which makes funding mandatory. Eligibility for
benefits is linked to employment in the upper tier but not in the lower;

TABLE 2.2
Cracks in the Tiers (Part 1)

Program Characteristics	Classic Distinctions		Major Exceptions	
	Upper	Lower	Upper	Lower
Eligibility and Benefits	Uniform	Vary by state	Unemployment insurance, workers' comp	EITC, SSI, Food Stamps
	Generous	Inadequate	Medicare vs.	Medicaid
			UI vs.	AFDC/TANF
Beneficiaries	Middle class	Poor	Social Security, Medicare	
	Men	Women	Social Security, Medicare	
	Elderly	Children	Workers' comp, UI, DI	
	White	Black, Hispanic	Survivors and disability insurance	
Growth	Faster	Slower	1980–2000	1980–2000; Medicaid, EITC

public support is supposed to be greater for programs that reinforce values of work and self-sufficiency. Of course, if outputs such as benefits and spending do not fit the two-tiered model, we might suspect that these explanations do not fit the facts, either.

Size

In a democracy, numbers matter. The sheer size of upper-tier programs is supposed to confer important political advantages. The more people who benefit, and the larger those benefits, then the greater the potential number of self-interested voters who are ready to defend those programs from attack and push for expansion. Lower-tier programs serve fewer citizens, many of whom are children who cannot vote. Moreover, upper-tier programs serve many members of the middle and upper classes, people with the resources needed to be effective in politics. Lower-tier programs serve the poor and near poor. These programs simply cannot compete with programs in the upper tier for public support and scarce resources.

In the year 2000, over 38 million Americans received Social Security benefits, at a total cost of over $350 billion. Social Security helped one out of every seven Americans and was the single largest item in the national budget, surpassing even national defense. That same year, only 5.8 million people collected welfare benefits. All of them lived in poverty, and a majority of them were children. Total spending on TANF, from national and state governments, was tiny ($22.8 billion) compared to Social Security.[46] The two programs, and by implication the two tiers, could not be further apart.

Within the upper tier, Medicare looks quite similar to Social Security. Total spending on Medicare surpassed $200 billion in 2000, making it one of the largest items in the national budget. There are actually more Medicare than Social Security beneficiaries, mostly because some of the nonelderly disabled are covered by Medicare. Within the lower tier, one can find a number of means-tested programs that are even smaller than welfare (e.g., Head Start, public housing, the State Children's Health Insurance Program, job training). So far, it makes sense to divide U.S. social programs into separate tiers of large and small programs.

But the exceptions soon start to pile up. Medicaid, for example, is supposed to belong in the lower tier, yet it costs almost as much as Medicare and serves more people than any program in the upper tier. Medicaid was approximately four times the size of disability insurance or workers' compensation in 2000. It cost ten times as much as unemployment insurance. That is one very large exception. Medicaid is also far bigger than anything else in the lower tier. It alone accounts for about one-half of all means-tested social spending in the United States, and about two-thirds of all means-tested social spending at the state level.[47] Medicaid is so important that any generalization about tiers that fails to account for it is, in my view, immediately suspect.

In terms of dollars spent, three programs in the upper tier (DI, workers' comp, UI) are closer in size to the larger lower-tier programs than they are to Social Security and Medicare.[48] In terms of beneficiaries, the three smaller upper-tier programs serve many fewer people than Medicaid, Food Stamps, or the Earned Income Tax Credit. In fact, the EITC (55 million) and Medicaid (42 million) have more beneficiaries than any upper-tier program. Even after subtracting the number of children, the EITC program benefits about as many adults as Social Security; the Food Stamps program benefits more adults than DI, UI, or workers' compensation; and Medicaid benefits many more adults than any of the latter three programs. These exceptions are even bigger problems for the two-tiered model.

The range in size within each tier of the American welfare state is enormous. Social Security and unemployment insurance are about as much alike as an SUV and a moped. Medicaid and public housing are about as much alike as Texas and Vermont. And the overlap between tiers is considerable. Four of the lower-tier programs are bigger than the smallest upper-tier program. Medicaid is much bigger than three out of five upper-tier programs.

Financing

According to Theda Skocpol, politically successful social programs must have reliable sources of funding.[49] What counts as reliable, she argues, has changed over time. Civil War pensions of the late nineteenth century were financed out of protective tariffs, which were then a major source of revenue. Since World War II, the recipe for success has been based on revenues from the national government as opposed to state governments, and in particular on earmarked payroll taxes and trust funds. This is the recipe created for Social Security and later copied for disability insurance and Medicare.

One advantage of this approach is that such revenues are more or less insulated from the often difficult choices elected officials must make among competing policy priorities. This is particularly important when officials feel pressured to clamp down on spending, as has been the case in recent decades. Another advantage is that citizens feel more protective of social programs when they see clearly how much they have paid to sustain them. They feel a sense of ownership. President Franklin Roosevelt clearly understood this feeling. Responding to criticisms about the regressive nature of the payroll tax, FDR said: "I guess you're right on the economics, but those taxes were never a problem of economics. They are politics all the way through. We put the payroll contributions there so as to give the contributors a legal, moral and political right to collect their pensions. . . . With those taxes in there, no damn politician can ever scrap my social security program."[50]

The financing of welfare makes it more vulnerable. For one thing, monies come from a combination of state and national coffers. Historically, states have paid for 40–50 percent of welfare costs.[51] Pressure to keep taxes low, in order to attract businesses and affluent individuals, gives states little room to raise taxes and increase benefits, as the national government has done many times with Social Security.[52] Moreover, funding for welfare comes from general revenues at the national and state levels, meaning that it must compete with national defense, space exploration, environmental protection, education, law enforcement, and a host of other priorities. Finally, welfare recipients are not required to pay income or property taxes in order to receive benefits. Compared to Social Security recipients, they may appear less entitled to benefits based on past contributions.

Not every social program in the lower tier relies as heavily on state governments for funding. Although Medicaid does, states pay a small fraction of the total cost of SSI and of Food Stamps, which are two of the larger means-tested programs. The same is true of smaller programs such as Head Start. The Earned Income Tax Credit and Section 8 rental vouchers are financed entirely by the national government.[53]

The variation among upper-tier programs is at least as large.[54] For example, the income subject to payroll taxation is capped in Social Security and disability insurance, but not in Medicare. All wage and salary income above $90,000 was exempt from Social Security taxes in 2005, making it a regressive tax. Someone earning $150,000 a year pays a lower effective rate than someone earning $30,000 a year. Among other things, this means that women and racial minorities typically pay a larger share of their incomes to Social Security than do men and whites, who are better paid. Everyone pays the same rate under Medicare, so it is financed by a flat tax.

Unlike Social Security or Medicare, unemployment taxes are experience rated. Employers who have fired many workers in the past are penalized with a higher tax rate. The UI tax is designed not only to raise revenues but also to discourage employers from engaging in socially undesirable behavior. It represents a cross between a traditional payroll tax and a "sin" tax on the consumption of alcoholic beverages or gasoline.

The most important deviations from Social Security occur with the financing of Medicare and workers' compensation. Part A of Medicare, which covers hospitalization and some nursing-home care, is compulsory and financed, like Social Security, out of payroll taxes. Part B, which covers more routine doctor care, is voluntary and financed by a combination of general revenues and monthly premiums paid by the elderly—but no payroll tax. Because these premiums cover about one-quarter of the cost of benefits, the vast majority of the elderly enroll. Medicare (B) cost $89 billion in 2000 (rising to $100 billion in 2001), making it one big exception.[55] The new prescription drug benefit, technically known as Medicare part D, will also be financed from a mix of general revenues and individual premiums, not payroll taxes. It is expected to cost $50–80 billion annually in the coming years.

Workers' compensation is structured much differently. About the only role for the national government is running workers' comp programs for its own employees. Otherwise, financing is handled at the state level, and not necessarily by state authorities. In a handful of states, employers are compelled to pay into a public compensation fund. Everywhere else, state governments compel employers to buy workers' compensation insurance but allow them to purchase from a private carrier or to self-insure. While employers in some of those states also have the option of buying insurance from a public fund, about half of the American states do not offer this option. Employers must work directly through the market. As a result, the financing of workers' compensation is more private than public: less than one-fifth of every dollar paid to injured workers in 2000 came from a public fund. In theory, workers' compensation is social insurance. In practice, it contains a large dose of social regulation.[56]

Relying on payroll taxes and trust funds is not the only way to protect the financing of social programs. They can also receive special treatment in the federal budget process. The key distinction is whether a program is classified as mandatory or discretionary spending. With mandatory spending, "Congress generally determines spending for those benefit programs by setting rules for eligibility, benefit formulas, and other parameters rather than by appropriating specific dollar amounts each year."[57] Budgetary entitlements are the largest component of mandatory spending, followed by interest on the debt. Mandatory spending is considered to be privileged. If legislators do nothing, the program will continue to be financed. For this reason observers sometimes refer to mandatory spending as automatic spending. Demographic trends and economic conditions largely determine the growth of mandatory spending. Discretionary spending, in contrast, must be appropriated every year or the program will cease to exist. Most agricultural, energy, environmental, and transportation programs fall in this category. In addition, budgetary rules adopted by Congress to limit the growth of spending in the 1990s usually imposed "softer" caps on mandatory than on discretionary spending. With such advantages, we might well expect mandatory spending to become a larger share of the federal budget, and we would be right. Mandatory spending accounts for almost two-thirds of the federal budget, up from one-third in the early 1960s.[58]

The national government classifies all the upper-tier programs except workers' comp as mandatory spending. TANF is classified as discretionary spending. These facts square with the classic two-tiered model. The problem is that the largest programs in the lower tier—Medicaid, Food Stamps, SSI, EITC—are also classified as mandatory spending.[59] Because so little means-tested spending is discretionary, the usual line separating the two tiers cannot hold.

Public Opinion

Americans hate welfare and have for a long time. Since at least the late 1960s, people have thought the country was spending too much on welfare rather than too little. In the mid-1990s, the ratio of people replying "too much" to "too little" when questioned by pollsters was four to one. Kent Weaver examined many opinion polls leading up to the historic 1996

TABLE 2.3
Cracks in the Tiers (Part 2)

Program Characteristics	Classic Distinctions		Major Exceptions	
	Upper	Lower	Upper	Lower
Size	Large	Small	DI, workers' comp, UI	Medicaid, EITC, Food Stamps
Financing	National	National + state	Workers' comp	EITC, Section 8 vouchers, SSI, Food Stamps
	Payroll tax	General revenues	Medicare B and D, workers' comp	
	Mandatory	Discretionary	Workers' comp	Medicaid, SSI, EITC, Food Stamps
Public Support	Strong	Weak	Middle class vs.	Poor
			Social Security vs.	SSI
			Medicare vs.	Medicaid

welfare reform law and discovered that Americans were ready to support all kinds of policy changes because they were so dissatisfied with the status quo. At bottom, people thought welfare was antithetical to core values of work and self-sufficiency. Their dissatisfaction paved the way for significant changes such as the addition of time limits and the loss of entitlement status. By the same token, Americans have consistently expressed strong support for Social Security. In the mid-1990s, almost seven times as many people said the government was spending too little on Social Security compared to those who said too much.[60] If we stopped here, the popularity of the two tiers would appear to be quite different.

Of course, we should not stop there. As Martin Gilens and others have shown, Americans support just about every part of their welfare state except welfare. Americans want to spend more on Social Security and Medicare—and more on Medicaid, child care for poor children, food programs for low-income individuals, programs to fight homelessness, and a number of other parts of the lower tier. When asked about "poor people" or "fighting poverty," Americans are much more supportive than when asked about "welfare." Gilens found that the ratio of people wanting to increase versus decrease spending on the poor is virtually identical to the ratio for Social Security. By examining comparable programs in the two tiers, he showed that SSI garners as much support as Social Security, and Medicaid just a bit less than Medicare. In each instance, clear majorities favor increased spending. Asked whether it was more important for government to spend money to help the poor or the middle class, more people sided with the poor.[61]

Much of Gilens's evidence is now ten years old, so we might wonder whether the public's views have changed. In 2005 large majorities of Americans said that Social Security (88%), Medicare (83%), *and* Medicaid (74%) were "very important" government programs—more so than defense and military spending (57%) or foreign aid (20%). Only 8 percent of respondents thought that their state government was spending too much on the means-tested Medicaid program, which was the same as the percentage for public education, a more inclusive program. Very few people thought that the national government was spending too much on Medicaid, Medicare, or Social Security. Comparable portions of the population felt that the government was not doing enough to help poor people (59%), children (61%), or seniors (64%) pay for health care. These results are quite similar to Gilens's. Except for welfare, the main story in public opinion is the similarities between the two tiers, not the differences.[62]

The survey data are consistent with prior findings that spending in the lower tier has grown faster than in the upper tier, and that benefits per person in the lower tier can be as large as those in the upper tier. These polls and surveys are a problem for those analysts who feel that only large, inclusive social programs are capable of winning public support. We will look more closely at public opinion in chapters 6 and 7. For now, public opinion does not appear to follow the traditional lines separating the upper and lower tiers.

Building a Better Model

No model in the social sciences has to be perfect to be useful. The two-tiered model of the American welfare state should be consistent with most of the evidence but not necessarily all. The question, then, is how good is good enough? The answer depends, of course, on the criteria. My first rule of thumb for evaluating any general claim about the American welfare state is this: if one of the "Big Three" programs (Social Security, Medicare, and Medicaid) does not fit the model, then we should probably try to create a better model. These three programs dominate the American welfare state, collectively accounting for two-thirds of total spending and most of the beneficiaries. You can not leave one of them out any more than you can leave Germany out of a discussion about Europe. My second rule of thumb is that two or more exceptions in the upper tier signal trouble, as do three or more moderate-size exceptions in the lower tier. A generalization that works for only three out of the five major social insurance programs is not terribly satisfying. Nor is a generalization that might work for Medicaid and a few of the smaller means-tested programs but not the ones in between.

Time and again, the two-tiered model fails these tests. Tables 2.2 and 2.3 capture the main flaws by describing what we expect to find in each tier and identifying the main social programs that run counter to expectations. The problem is not Social Security or welfare. Social Security consistently displays all the advantages and welfare all the disadvantages that are supposed to characterize the two tiers. The most common problems are Medicaid and EITC in the lower tier and workers' compensation and unemployment insurance in the upper tier. The first pair of programs is more advantaged and the second pair more disadvantaged than we expect. Unlike a classic means-tested program, Medicaid is enormous, whether measured in dollars or people, and is classified as mandatory rather than discretionary spending in the federal budget process. Spending per patient is significantly higher in Medicaid than in Medicare. Public support for Medicaid is much closer to support for Social Security and Medicare than to support for welfare. The Earned Income Tax Credit is a fast-growing income transfer run entirely by the national government and administered uniformly across the states. It, too, enjoys protection in the budget process. In several respects the EITC looks more like Social Security than welfare. Compared to Social Security and Medicare, workers' comp and UI are small programs whose benefits vary considerably by state. The financing of workers' compensation hardly qualifies it as social insurance. Most of the unemployed do not collect UI benefits, and those who do cannot receive benefits for very long.

In short, if you want to argue that the American welfare state is two-tiered, you must first limit your discussion to Social Security and welfare, then ignore all the other social programs; or you must emphasize selective features of social programs and hope that readers make the (faulty) inference that all the other features follow the same pattern. Neither option seems terribly attractive. This is not to say that a two-tiered model has always been inaccurate. By the end of the twentieth century, though, it was.[63]

I am less certain what ought to replace the two-tiered model. Ideally, I would like to offer readers something to take its place, something more than a laundry list of the unique features of individual programs. The idea of creating a typology appeals to the part of me that wants to see patterns in politics. It need not be separate tiers; a continuum of social programs might be more appropriate. The idea of thinking in terms of social programs that are more or less advantaged is also appealing. What follows, then, is closer to informed speculation than to well-developed argument.

How we categorize social programs depends on what features we deem important. If our ideal is large, generous programs that enjoy popular support and can expand over time (i.e., something like the classic European model), then we might rank Social Security and Medicare at the top, Medicaid close behind, and welfare at the bottom. The main categories are not social insurance and public assistance; they are elderly and nonelderly. Granted, the three top programs serve a variety of clients: Social Security benefits go to surviving spouses and children; Medicare covers some of the disabled; and Medicaid covers millions of poor children and poor disabled. Nevertheless, the elderly are major beneficiaries of each program and receive most of the benefits. The U.S. Congressional Budget Office (CBO) calculated in 2000 that the national government spends four times more on the elderly than on children. Almost all of that spending occurred through Social Security, Medicare, and Medicaid. Even when the parents of children were included, spending favored the elderly by more than three to one. The CBO projected that the gap between the elderly and families with children would grow larger in the coming decades.[64] In other countries, this gap is smaller. Using data from the 1980s and early 1990s, Julia Lynch found that the ratio of elderly to nonelderly social spending is higher in the United States than in most OECD countries.[65]

Grouping social programs according to the age of beneficiaries does a better job of dealing with the major outliers in the two-tiered model. It drops UI and workers' compensation out of the old upper tier and elevates Medicaid out of the old lower tier. To refine this alternative model, we might distinguish among the nonelderly, perhaps placing the handicapped ahead of working families, with nonworking families at the very bottom. Just below the Big Three would be disability insurance, workers' comp, and SSI. Below them would be the EITC and unemployment insurance. Public housing and Food Stamps would be further down. This ranking is by no means perfect, but it does seem to be a step in the right direction. In this case, we might step back and conclude that the American welfare state offers the most help to people who are deemed unable to support themselves through wage labor (the elderly and the handicapped) and the least help to people who could be employed but are not.

Before readers become too enamored with this alternative, allow me (once again) to muddy the waters. One possible complication is education, which some scholars consider to be part of the welfare state and others do not.[66] When the Congressional Budget Office calculated spending on the elderly and on children, it included education spending by the national government ($20 billion for kindergarten through twelfth grade, or K–12). State and local governments, however, provide the majority of educational funding. In 2000 governments spent a total of $388 billion on public elementary and secondary education in the United States, and almost $170 billion on public colleges and universities. If one includes all that spending, then the gap between the elderly and children starts to disappear. When Lynch incorporated education into her cross-national comparisons, the ratio of elderly spending to nonelderly spending in the United States was no longer high, just average.[67]

A second complication is race. As mentioned before, a bias in favor of the elderly is a bias against African-Americans. Blacks are less likely to receive retirement benefits and Medicare than are whites, and they are more likely to receive welfare. The third quotation at the start of the chapter, stressing the importance of age and race, appears to be on target. At least, it is on target with respect to the high and low ends of my scale. To be more certain, it would help to know how race intersects with many of the programs in the middle—workers' compensation, unemployment insurance, and the EITC, for example. To my knowledge, racial data on those programs are scarce or nonexistent. To get a better sense of the impact of race on social policy, we may need to gather different kinds of data and analyze them in a different way.

Finally, everything said so far in this chapter has been based on the traditional tools of social policy. Having stressed the significance of non-traditional tools in chapter 1, I cannot finish without bringing some of them back into consideration. Even a cursory examination of tax expenditures, loan guarantees, and social regulation reveals interesting countertrends. The more inclusive tax expenditures, for instance, are financed not out of payroll taxes but out of general revenues (as are all tax expenditures). The largest of these, however, are not available to as many people as Social Security and Medicare. They tend to benefit anywhere from one-half to two-thirds of the population that receives health insurance or retirement pensions from employers, or that owns a home. In terms of scope of coverage, the largest tax expenditures are smaller than the largest social insurance programs but bigger than almost everything else. The home mortgage interest deduction, for example, was claimed on over 37 million tax returns in 2004, to the tune of $70 billion. Other tax expenditures, such as the deduction for charitable contributions, and some social regulations are effectively targeted at the well-to-do.[68] None of these features conforms well with a two-tiered model. (I will say more about the distribution of benefits in chapter 10.)

Moreover, many of these latter tools of U.S. social policy do not benefit the elderly. They benefit adults in their working years and their children—the same people who look like second-class citizens in the traditional wing of the American welfare state. About two-thirds of the U.S. population is covered by private health insurance. These people are not old enough for Medicare or poor enough for Medicaid. The vast majority are between the ages of eighteen and sixty-four. Their coverage is not entirely private, because companies get to deduct the cost of health insurance from their taxable income. This tax expenditure cost the government $75 billion in 2005.[69] The Child Tax Credit (CTC), a de facto family allowance, has already grown larger than TANF or any of the major food programs. Among the major social regulations, minimum wage laws and the Americans with Disabilities Act are both aimed at helping workers and their families. The same goes for the Family and Medical Leave Act. Regulations known as COBRA and HIPAA laws are designed to make private health insurance easier to get and keep. Federal loan guarantees for housing are targeted at first-time buyers with average or below-average incomes, typically adults in their twenties and thirties.

These tools serve the elderly as well. Tax expenditures for retirement pensions are every bit as large as for health insurance. One of the government's major insurance programs, the Pension Benefit Guaranty Corporation, exists to protect workers against the loss of their company pensions. Some scholars argue that tax breaks for home owners are a large if indirect subsidy to the elderly, considering that homes are often their single largest asset.[70] In the United States, the various tax expenditures for home owners cost over $100 billion in 2005. If we assume that most of the elderly have paid off most or all of their mortgages, then we can reasonably expect that most of the beneficiaries of the home mortgage interest deduction are adults in their working years. Here is one policy that seems to bridge generations, which may help explain its popularity and growth.[71]

In short, these nontraditional tools may balance out, to some degree, the age bias we observe in the traditional welfare state. The mix of social policy tools targeted at people of different ages varies over an individual's life cycle. The United States leans heavily on grants for children (TANF, Food Stamps, Medicaid, K–12 education) and on social insurance (Social Security, Medicare) for the elderly. In the middle years, workers and their families are subsidized through the tax code or helped by regulations affecting their wages and benefits. Thus, no national health insurance for them, but tax subsidies and regulations for medical care. No European-style family allowances, but tax credits for children and tax deductions for child care expenses. Not much job training or retraining to boost workers' incomes, but minimum wage laws and the EITC.[72] Compared to other nations, the United States may be distinctive in the mix of policy tools it uses to address various social needs over the course of individual lives. We will not see much family policy or housing policy in the United States if all we look for are social insurance programs or grants. Analysts ought to incorporate these alternative tools into their models of the American welfare state before offering any definitive judgments about winners and losers.

CHAPTER 3

Twice in a Lifetime

THE FIRST TWO CHAPTERS OF THIS BOOK have been designed to help readers understand the current size and shape of the American welfare state. This chapter identifies key moments in its historical development. The story we usually hear is that the American welfare state emerged late, years after welfare states took root in Europe. The major parts originated during the New Deal and the Great Society. The changes were so sudden and dramatic that some scholars refer to these periods as the two "big bangs" of the American welfare state.[1] Not coincidentally, these same two periods represent the high-water marks of Democratic Party power in the twentieth century. The first part of this chapter develops this traditional account of the origins of the American welfare state with an emphasis on party politics.

This is not the only way to tell the story. A much different narrative emerges if we broaden our vision beyond the classic social insurance and public assistance programs. New tax expenditures, loan guarantees, and social regulations emerged steadily throughout the twentieth century. Some even began before the 1930s, which cuts down the time lag separating the birth of the American welfare state from its European counterparts. Consequently, huge Democratic majorities were not always necessary to produce new social programs in the United States. A number of new social programs originated under divided government. The second part of this chapter develops an alternative chronology of the American welfare state, based on a wider range of policy tools.

ORIGINS (TAKE 1): THE TWO BIG BANGS

The defining feature of modern welfare states is usually thought to be social insurance (chapter 1). Before such programs emerged, local governments in many countries had long offered some aid to the poor through a combination of cash relief and forced labor. In the late nineteenth and early twentieth centuries, several nations started to add social insurance programs to cover sickness, disability, unemployment, and old age. Germany pioneered social insurance in the 1880s, and many other European countries followed suit by 1920. The United States did not adopt old age and unemployment insurance until 1935, and it has never enacted national health insurance. This is another sense, apart from size, in which the United States is supposed to be a welfare state laggard.[2]

Most of the programs we typically associate with the American welfare state became law in the 1930s and 1960s. President Franklin Roosevelt signed the historic Social Security Act on August 14, 1935. This Act was the epicenter of the first big bang, in large part because it marked the debut of social insurance at the national level. Title II of the Act created old age insurance; Title III created unemployment insurance. In addition, the Social Security Act federalized programs that had previously been exclusive responsibilities of state and local governments—cash grants to the poor blind, the poor elderly, and the children of poor single-parent (i.e., single-mother) families.* This last program, Aid to Dependent Children, is what many people think of as the national government's first "welfare" program. The other legislative milestones of this era include the Housing Act of 1937, which authorized construction of low-income public housing units. The Social Security Amendments of 1939 added survivors benefits to Old Age Insurance, creating what we now call Social Security. Thus, the 1930s gave us Social Security, the largest piece of the American welfare state (and for many years the largest item in the national budget), and welfare, historically the most contentious piece of the American welfare state.

The 1940s and 1950s are usually portrayed as a time of incremental expansion to existing programs. Social Security was extended from industrial workers to agricultural and domestic workers in 1950, paving the way for many more African-Americans to receive benefits. With the exception of disability insurance (1956), no major social programs were enacted. Our understanding of this era might be different had President Truman won more support for national health insurance in the late 1940s, but he was unable to overcome opposition by the American Medical Association and congressional conservatives. A partial substitute for national health insurance arrived in 1965 with the enactment of Medicare for the elderly and Medicaid for the poor. This was the peak of the second big bang, which also produced Food Stamps and a variety of means-tested job training and social service programs. Most of these programs were part of President Johnson's Great Society, which he envisioned as the worthy successor to President Roosevelt's New Deal.

---

* By "federalized," I mean that national and state governments shared responsibility for financing and administration. If the programs were "nationalized," then responsibility would belong solely to the national government.

In both the 1930s and the 1960s, the new programs included some that were truly national in their financing and administration (Social Security, Medicare) and some that were truly federal (Aid to Dependent Children, unemployment insurance, Medicaid). In both eras, the main beneficiaries were the elderly and the poor. They were helped, however, in different ways in each era. Whereas most of the new social programs of the 1930s offered income support, programs created in the 1960s usually offered some kind of service like medical care or job training. In most cases these services were financed by government but provided by third parties from the private or nonprofit sectors. The doctors and nurses who treat Medicare and Medicaid patients, for example, are not government employees. Nevertheless, national and state governments do provide much of their income, and we would expect them to become an important constituency for Medicare and Medicaid.

Scholars have devoted considerable energy toward trying to understand why the American welfare state emerged in two brief but dramatic spasms. What happened in the 1930s and 1960s that did not during the rest of the twentieth century? The answer is not economic crisis: the 1930s featured a prolonged depression, but the 1960s were a generally prosperous decade. Explanations rooted in national values do not seem terribly satisfactory, either, considering that values change gradually and these new social programs appeared quite suddenly. The most obvious thread linking these two periods is Democratic control of government.[3]

More precisely, the thread involves Democratic presidents who won election by large margins and who worked with Congresses in which Democrats enjoyed huge majorities. The 1932 election brought Franklin Roosevelt into the White House and gave Democrats unified control for the first time in almost two decades. Roosevelt won approximately 60 percent of the popular vote and a whopping 90 percent of the Electoral College vote in 1932 and 1936. The elections from 1932 to 1936 produced some of the most one-sided Congresses in U.S. history. After the 1934 midterm election, Democrats outnumbered Republicans by a three to one margin in the House and enjoyed almost as large a lead in the Senate. Between 1928 and 1936, Democrats essentially doubled their numbers in the House and the Senate, a truly historic surge. If anyone had a mandate for change, it was the Democratic Party of the 1930s.

Almost all these gains came from outside the southern and border states. In the mid-1920s, more than half of congressional Democrats were from the South, and two-thirds were from southern or border states. By the mid-1930s, fewer than a third of the Democrats in Congress were from the South and fewer than half were from the southern and border states. The conservative coalition of Republicans and Southern Democrats, previously a dominant majority in Congress, had been weakened to a point where new social programs were now possible. The Roosevelt administration still had to make concessions because longtime Southern Democrats still controlled important committees in Congress. But the policy changes that Roosevelt and the more liberal Democrats in Congress did bring about were unprecedented. The Democrats' advantage started to erode when the party lost over seventy House seats in the 1938 midterm election, almost all of which were outside the South.[4] The window of opportunity for Roosevelt and the left wing of the Democratic Party had started to close. The peak of their power, however, overlapped almost perfectly with the first big bang of the American welfare state.[5]

The story for the 1960s is similar, though a bit less dramatic. Lyndon Johnson won a larger share of the popular vote in 1964 than any president in American history. Like FDR, he also won 90 percent of the Electoral College vote. Democrats outnumbered Republicans by more than two to one in the House and Senate during the pivotal Eighty-ninth Congress, which passed Medicare and Medicaid.[6] True, Democrats enjoyed a sizable advantage in Congress starting in 1958, which helps explain some of the smaller social policy innovations that occurred before the Johnson administration.[7] But they did not have such a popular president until LBJ (after all, Kennedy beat Nixon by the slimmest of margins in 1960), and their advantage in Congress reached its peak in the 1965–66 term. The 1966 election was akin to that of 1938, producing large losses for congressional Democrats and helping to close the window for new social programs. Once again, the party's fortunes coincided nicely with a big bang of the American welfare state.

No other comparable period of Democratic power existed in the twentieth century. Democratic Presidents Woodrow Wilson, Harry Truman, John Kennedy, and Bill Clinton all failed to win 50 percent of the popular vote. Jimmy Carter managed but 50.1 percent in 1976, and he is widely regarded as the most conservative Democratic president of the twentieth century. Truman and Clinton had to contend with divided government for some part of their administrations. For two brief moments (1949–50 and 1993–94), these presidents enjoyed fairly large Democratic majorities in Congress. Not surprisingly, these were also the two times when national health insurance came closest to passage. Both times, the Democrats' margin in the House was smaller than in the mid-1930s or the mid-1960s, and perhaps more important, there were fewer than sixty Democrats in the Senate—the number needed to stop the opposition from filibustering a bill to death.

Election results are not the only way to demonstrate the significance of political parties. The public statements of leading politicians give us more evidence for the stark differences between Democrats and Republicans.

On the day he signed the Social Security Act into law, President Franklin Roosevelt declared:

> Today a hope of many years' standing is in large part fulfilled. The civilization of the past hundred years, with its startling industrial changes, has tended more and more to make life insecure. Young people have come to wonder what would be their lot when they came to old age. The man with a job has wondered how long the job would last.
>
> This social security measure gives at least some protection to thirty millions of our citizens who will reap direct benefits through unemployment compensation, through old-age pensions and through increased services for the protection of children and the prevention of ill health.
>
> We can never insure one hundred percent of the population against one hundred percent of the hazards and vicissitudes of life, but we have tried to frame a law which will give some measure of protection to the average citizen and to his family against the loss of a job and against poverty-ridden old age.
>
> This law, too, represents a cornerstone in a structure which is being built but is by no means complete.[8]

One year later Alf Landon, the Republican candidate for president, offered a blistering attack on Roosevelt's policies. Campaigning before an audience in Milwaukee, Landon declared that the Social Security Act "assumes that Americans are irresponsible. It assumes that old-age pensions are necessary because Americans lack the foresight to provide for their old age. I refuse to accept any such judgment of my fellow-citizens. . . . To get a workable old-age pension plan we must repeal the present compulsory insurance plan. The Republican party is pledged to do this."[9]

If we fast-forward to the 1960s, we can hear President Lyndon Johnson promoting Medicare in words that echo Roosevelt's: "No longer will older Americans be denied the healing miracle of modern medicine. No longer will illness crush and destroy the savings that they have so carefully, put away over a lifetime so that they might enjoy dignity in their later years. No longer will young families see their own incomes, and their own hopes, eaten away simply because they are carrying out their deep moral obligations to their parents, and to their uncles, and their aunts."[10] Donald Rumsfeld, the current secretary of defense but in 1965 a young House Republican, voiced a much different opinion. He found it "regrettable that the majority of the committee on Ways and Means has felt it necessary to institute a program which is just another step toward Government management of individual income."[11]

If we fast-forward again to the mid-1990s, we see a similar gulf regarding government aid to the poor. At one point in the congressional debate over welfare reform, Rep. John Mica (R-FL) held up a sign that read, "Do Not Feed The Alligators." He explained that just as tourists in his home state had to be reminded that feeding alligators fostered a dangerous sort of dependence, policy makers should remember not to treat welfare recipients too well. His Republican colleague, Rep. Barbara Cubin, preferred to think in terms of wolves (probably because she hailed from Wyoming). Welfare recipients were liked caged wolves that had to be coaxed and pushed to return to the wild. Not surprisingly, a number of Democrats took exception to these comparisons. "Don't feed the alligators, feed the children," retorted Eleanor Holmes Norton (D-DC).[12] Congressional Democrats offered their own vivid images of Republican plans for welfare reform, the most controversial of which involved Nazi Germany.[13]

All these statements illustrate well-known ideological differences between the two parties over the proper role of government. Whereas Republicans see inevitable trade-offs between government involvement and individual liberty, many Democrats believe that government can foster liberty. Democrats believe that decent Social Security benefits give the elderly a chance to live independently, enhancing both their liberty and that of their grown children. More Democrats than Republicans believe that government is needed to create true equality of opportunity. Head Start is a good example.

Of course, moments as rich and historic as the mid-1930s and mid-1960s cannot be explained solely with reference to political parties. The tragic assassination of President Kennedy in 1963 certainly helped build momentum for Johnson's new social programs. And the Democratic Party under Roosevelt and Johnson will never be mistaken for Sweden's Social Democratic Party or Britain's Labour Party during the same period. Even at their peak, America's Democrats were more willing to means-test, less willing to redistribute income, and more willing to work around existing benefit programs offered in the private sector. Nevertheless, the ebb and flow of Democratic Party power matches up so well with the formative moments of the American welfare state, and the causal connection with political power seems so well established in other nations and so plausible here, that it is hard to avoid the conclusion that the balance of power between Democrats and Republicans has been an important influence on the formative moments of the American welfare state.[14]

ORIGINS (TAKE 2): MORE TOOLS, LESS DRAMA

Assuming that you are convinced about the wisdom of including a variety of policy tools to arrive at a workable understanding of the American welfare state, I will now offer a more complete chronology of new U.S. social programs in the twentieth century. In effect, I am running the camera over the same historical landscape included in the "two big bang" version but pulling back to capture more of the terrain. The relevant functional categories used here—retirement pensions, medical care, housing, social services, family allowances, job training, and income support for the poor, the disabled, and the unemployed—are those commonly associated with the modern welfare state. In addition, I have included education, which past studies of the welfare state have sometimes included and sometimes excluded. Because I believe that national government involvement defines the welfare state, I have generally omitted programs that operate solely at the state and local levels.[15] Examples include general assistance/general relief and state-level versions of the Earned Income Tax Credit, and they are generally quite small. For ease of presentation, I include only the larger national programs, leaving aside dozens of relatively small grants and tax expenditures that also dot the landscape. I define "large" as any social program costing $5 billion or more in 2000. This means excluding smaller programs such as grants for job training and the tax deduction for child and dependent care expenses. Collectively, these smaller programs account for less than 10 percent of social spending, so we are not missing much.

Not every social program can be measured by dollars spent. Determining which loan and loan guarantee programs, insurance programs, and social regulations to include is therefore more difficult. I have relied in part on objective measures such as the total size of loan obligations (eliminating the smaller loan and loan guarantee programs) and in part on the judgments of other scholars who have studied these tools. The insurance tool is fairly straightforward because only one program, the Pension Benefit Guaranty Corporation, clearly has social welfare objectives, and it is also one of the largest insurance programs run by the national government. Altogether, I have identified about fifty major social programs created during the twentieth century (half a dozen of which involve education). They are grouped into two categories, traditional and nontraditional. The former includes social insurance, grants, and vouchers; the latter includes tax expenditures, social regulation, loans, loan guarantees, and insurance.

Missing, however, are social programs that may have been large at some earlier point in time but were later eliminated or replaced. Prominent examples include Civil War pensions of the late nineteenth and early twentieth centuries, the public works programs of the 1930s, the Kerr-Mills program providing medical care to the elderly poor (early 1960s), and the Medicare Catastrophic Coverage Act (late 1980s). My main interest is in large, durable social programs; other scholars may be more interested in policy dead ends and reversals, and that kind of history certainly has value as well.[16]

Because I want to know if including a wider range of policy tools changes our views about the importance of the 1930s and the 1960s, I have divided the twentieth century into five eras: pre–New Deal (1900–1932), New Deal (1932–40), 1940s and 1950s, Great Society (1960s), and post–Great Society (1970s–90s).[17] This way we can see which new programs have coincided with the classic big bangs of the American welfare state (and peaks of Democratic Party power) and which have not.

A couple of patterns in table 3.1 stand out immediately. The first is that the significance of the 1930s and 1960s goes beyond the traditional tools of social policy. A year before the landmark Social Security Act, the Roosevelt administration tried to increase home ownership by creating loan guarantees for individuals who might not otherwise qualify for loans at a private bank. At the time, lenders typically required a 50 percent down payment and full repayment of the loan within five years; given those terms, most people rented. Known as FHA loans, this program still serves a large number of first-time home buyers and a disproportionate share of racial minorities. In the process, the government helped to reshape the market for housing credit by showing lenders in the private sector that they could demand smaller down payments and longer loan periods and still stay in business.[18] In 1938, just before the decisive midterm elections, Roosevelt won passage of the Fair Labor Standards Act, establishing the first national minimum wage law. The Johnson administration likewise deployed a variety of policy tools while building its Great Society. The Higher Education Act (1965) created guaranteed student loans for college, and the Fair Housing Act (1968) included regulations aimed at ending racial discrimination in housing.[19] The 1930s and the 1960s were indeed two very fertile periods for the American welfare state.

Nevertheless, fewer than half of the new social programs identified in table 3.1 originated during the New Deal and the Great Society. This figure is a little misleading: not all programs are created equal, and the enactment of Social Security, unemployment insurance, Aid to Dependent Children, Medicare, and Medicaid were clearly pivotal moments. But the fact remains that important pieces of the American welfare state appeared before the New Deal; other important pieces appeared between the New Deal and Great Society, and still others after the Great Society. New social programs do not appear once in a lifetime, or even twice. They happen all the time.

Scholars usually portray the pre–New Deal period as a time when state and local governments accomplished more than the national government.[20] National health insurance made some headway in Washington during the 1910s but ultimately failed by 1920. Among other reasons, the idea of imitating Europe, and in particular Germany, lost its appeal after World War I. Other forms of social insurance (e.g., retirement

TABLE 3.1
Timing of Major New Social Programs during the Twentieth Century

Major Era	Traditional Programs (social insurance, grants)	Nontraditional Programs (tax expenditures, loan guarantees, social regulation, insurance)
Pre–New Deal (1900–1932)	1910s–1920s: workers' compensation (social insurance in some states)*	1910s–1920s: workers' compensation (social regulation in most states)*
		Tax expenditures for home mortgage interest, property taxes on homes, interest on life insurance (all 1913); employer pensions (1914–26); charitable contributions (1917); workers' compensation benefits (1918); capital gains at death (1921)
New Deal (1932–1940)	1935: Social Security Act creates Old Age Insurance, unemployment insurance, Aid to Dependent Children, Old Age Assistance, and Aid to the Blind	1934: FHA loan guarantees for housing
	1937: public housing 1939: survivors insurance	1938: Minimum wage, maximum hours laws (social regulation)
1940s and 1950s	1944: GI Bill (grants for college education) 1946: subsidized school lunches 1956: disability insurance	Tax expenditures for Social Security benefits (1941) and extraordinary medical expenses (1942) 1944: GI Bill (VA loan guarantees for housing) Tax expenditures for capital gains on home sales (1951) and employer health insurance (1954) 1958: National Defense Student (Perkins) Loans
Great Society (1960s)	1964: Food Stamps 1965: Medicare, Medicaid, Head Start, Elementary and Secondary Education Act	1962: Tax expenditure for Keogh retirement plans (self-employed) 1965: Guaranteed student loans, Stafford loans 1968: Fair Housing Act (social regulation re racial discrimination)

* Never enacted by national government.

TABLE 3.1 (*cont'd*)

Major Era	Traditional Programs (social insurance, grants)	Nontraditional Programs (tax expenditures, loan guarantees, social regulation, insurance)
Post–Great Society (1970s–1990s)	1972: Supplemental Security Income; Pell grants (higher education) 1974: Section 8 housing 1980: Adoption assistance and foster care	1970: Tax expenditure for Medicare benefits 1974: ERISA creates new regulations re company retirement and health plans; Pension Benefit Guaranty Corporation (insurance); and a new tax expenditure for Individual Retirement Accounts 1975: Earned Income Tax Credit 1980: PLUS loans (education) 1985: COBRA regulations (health insurance)
	1990: Child care block grant	1990: Americans with Disabilities Act (social regulation) 1993: Family and Medical Leave Act (social regulation); direct student loans 1996: HIPAA regulations (health insurance)
	1997: State Children's Health Insurance Program	1997: Child Tax Credit

* Never enacted by national government.

pensions) never got this close. The American states proved more receptive. Almost every state enacted a workers' compensation law during the 1910s and 1920s.[21] Some laws established a monopoly state fund and were financed along traditional social insurance principles. Most states, however, opted to rely on social regulation and tort law to handle workplace accidents. They required employers to make some provision for injured workers, either by buying a private insurance policy or setting aside some of their own funds. And they often allowed injured workers to retain the option of seeking compensation through the courts. Workers' compensation thus relied on different tools in different states, which is why the program appears in two different columns in table 3.1. For a variety of reasons, workers' compensation remained at the state level during the New Deal, untouched by the Social Security Act or any other national legislation. The failure to establish a single, nationwide workers' compensation program proved remarkably durable. As mentioned in chapter 2, the U.S. government still plays virtually no role in workers' compensation, which is highly unusual among welfare states around the world.[22] I will have more to say about this anomaly in chapter 8, where I consider it in the context of states as policy laboratories.

Despite the failure of national health insurance, some national social programs did emerge in the first decades of the twentieth century. They just were not the usual suspects. The evidence in Table 3.1 indicates that tax expenditure, not social insurance or grants, was the first policy tool deployed by the national government. Some of the largest tax expenditures with social welfare objectives, such as the deductions for home mortgage interest and property taxes on homes, were enacted when the individual income tax became permanent in 1913.[23] The favorable tax treatment of employer pensions developed gradually, first via administrative rulings by the Treasury Department and later by the Revenue Acts of 1921 and 1926. Although it is tempting to view the Social Security Act as the starting point for a national retirement policy, we can see that public support for private pensions came first. In short, the New Deal appears to lose absolute title to the birth of the American welfare state. The right year might be 1913, not 1935, and if that is the case, then there is no meaningful gap between the start of the American welfare state and the start of many European welfare states. Once again, the "laggard" label so often applied to the United States seems undeserved.[24]

The period between the New Deal and the Great Society is generally understood as a time when national health insurance failed again and when the new tier of social insurance programs grew larger than the old tier of public assistance. Spending on Social Security, which was initially a modest program, surpassed spending on the means-tested Old Age Assistance program for the first time in the 1950s.* Disability insurance was added to Social Security in 1956. What also becomes clear is that other kinds of social programs continued to emerge. Unlike the 1930s, the 1940s and 1950s produced important tax expenditures in health care, housing, and retirement income. The most important innovation was the favorable tax treatment of employer health insurance (1954). It and the similar treatment of employer pensions are now the largest tax expenditures in the budget, together costing close to $200 billion per year. The GI Bill (1944) offered veterans loan guarantees for home purchases and grants to finance their college education. The terms of these VA home loans were often even more favorable than those of the FHA loans, and

---

* Old Age Assistance later became part of Supplemental Security Income (SSI).

40 percent of World War II veterans eventually took advantage of the program.

Perhaps the most interesting period is the most recent. The decades since the Great Society are widely believed to be an era of welfare state retrenchment, not only in the United States but in other affluent democracies as well. Shortly after the demise of the Clinton health plan, one respected political scientist declared that "American social policy seems to have reached a dead end: there has been no real innovation since the 1960s."[25] Scholars, most notably Paul Pierson, have started talking about a "new politics" of the welfare state, in which austerity and blame avoidance predominate. Expansion is supposed to be a thing of the past; deliberate cutbacks are more likely. The central issue is how policy makers cope with fiscal and demographic pressures on popular programs. Cuts to various antipoverty programs in 1981, the growing prominence of plans to privatize Social Security, attempts to slow the growth of Medicare, and the passage of welfare reform in 1996 all fit this pattern.[26]

Dividing the history of the American welfare state into periods of growth and retrenchment makes sense if we focus on social insurance, grants, and vouchers.[27] It makes less sense if we examine other policy tools. In the latter decades of the twentieth century, public officials rolled out new tax expenditures to promote retirement pensions, boost the income of the working poor, and defray the costs of raising children. The Earned Income Tax Credit (created in 1975) has become the single largest cash transfer to the poor and near poor. The Child Tax Credit (1997) has quickly become a major part of U.S. family policy.[28] Public officials issued hundreds and hundreds of pages of new regulations governing health and pension benefits for workers (ERISA, 1974) and working conditions for the disabled (ADA, 1990). They created the Pension Benefit Guaranty Corporation (1974) to protect workers against the risk that companies might terminate their pension plans. They created new loan programs for college students (1980). If you think of the American welfare state as a building under construction, then policy makers at the end of the twentieth century were arguing over whether certain rooms were too big at the same time that they were adding a new wing. The last decades of the twentieth century were in fact a creative period in U.S. social policy (for another twist on this history, see box 3.1).

Seen from this wider angle, the origins of the American welfare state do not translate so easily into a story of profound, episodic change. The mid-1930s and mid-1960s no longer figure so prominently. Public officials may reach for different kinds of policy tools in different eras, but they are usually reaching for something. The sheer proliferation of new social programs means that Democratic Party control may not be essential, either. To test this possibility, I will categorize the programs featured

BOX 3.1

Origins: Laws Passed or Lives Touched?

In tracing the history of the American welfare state, I have emphasized when new laws hit the books. That is standard practice among social scientists. It is quite possible, however, that those laws did not touch many lives for many years. If, at the end of the day, we care about social programs because of what they do for people, then it makes sense to trace the impact of these new laws and programs (a point that will be developed more fully in part 3 of the book). From this perspective, several key pieces of the contemporary American welfare state that became law before or during the 1930s did not affect many people until after World War II.

Some of the largest tax expenditures today appeared as early as 1913, which undercuts claims about the late development of the American welfare state. Nevertheless, few people actually benefited from those tax expenditures. The original income tax applied only to the wealthiest 2 percent of Americans. By the late 1930s, only about 6 percent of Americans paid income tax. Most individuals could not benefit, for example, from the tax deductions available to home owners. This situation changed dramatically during World War II when officials expanded the income tax to finance the war. By 1945, over 70 percent of Americans paid some income tax, which meant that many more could benefit from tax deductions and tax credits. The home mortgage interest deduction was no longer targeted at the rich.

Similarly, few companies offered pensions before the 1930s, and many of those who did made it hard for workers to qualify. Fewer than one in twenty workers had any reasonable hope of receiving a pension in the first decades of the twentieth century, so the tax expenditure for employer pensions could not have had much impact initially. Company pensions became much more common in the 1940s and 1950s. Two of the largest tax expenditures today thus conveyed few benefits during the 1910s, 1920s, and 1930s. From the standpoint of impact, the New Deal reemerges as the starting point of the American welfare state.

To be fair, we ought to examine the impact of the more traditional social programs as well. Social Security was not designed to pay monthly benefits until 1942, seven years after enactment. The program's architects wanted to collect revenues without paying benefits in order to put the program on a sound fiscal footing. The 1939 amendments moved the date up to 1940, and by 1941 a tiny fraction of individuals over the age of sixty-five were receiving monthly Social Security checks. By the end of the decade, the figure was still under 10 percent. Social Security benefits initially failed to keep pace with inflation. By 1950 the average monthly benefit check was only 19 percent of the average monthly wage, down from 30 percent in 1940. Not until the 1950s and especially the 1960s did Social Security become an important source of income for many retirees.

(boxed text continued on following page)

The more immediate impact of the Social Security Act came from Old Age Assistance (OAA) and Aid to Dependent Children (ADC), both targeted at the poor. Before regular Social Security benefits had started, OAA spending had grown to almost $500 million per year, and ADC spending was over $125 million. In 1948 the average OAA recipient received a monthly check that was 50 percent larger than the one sent to the average Social Security recipient. There were roughly 50 percent more OAA recipients as well, even if you combine all the retirees and survivors receiving Social Security. This pattern held until the historic 1950 amendments that expanded Social Security. Spending on unemployment insurance (UI) varied with the economy, making the program large in the late 1930s but small during World War II. The average UI benefit in the late 1940s was not much higher than ADC families were receiving. Based on aid given and not laws passed, the 1930s probably deserve to be called the starting point of the American welfare state, though less for the introduction of social insurance programs and more for the introduction of means-tested grants.

If the impact of nontraditional tools was quite modest prior to the 1940s, their impact since then, and particularly in recent decades, has been substantial. Switching the perspective from laws passed to lives touched does not diminish the remarkable record of new tax expenditures, social regulations, and the like since the 1970s. A number of these new social programs affected millions of individuals and families very soon after their enactment. Thus, we need not look solely at the 1930s and the 1960s for social programs that made a difference in the lives of ordinary Americans.

Sources: The figures for Social Security come from the Annual Reports of the Trustees of the Social Security program, available at http://www.ssa.gov/history/reports/trust/trustyears.html. The UI-ADC comparisons come from the 1948 Report of the Advisory Council on Social Security, available at http://www.ssa.gov/history/reports/48advisegen.html. See also Christopher Howard, *The Hidden Welfare State: Tax Expenditures and Social Policy in the United States* (Princeton, NJ: Princeton University Press, 1997), and Steven A. Sass, *The Promise of Private Pensions: The First Hundred Years* (Cambridge, MA: Harvard University Press, 1997).

in table 3.1 based on party control of government at the time of enactment. The four main categories are unified Democratic control, divided government with a Democratic president, divided government with a Republican president, and unified Republican control.

Table 3.2 summarizes the results, some of which are consistent with patterns noted earlier in the chapter. For one, unified Democratic Party control is still the most conducive environment for new social programs.

TABLE 3.2
Political Parties and New Social Programs in the Twentieth Century

Party Control	Traditional programs	Nontraditional programs	Total
Unified Democratic Party control (36 yrs.)	15	13	28
Democratic president, divided govt. (12 yrs.)	1	4	5
Republican president, divided govt. (28 yrs.)	5	8	13
Unified Republican Party control (24 yrs.)	0	3	3
Total	21	28	49

Note: Traditional programs equal social insurance and grants; nontraditional programs equal tax expenditures, loans and loan guarantees, insurance, and social regulation. Workers' compensation is omitted for reasons discussed in the text; the tax expenditure for company pensions is classified as originating under unified Republican control because the key legislation occurred in 1921 and 1926.

Over half of the programs in this study were enacted when Democrats controlled the White House and Congress. The rate of innovation was decidedly higher as well, with twenty-eight new programs in thirty-six years of Democratic control. Unified Republican control is still the most hostile environment for new social programs. In more than two decades of Republican rule, only three major social programs became law, all of them tax expenditures. Of all the decades, the 1920s was the least productive with respect to new social programs, and not surprisingly it was a high point of Republican power.

Between these two extremes are the equivalent of four decades of divided government. These years produced eighteen new social programs, or a little over one-third of the total. That is not a trivial number. Nor are the individual programs insignificant. Included in this group are Section 8 vouchers, the largest low-income housing program; the Earned Income Tax Credit; major additions to pension regulations (ERISA); as well as disability insurance and the Americans with Disabilities Act. Divided governments led by Republican presidents were just as likely to produce new social programs as divided governments led by Democratic presidents. Divided governments, regardless of the president's party, were almost as likely to produce new social programs as were unified governments.[29] All of which indicates that proponents of new social programs do not need lots of Democrats in office to succeed.

Instead, table 3.2 suggests that different combinations of party control may be associated with different tools of social policy. Fully three-quarters of the main social insurance and grant programs originated under unified Democratic control, and most of these came during the mid-1930s and mid-1960s. These are the tools Democrats reach for when they enjoy overwhelming majorities in government. (Democrats also appear to have an affinity for loan and loan guarantee programs.) When Democrats and Republicans share power, tax expenditures and social regulation become more likely. Although the contrast is not black-and-white, it does seem to be a general tendency. Rather than ask why new social programs are so hard to enact, we might ask why policy makers reach for different tools at different points in time.

CONCLUSION

If we march along the usual path of social insurance and grants, we see a clear relationship between party control and new social programs. The mid-1930s and mid-1960s were the high points of Democratic power in the twentieth century, and they featured the two big bangs of the American welfare state. Put a Democrat in the White House, give him a large margin of victory, surround him with loads of Democrats in Congress, and watch them generate programs like Social Security, welfare, Medicare, and Medicaid. It is a simple but powerful formula. Race, gender, federalism, policy experts, business, labor—all these factors and more no doubt helped define the precise shape of new social programs. Yet without strong Democratic Party control, significant new social insurance and grant programs seldom appear.[30]

This is not the way we are usually told to think about parties and the American welfare state. Most scholars, again with an eye toward Europe, emphasize the weakness of American parties. In particular, they have noted the absence of any significant labor or socialist party in the United States. The Democratic Party, the leftmost of the two major parties, does not qualify as a genuine left party in the eyes of most experts. Democrats have rarely embraced national ownership of industry, have often supported large increases in military spending, and have relied too much on the support of the have-lots to engage in much redistribution to the have-nots. Placed on the spectrum of European parties, the American Democratic Party belongs closer to a centrist liberal party than to labor or social democratic parties. One of the most important agents responsible for building modern welfare states is therefore missing in the United States. This fact is supposed to help explain why the American welfare state never achieved the size and scope of European welfare states, or made much progress in reducing inequality.[31] Nevertheless, when we shift our atten-

tion to what has happened in U.S. social policy, we gain a new appreciation for the importance of parties and party control of government.

On the other hand, if we march down a different path, one that takes
us past a wider range of policy tools, then we have to rethink the timing
of new social programs and the relationship between parties and social
policy. The 1930s and the 1960s are no longer exceptional periods. Important social programs were initiated in virtually every decade of the
twentieth century, from the home mortgage interest deduction (1913) to
the Family and Medical Leave Act (1993) and Child Tax Credit (1997).
Sometimes they were new tax expenditures, sometimes loan guarantees
or social regulation, sometimes grants or social insurance. This is a much
different portrait of the American welfare state than we commonly see.
From this perspective, Democratic Party control is no longer essential to
enact new social programs. It certainly helps—unified Democratic governments created more new programs than any other combination of party
control—but it is not essential.

A significant number of social programs, employing a variety of policy
tools, originated under divided government during the last century. They
continued to appear in the 1970s, 1980s, and 1990s, despite mounting
fiscal pressures and the greater success of Republicans running for national office. The political environment in the United States may not be
as conducive to social insurance as the environment in many European
nations. But it provides fertile ground for other kinds of social programs.
The next chapter investigates how three recent social programs took root
without unified Democratic control of government.

PART II

New Horizons

CHAPTER 4

Ogres, Onions, and Layers

(OR, HOW REPUBLICANS BUILT THE AMERICAN WELFARE STATE)

THE PREVIOUS CHAPTER OPENED with a fairly simple account of party politics and social policy. If the American welfare state were a machine, then Democrats would be the gas pedal and Republicans would be the brake. Electing more Democrats in the mid-1930s and mid-1960s meant that government churned out new social programs at a faster speed. That chapter ended with the rather intriguing finding that certain kinds of social programs have been enacted when Democrats were not particularly powerful—even when they had to share control of government with Republicans. The possibilities for expanding the welfare state do not end when Democrats lose power. To understand these possibilities more fully, I will analyze in more depth three social programs that were enacted in recent decades under divided government. Those programs are the Employee Retirement Income Security Act, the Americans with Disabilities Act, and the Child Tax Credit.

What makes these programs particularly interesting is that they originated as the ideological gulf separating congressional Democrats and Republicans widened. For reasons that go well beyond this study, the Democratic Party in Congress has become more homogeneous and more liberal over the last few decades. One reason is that the conservative southern wing of the party converted to the Republican Party or was replaced by more liberal Democrats. In 1960, for example, all twenty-two senators from the former Confederate states were Democrats. By the 1990s about one-third of them were Democrats and two-thirds were Republicans. Similarly, the House delegation from Georgia consisted of eight Republicans and three Democrats by the late 1990s. Their Americans for Democratic Action scores, which reflect their support for liberal causes, could not have been more different. The Republicans' scores ranged from several zeros to a high of 10; the Democrats scored 70, 90, and a perfect 100. Georgia's two senators, one a Republican and the other a Democrat, scored 0 and 85, respectively. Another way to appreciate the change is to examine party unity scores in Congress, which reflect how often a majority of one party opposes a majority of the other party on important votes.

In the late 1960s and early 1970s, Southern Democrats joined with the rest of their party to oppose Republicans on about half of these votes. In the 1990s, Democratic Party unity was closer to 80 percent.[1] Defections were less common because Southern Democrats had become similar to Democrats in other parts of the country.

The transformation of the South helped move the Democratic Party a bit to the left. One widely used measure of party ideology is the DW-NOMINATE scores calculated by political scientists Keith Poole and Howard Rosenthal. These scores reflect all roll call votes taken in each chamber for a given session of Congress. An overall score of zero denotes a pure moderate, with negative scores denoting liberals and positive scores conservatives. During the Eighty-ninth Congress (1965–66), at the height of the Great Society, the median score for House Democrats was –0.312. Thirty years later, the House Democrat median was –0.407. House Democrats were more liberal in the 1990s than at any other time in the twentieth century. Over the last few decades, Senate Democrats have become a bit more liberal as well.[2]

For their part, congressional Republicans became more unified and moved to the right—and faster than Democrats moved to the left. During the Eighty-ninth Congress, the average score was 0.267 for House Republicans and 0.304 for Senate Republicans. By the time of the 104th Congress (1995–96), when Republicans controlled both houses for the first time in decades, the average House Republican score was 0.429 and the average Senate score was 0.372. Not surprisingly, Republican leaders moved right along with their party. The top-ranking House Republican in the mid-1960s was Gerald Ford (0.271). His counterpart in the mid-1990s was the more conservative Newt Gingrich (0.471). One would have to go back to the Roaring Twenties to find so many Republicans as conservative as Gingrich, Tom DeLay, Jesse Helms, and company. The ideological divide separating the two major parties was larger in the 1990s than at any point since before the New Deal.

Polarization would not matter as much if one party dominated, which might produce a clear direction in policy, or if the two parties alternated in firm control of government, which might cause policy to zigzag. When the two parties remain evenly matched, as they have been in recent decades, the more likely result is legislative gridlock. There is less overlap in the "zones of acceptable outcomes" between Democrats and Republicans.[3] The combination of polarization and divided government, not to mention slower economic growth, should have made the years since the Great Society a terrible time for new social programs, yet elected officials created a number of them. How did this happen? What kind of social policies managed to take root in an environment that seemed so hostile?

TABLE 4.1
Policy Innovation under Divided Government

	ERISA	ADA	CTC
Year enacted	1974	1990	1997
Policy tool(s)	Social regulation, insurance, tax expenditure	Social regulation	Tax expenditure
Target group	Retirees	Disabled	Families with children
President	Republican	Republican	Democratic
Congress	Democratic	Democratic	Republican

ERISA: Employee Retirement Income Security Act
ADA: Americans with Disabilities Act
CTC: Child Tax Credit

To address these questions, I switch from a broad overview to a comparison of three legislative milestones enacted since the last "big bang" of the American welfare state. These cases were not selected at random. Because we already know a fair amount about grants, and because no major social insurance programs were created between 1965 and 2000, I decided to focus on some of the less traditional tools of social policy. All three programs are substantively important, affecting millions of people and costing billions of dollars. None of them has received much scholarly attention from students of the American welfare state.[4] Apart from these similarities, each used different policy tools, targeted different populations, and appeared under different versions of divided government (table 4.1). To the extent that one can use three cases to generalize about the origins of social programs since the Great Society, these are good choices.

My main objective is to analyze the role of Republicans and Democrats in the process of creating each law or program. The most likely outcome is that Republicans offered little support for new social programs but acquiesced in order to win Democrats' support for some other policy that Republicans genuinely favored. This would qualify as classic logrolling behavior, a staple of the congressional literature. In that event, Democrats would retain their title as The Party That Built the American Welfare State. Alternatively, support might have been genuinely bipartisan. The possibility that Republicans were the prime movers is unlikely but cannot be ruled out. To the extent that Republicans were involved, a second objective of these case studies is to identify reasons why.

Employee Retirement Income Security Act

Social Security is the single most important source of retirement income in the United States. More than half of the elderly rely on Social Security for more than half of their income. About a quarter of the elderly rely on Social Security for at least 90 percent of their income. This last group does not necessarily live well, for Social Security was never designed to provide an adequate income for all retirees. Indeed, many of the elderly who depend so heavily on Social Security live below the poverty line. Policy makers have long encouraged individuals to think in terms of a multilegged stool of retirement income, with Social Security as one leg and public assistance, personal savings, earnings, and employer pensions as the other major legs. The most affluent elderly are those who depend a little on Social Security and public assistance and a lot on the other sources of retirement income.[5]

It would be misleading, however, to think of these other sources as wholly "private." In particular, the U.S. government has created an intricate network of public programs designed to enhance and protect the retirement pensions offered by employers to their employees. Although public support for company pensions antedated the New Deal (via tax expenditures), the single most important milestone was passage of the Employee Retirement Income Security Act (ERISA) in 1974. ERISA relies on a combination of policy tools. Much of the legislation qualifies as social regulation, with detailed and often complex rules governing eligibility, financing, disclosure, and benefits for private pension plans. These regulations are administered by the Departments of Labor and Treasury and have prompted a veritable flood of court challenges and legislative amendments. Another part of ERISA established the Pension Benefit Guaranty Corporation (PBGC) to shield private pensions from collapse and termination.[6] With respect to personal savings, ERISA created a tax expenditure for individual retirement accounts (IRAs).

While ERISA may not affect as many individuals as Social Security, its scope is still impressive. Close to one-half of all employees participate in a retirement plan offered by their employer and regulated by the government. Forty percent of the elderly currently receive a pension from their former employers, a figure that climbed steadily between the 1970s and 1990s. Almost 40 percent of all households own an individual retirement account, and that figure has also grown in recent decades.[7] Employers who operate a defined benefit retirement plan* are required to buy

---

* Defined benefit plans promise workers a certain pension amount when they retire. Defined contribution plans, in contrast, promise workers only that a certain amount will be invested in their pension. Defined contribution plans shift risk (e.g., of inflation or stock

termination insurance from the Pension Benefit Guaranty Corporation. This insurance extends to almost 45 million workers and thirty-one thousand different pension plans. The U.S. government, through the PBGC, is currently responsible for paying out pensions to over one million workers and retirees whose plans failed. Its single largest "account" is Bethlehem Steel, whose recent bankruptcy affected 95,000 individuals. Difficulties facing major airlines and the scandal-ridden Enron Corporation, as well as underfunding of hundreds of pension plans, threaten to swamp the agency.[8] Other parts of ERISA, not discussed in this chapter, affect employer-provided health insurance. Based on the sheer number of lives touched, the passage of ERISA is arguably the third "big bang" of the American welfare state, and its origins deserve closer scrutiny.[9]

Politicians did not pay much attention to company pensions in the first half of the twentieth century. A few pieces of minor legislation, passed in the late 1950s and early 1960s, were designed to minimize fraud and limit the role of organized labor in administering pension funds. For his part, President Kennedy established a cabinet-level Committee on Corporate Pension Funds. Official interest in the subject grew dramatically, however, with the bankruptcy of the Studebaker automobile company and subsequent termination of the company's pension plan in 1963. Suddenly, seven thousand workers lost hope of receiving their full pension at a time when Social Security benefits were nowhere near as large as they are today. Studebaker's collapse had the same effect on policy makers that a mining accident or an oil spill can have. It was what political scientists call a "focusing event" (and what everyone else calls a disaster). Once it became obvious that Studebaker was in deep trouble, Senator Vance Hartke (D-IN) sponsored a bill creating pension insurance. Because Studebaker was based in his home state of Indiana, Hartke's interest was understandable. He was also strongly encouraged to act by the United Auto Workers, whose members were directly affected by Studebaker's collapse.

This event spurred wider interest in private pensions. During the mid-1960s, members of Congress introduced a number of bills and held hearings dealing with pension fund mismanagement and outright fraud, vesting standards, portability, and the tax benefits given to companies offering pensions. Hartke's interest in pension reform did not extend in all these directions, partly because some of them posed a threat to labor. The one person who tried to pull these different pieces together into a single comprehensive bill was Republican senator Jacob Javits of New York. From 1967 to 1974, Javits was the driving force behind pension reform.

---

market decline) from employer to worker, which is one reason why new defined benefit plans seldom appear anymore. This is also one reason why employers offering defined contribution plans are not required to buy government pension insurance.

The chances of something like ERISA passing were slim. Senator Javits was a member of the minority party and thus at an immediate disadvantage. He was not entirely popular in his own party, either, given how often he voted against the majority of his fellow Republicans. With business groups such as the Chamber of Commerce and the National Association of Manufacturers expressing serious reservations about pension reform, Republican support was even more doubtful. In the words of one business representative, pension reform went "too far, too fast, with too many proposals. . . . [It was] a straitjacket of controls that would slow down pension growth."[10] Democrats, who controlled Congress, were more likely allies, but even there Javits ran into trouble. Two of the leading power brokers, House Ways and Means chairman Wilbur Mills (D-AR) and Senate Finance chairman Russell Long (D-LA), feared that Javits's proposals would stir up intense business opposition. More liberal Democrats were receiving mixed signals from their labor allies who very badly wanted pension insurance but had misgivings about some of the other proposed reforms. Moreover, when most Democrats thought of retirement income, they thought first about increasing Social Security benefits. To compound these difficulties, the broad scope of pension reform triggered jurisdictional fights between congressional labor and revenue committees, and the technical complexity of the issue left many legislators unsure about the ultimate effects of reform.

To make matters worse, the White House was neither a leader nor an ardent follower. When the United Auto Workers pressed President Johnson to take up pension insurance in 1964, he refused, fearing that it might cost him business support in the upcoming election. When a comprehensive bill took shape in 1967, Johnson withheld support as a way of striking back at his secretary of labor, who had publicly criticized the administration's conduct of the Vietnam War.[11] The basic attitude of the Nixon administration was to make pension reform as toothless as possible.

Still, Javits had a few things going for him. He was the ranking Republican on the Senate Labor and Public Welfare Committee, giving him some measure of clout. He gained national visibility after appearing on the cover of *Time* magazine in 1966, with a story touting him as a legitimate vice presidential candidate in the next election. He knew that pensions mattered to his constituents, who wrote more angry letters to him about their company pensions than almost any other topic. As a member of the Senate Government Operations Committee, Javits had seen dramatic examples of fraud in union-run benefit plans, none of which existing laws could prevent. Javits had a close working relationship with two experts in the field. Frank Cummings had been a labor lawyer specializing in cases where workers lost their pensions (including Studebaker), was later a member of the Senate labor committee staff, and then became Javits's administrative assistant. Michael Gordon, a lawyer who had dealt with pension issues in the Labor Department, had been an adviser to President Kennedy's committee on pension reform and later joined Javits as counsel for pensions on the Senate labor committee staff. It was Cummings who first persuaded Javits that comprehensive reform was needed, and Gordon who drafted the bill that became ERISA.

By 1971 Javits also had new and startling information about pensions that he used to attract attention. A congressional study of the period between 1950 and 1970 found that the vast majority of people who worked in firms that offered pensions never received a penny in benefits. Many workers never qualified for pensions because of extraordinary vesting requirements, and some who did qualify were victimized by badly managed or corrupt plans. "Javits then followed up with a series of [congressional] hearings featuring individuals who had lost their pension benefits. Simultaneously, the media began to highlight specific cases of lost benefits, and Ralph Nader launched an attack on pension plans, calling them consumer fraud on a grand scale."[12] The senator shrewdly held these hearings in major cities around the country to maximize their impact. Javits recalled later in his autobiography that his office received twenty thousand letters supporting reform during a two-week period in 1972.

Pension reform soon grew more visible in Washington, with more congressional hearings and bills. It was not exactly front-page news—not with the Vietnam War, the Cold War, new regulatory agencies, wage and price controls, the first OPEC oil shock, and later Watergate vying for attention—but serious debate over comprehensive reform began for the first time. Javits gained more support in Congress, usually from legislators who represented the more industrial, unionized states, where company pensions were more common. His most important ally was Harrison (Pete) Williams (D-NJ), who became chairman of the Senate Labor and Public Welfare Committee in 1971. The two men submitted a joint bill in 1972 that replaced Javits's earlier proposals. But the odds were still against passage. The bill touched on so many features of pensions that almost any legislator, union, or business group could (and did) find something it disliked. Jurisdictional battles among congressional committees persisted. Senate Finance chairman Long managed almost single-handedly to stop the bill in 1972. The Nixon administration came out strongly against pension insurance, the one provision that labor wanted most.

At this point, advocates of pension reform caught a break (or two or three). First, the growing Watergate scandal diminished the power of President Nixon and forced White House officials to devote less time and energy to undermining the Javits-Williams bill. To placate the administration, a new tax break for individual retirement accounts was added. Second, a major wave of congressional reform was about to crest, one that would among other things reduce the power of committee chairs. Leaders such as Representative Mills and Senator Long were therefore generally on the defensive and less able to block pension reform. Third, a series of remarkable amendments to Social Security in the late 1960s and early 1970s, generating the largest increase in benefits in the program's history, had a major effect. This upward trend was particularly upsetting to a number of congressional Republicans, who started to view pension reform as a way to solidify company pensions and curb demand for future expansions of Social Security. Seen in this light, greater regulation of company pensions and creation of a new government bureaucracy (PBGC) looked a little less objectionable. The combination of these trends helped pave the way to enactment. On Labor Day 1974, less than a month after becoming president, Republican Gerald Ford signed the comprehensive Employee Retirement Income Security Act into law.

The origin of ERISA, then, was largely a top-down effort by a handful of politicians. The law expanded government's role in company pensions well beyond what major business groups favored. Political entrepreneurs, Senator Javits foremost among them, cultivated public opinion as much as they responded to it. In these ways, ERISA resembled the Social Security Act. One difference, of course, is that members of Congress took the lead in crafting ERISA and had to overcome presidential objections, whereas President Roosevelt was instrumental in passing the Social Security Act. The other key difference relates to the party affiliations of the main architects. Put simply, no Republican like Senator Jacob Javits was involved in the design and passage of the Social Security Act. Javits is widely credited with being the father of ERISA, and that title is well deserved. He was the first to sponsor a comprehensive bill in Congress, he championed the cause of pension reform when few others did, and he successfully generated support among officials and the general public. While it would be inaccurate to portray ERISA as a Republican initiative—after all, Nixon was little help and many congressional Republicans remained skeptical until the very end—it would be fair to say that ERISA was a bipartisan effort led by a Republican legislator.

By itself, this case does not help us unravel the puzzle described at the start of the chapter. The ideological gulf separating the two parties was considerably smaller when ERISA was debated than it was in the 1980s and 1990s. Bipartisan agreement was less remarkable in the 1970s than it would be in later years. Likewise, one might be inclined to dismiss Jacob Javits as part of a dying breed of liberal Republicans. As senator, he voted for the Civil Rights Act of 1964, the Voting Rights Act of 1965, Medicare, and the Equal Rights Amendment. He voted to increase funding for Food Stamps and Head Start. He voted more than half the time against bills that President Nixon endorsed. Republicans like Javits rarely exist in

Washington anymore, much less wield power. If ERISA is part of some new pattern of party politics, then conservative Republicans would have to be involved in subsequent additions to the American welfare state, and that seems unlikely. The next case will test that notion by starting several years after ERISA was enacted, when friction between the two parties reached a new level.

AMERICANS WITH DISABILITIES ACT

The history of the Americans with Disabilities Act (ADA) is filled with surprising twists.[13] Some scholars have traced the ADA's origins back to the civil rights movement of the 1960s. For the sake of brevity I focus on the 1980s, when the first specific proposals emerged. At this point, Republicans controlled both the White House and the Senate, the most power they had enjoyed since the early 1950s. Ronald Reagan campaigned on a pledge to rein in the national government, and he delivered major cuts in taxes and domestic spending in his first year as president. Realizing that government does more than tax and spend, President Reagan created a Task Force on Regulatory Relief, led by Vice President George Bush. The task force was designed to cut back on regulations, and in areas such as environmental protection it made significant changes. Another target was Section 504 of the Rehabilitation Act (1973), which prohibited organizations that contracted with the federal government from discriminating against the handicapped.

The more that members of the task force learned about the handicapped, the more they became convinced that the national government ought to do *more*, not less. In particular, the government needed to do more to help the handicapped become self-sufficient. According to C. Boyden Gray, counsel to the task force, the goal of public policy ought to be "to turn as many of the disabled as possible into taxpaying citizens."[14] At the time, there were roughly 13 million adults with a work disability. About 2.5 million of them received Food Stamps and Medicaid.[15] While it was foolish to think that all these individuals might be gainfully employed and disqualified from means-tested benefits, officials hoped to reduce their numbers. In 1983 Vice President Bush declared that Section 504 was no longer a target for regulatory relief.

The task force was responding in part to pressure from the disability rights movement. In addition to letter-writing campaigns, organizations representing the handicapped managed to develop a close relationship with Bush's task force. The most important link was Evan Kemp, director of the Disability Rights Center. "Kemp told Gray that disabled people didn't want the paternalistic heavy hand of government doling out welfare to them. The disability regulations were not handouts, Gray argued, but accommodations made so that people with disabilities could become independent and support themselves with jobs."[16] Bush was so impressed that he later asked Kemp to draft speeches on disability issues. On Bush's recommendation, Kemp gained a seat on the Equal Employment Opportunity Commission in 1987 and became chair of the commission during the Bush administration.

The Reagan administration's reversal was also prompted by developments in other disability programs. Toward the end of the 1970s, policy makers were starting to worry about the rapid growth of disability insurance and Supplemental Security Income (SSI), both driven by a sizable increase in the numbers of the disabled. Legislative amendments passed in 1980 included a provision to review the status of disabled beneficiaries at least once every three years, with an eye to identifying individuals who might have regained the ability to earn a living and thus no longer qualified for public benefits. The General Accounting Office issued a report in 1987 indicating that one out of every five individuals might have been incorrectly certified as disabled. Reagan officials were already looking for ways to cut domestic spending, and they saw disability programs as a good target. They accelerated the review of disability determinations. Between March 1981 and April 1982, the administration declared ineligible almost half of the 400,000 cases reviewed. The final tally of disenrolled beneficiaries approached half a million people.

In their haste to purge the rolls, however, officials triggered a firestorm of protests. Congress held multiple hearings, many featuring individuals who were clearly disabled and had been purged by mistake. Many of these individuals started to appeal their cases in court, and by 1984 they were winning on a regular basis. The administration subsequently backed off its aggressive plans and stopped the purge.[17] In this context, any attempt to cut back on regulations that helped the handicapped must have been politically unappealing. It seems likely that the whole episode left officials looking for ways to repair the administration's image.

During the mid-1980s, Reagan appointees to the National Council on the Handicapped produced a few surprises of their own. The most visible member of the council was Justin Dart, Jr., son of a prominent GOP donor and himself a successful businessman. Dart had worked tirelessly for disability rights since the mid-1960s, and he helped push the council to advocate for major changes in public policy. In 1983 the organization issued its National Policy for Persons with Disabilities, which called for realizing the "maximum life potential, self-reliance, independence, productivity, and equitable mainstream social participation in the most productive and least restrictive environment." The council's landmark report, *Toward Independence* (1986), challenged Congress to "enact a comprehensive law requiring equal opportunity for individuals with disabilities," extending to public accommodations, employment, housing, travel, and the functions of state and local governments. It suggested that such a law be titled The Americans with Disabilities Act.[18] The council issued a follow-up report in January of 1988 with more detailed legislative language.

The council's recommendations went too far for members of the Reagan White House, who reacted with the mildest words of encouragement and failed to develop any serious legislative proposals. The reception was warmer in Congress. The first to build on *Toward Independence* were Senator Lowell Weicker (R-CT) and Rep. Tony Coelho (D-CA), who introduced legislation in April of 1988. After Weicker lost his reelection bid in November, Senators Ted Kennedy (D-MA) and Tom Harkin (D-IA) took the lead. Their main objective was to create a bill that was more modest than the council's report. They worried especially about business opposition. They favored making accessibility standards more flexible and giving businesses more time to comply. In other words, two of the Senate's leading liberals were backing away from regulation-expanding recommendations made by Reagan appointees.

The political environment in Washington became more favorable for disability legislation once Bush started running for president. In creating some distance between himself and Reagan, Bush made disability rights an important part of his 1988 election campaign. He endorsed the general principles of the Weicker-Coelho bill, and during his acceptance speech at the GOP convention Bush pledged to "do whatever it takes to make sure the disabled are included in the mainstream."[19] Surveys taken around the November election reinforced the importance of the issue. The Louis Harris polling organization estimated that disabled Americans who usually voted Democratic but in 1988 voted Republican accounted for up to one-half of Bush's winning margin. Two days before his inauguration, Bush repeated his promises to the disabled and vowed to deliver on them.

The final steps of the legislative process were, at least in comparison to ERISA, relatively straightforward. One sticking point was punitive damages for violations, which many congressional Republicans and the Justice Department objected to strongly. In exchange for dropping this provision, the ADA's coverage was expanded to a larger number of private businesses. The final major bone of contention was the Chapman amendment, which would have excluded individuals with HIV/AIDS from the bill's protections.[20] After much wrangling, it was defeated. Otherwise, support was genuinely bipartisan. The final bill passed 377 to 28 in the House and 91 to 6 in the Senate, meaning that large majorities of both parties voted yes. In addition to President Bush and Democrats Kennedy, Harkin, and Coelho, Republican senators Robert Dole and Orrin Hatch played important leadership roles. GOP support in the House was less enthusiastic, but the same was true of Democratic support. Representative Coelho had considerable difficulty getting Speaker Jim Wright (D-TX) and Majority Leader Tom Foley (D-WA) to make the ADA a priority; they thought the bill tried to do too much. Most of the forward momentum, then, was provided by a Republican president and senators from both parties.

President Bush signed the ADA into law on July 26, 1990. Some three thousand individuals gathered on the South Lawn of the White House in what was at the time the largest signing ceremony in American history. In his remarks, Bush proclaimed a "long overdue" Independence Day: "every man, woman and child with a disability can now pass through once-closed doors into a bright new era of equality, independence and freedom."[21] He also took some pains to downplay the potential cost, noting that governments and charities were already spending upward of $200 billion each year on the disabled. The ADA would make it easier for the disabled to find work, earn a paycheck, pay taxes, and reduce their dependence on others. This argument was more an article of faith than anything else, for no one produced a decent cost-benefit analysis of the ADA during the entire legislative process. Given Republicans' traditional sensitivity to the cost of government regulations, this omission added yet another irony to the entire tale.[22]

The ADA effectively added a large third layer to U.S. disability policy. The first two layers consisted of disability insurance and vocational rehabilitation, representing social insurance and grants, respectively. The ADA created a new series of mandates on employers, state and local governments, and public accommodations. Employers, for example, must provide "reasonable accommodations" to "otherwise qualified" workers, such as making changes to their physical work space (e.g., ramps, elevators, bathrooms). Employers may also be expected to adjust normal work hours and make allowances for prolonged illness. Individuals who feel that employers are failing to live up to these requirements can file a claim with the U.S. Equal Employment Opportunity Commission; they also have a right to take employers to court and seek damages.[23]

This new layer was distinctively American. At the time, employment of the disabled in many European countries was promoted through hiring quotas. Employers who failed to meet their quota paid a "compensation contribution" to the government, which was then used to finance other programs for the disabled. Alternatively, a number of countries directly subsidized employers who hired the handicapped. Both of these approaches, it should be noted, relied on policy tools whose costs were fairly visible. The ADA, in contrast, shifts the costs to the private sector and to lower levels of government in ways that are hard to quantify but nevertheless quite real.[24]

Child Tax Credit

Most of the largest tax expenditures today, such as the home mortgage interest deduction, are very old and took decades to reach any significant size. The Child Tax Credit (CTC) is much different. Within a few years, the CTC has become one of the largest income support programs for families with children in the United States. It has become a key instrument of family policy. The Child Tax Credit cost the national government $27 billion in 2002—$22 billion in forgone tax revenues plus $5 billion in tax refunds.[25] It ranks among the dozen largest tax expenditures in the entire U.S. tax code, and it will move even higher up that list as its scheduled increases take effect. The national government spends more on the CTC than it does on the classic "welfare" program, TANF (Temporary Assistance for Needy Families). It spends almost ten times as much on the CTC as on the tax deduction for child and dependent care expenses or on the child care block grant. Spending on the State Children's Health Insurance Program, one of the largest of the new grants, is but a fraction of the CTC. Unlike the Earned Income Tax Credit, which is targeted at the working poor, the Child Tax Credit is also available to middle- and upper-middle-income families. In 2000 the CTC was claimed on 26 million tax returns compared to 18 million for the EITC.[26]

The origins of the Child Tax Credit date back to the mid-1980s. Republicans and Democrats at the time were competing to be the "pro-family" party. This label applied to a variety of issues, ranging from homosexuality and abortion to prayer in school. It also applied to the financial pressures facing families with children. Opinion polls showed that child care ranked high among voters' concerns, and there was considerable attention in the media to the growing numbers of working mothers and "latchkey" children. One in five American children lived in poverty. To demonstrate their concern and, perhaps more important, to buy enough time to work out their differences, elected officials created a bipartisan National Commission on Children in 1987.

The two parties disagreed about how the government should help families with children. The liberal wing of the Democratic Party favored more grants for child care and more regulation of child care providers. So did liberal interest groups such as the Children's Defense Fund. The less liberal, more centrist wing of the party (the so-called New Democrats) and virtually all Republicans disagreed. They felt that public policy already favored families who paid others to care for their children and that government should do more to help parents who stayed home with their children.[27] Doing nothing was not a good option, because it would signal indifference on an issue that was important to many voters. Instead, moderates and conservatives proposed new tax expenditures for families with children.

Republicans took the lead. During the 1988 presidential campaign, Democrat Michael Dukakis embraced the grant-and-regulate approach to child care. George Bush countered with a proposed $1,000 tax credit for families with children, regardless of whether their parents paid for child care. The logic was stated clearly in the 1988 Republican Party platform: "The more options families have in child care, the better. Government must not constrain their decisions. Individual choice should determine child care arrangements for the family. The best care for most children, especially in the early years, is parental. Government must never hinder it. Public policy must acknowledge the full range of family situations. Mothers or fathers who stay at home, who work part-time, or who work full-time, should all receive the same respect and consideration in public policy."[28] After Bush's election, a number of Republicans in the House and Senate introduced similar proposals. Senator Dan Coats wanted to make the credit refundable. Senator Pete Domenici and Rep. Tom Tauke wanted to increase the credit's value. Senator Bob Dole's "Working Family Child Care Assistance Act of 1989," which included a tax credit like Bush's, gathered twenty-six cosponsors in the Senate, all of them Republicans. These were not just the moderate Republicans. Coats and Dole were ideologically to the right of the average GOP senator at the time.[29]

Liberal Democrats and liberal interest groups vigorously opposed the tax credit approach. They felt that it would do nothing to improve the quality or availability of child care and, like most tax expenditures, would invariably favor the middle class over the poor. But these Democrats faced a Republican president, and they lacked the numbers to override a veto. Believing that something was better than nothing, a number of liberal Democrats allied with congressional Republicans and President Bush on this issue. The final version, incorporated into the omnibus 1990 budget bill, included a total of $15 billion in tax expenditures and only $4 billion in grants. Greater regulation of day care providers was dropped. The key tax measures included an increase in the Earned Income Tax Credit, a new tax credit to help working poor families buy health insurance for their children, and a new Young Child Tax Credit, available to parents of children less than one year old. The Bush White House referred to this last item as "non-negotiable." Though definitely smaller in value and scope than Republicans' earlier proposals, the Young Child Tax Credit was undeniably their baby.

Unlike most tax expenditures, the Young Child Tax Credit had a very short life. The Clinton administration terminated it in 1993. One rationale for doing so was that the credit was unwieldy: eligibility and benefits were linked to the Earned Income Tax Credit in complicated ways that confused taxpayers and led to erroneous tax returns. Moreover, Clinton felt strongly that expanding the EITC was just better policy, and the 1993 budget gave that program a substantial increase.[30]

Republicans resurrected the idea in their Contract with America. A $500 per child tax credit, available to all families earning up to $200,000, was the first item in their proposed American Dream Restoration Act. After Republicans won control of Congress in 1994, President Clinton became more receptive to the idea as well. Clinton was not the only Democrat to support the idea. Senator Jay Rockefeller (D-WV) introduced a bill in 1992 and 1993 that would have created a refundable child tax credit, and Rep. Martin Sabo (D-MN) offered a variation in 1994.[31] For the most part, though, congressional Democrats were cool to any child tax credit proposal.

That did not stop Clinton. During the 1996 presidential campaign, President Clinton came out in favor of a $500 per child tax credit. He was reelected and the Republicans retained control of Congress, making passage of such a tax credit highly likely. The odds improved even more when some of the GOP's top priorities, such as cuts in capital gains and estate taxes, triggered intense opposition from the more liberal Democrats. In this context, the proposals for a child tax credit looked more attractive, for it would balance some of the tax relief aimed at the upper classes. It would also be more progressive than an expansion of the personal exemption, which some analysts and politicians favored. There were disagreements over how large the tax credit should be and which families should benefit, but ultimately a $500 per child tax credit passed as part of the massive Taxpayer Relief Act of 1997.[32]

With omnibus measures like this one, it is tempting to imagine that Republicans accepted a new benefit for families with children as the price of winning approval for tax cuts aimed at businesses and the rich. That is not what happened. Republicans were the earliest and strongest supporters of the Child Tax Credit, and the reasons are not hard to understand. Republicans wanted to help "traditional" families with stay-at-home moms, families that could not benefit from existing tax deductions or from grants for families who paid for child care. These families were (and are) a major source of votes for the party. More organized voices on the right, namely interest groups such as the Christian Coalition and the Family Research Council, endorsed the CTC.[33] In addition, Republicans could take advantage of the ambiguity of tax expenditures by portraying the CTC as tax relief rather than social spending. While President Clinton deserves some credit for creating this program, Republicans deserve more.

Conclusion

The Republicans we usually hear about are the ogres who compare poor people to wild animals (chapter 3). They think that a major problem with social policy is, to quote Senator Phil Gramm, too many folks riding in the wagon and not enough folks pulling the wagon. These Republicans definitely do exist. But there is another side to the Republican Party, one that has played an instrumental role in expanding and reshaping the American welfare state.

We already know some of this history. In his study of social policy between the late 1940s and the early 1980s, Robert Browning calculated that annual social welfare expenditures increased more during the GOP Eisenhower, Nixon, and Ford administrations than under Democrats Truman, Kennedy, and Carter.[34] In some cases, the growth was fueled by Democrats in Congress. But after comparing the presidents' initial budget proposals, Browning still found that both the Nixon and the first Eisenhower administration asked for larger increases in social spending than did Kennedy or Carter. The main category of social spending consists of payments to individuals, and they revealed a similar pattern. In real terms, these payments increased most under Eisenhower (even more than Johnson) and least under Kennedy and Carter.[35] Thus, although Republicans often opposed creation of new social programs in the 1930s and the 1960s, they did not necessarily offer less support than Democrats for existing social programs in the middle of the twentieth century.

The new part of this story is the leadership role that Republican officials have taken in creating social programs. Historically, this role appears to be fairly recent and more evident with the less traditional tools of social policy. It is, nevertheless, quite significant. ERISA, the ADA, and the Child Tax Credit are three of the most important additions to the American welfare state since the Great Society. In each case, spanning a variety of policy tools and target groups, a bipartisan coalition led by a Republican politician was responsible. Senator Javits and the first President Bush were no less instrumental to social policy in the 1970s and 1980s than Representative Mills and President Johnson were in the 1960s. They may have chosen different tools, but all these officials deliberately and energetically expanded the role of government to promote social welfare.

One irony is that Republicans have been expanding some parts of the American welfare state at the same time that they have been launching vigorous attacks on other parts. In addition to making it harder to qualify for welfare benefits, Republicans tried to cut back on the growth of Social Security, Medicare, Medicaid, and disability insurance in the 1980s and 1990s. More often than not, they failed. Democrats still managed to control either the White House or Congress as the partisan balance in Washington achieved first a rough and then a razor-sharp parity. Organized groups representing beneficiaries stood ready to defend these programs from attack. The reaction to cutbacks in disability programs in the early 1980s, though impressive, was actually less dramatic than the reaction to proposed cuts in Social Security during that same period. Republicans learned from experience that retrenchment could be very painful, not just to beneficiaries but to their own political careers.

Faced with these obstacles, a number of Republicans reverted to plan B, which meant creating a different kind of social program. In all three cases studied here, Republicans designed new social programs in order to curb existing programs. Those who felt that Social Security was growing too fast in the 1960s and 1970s took steps to slow it down. One step was indexing benefits to inflation, which a number of Republicans agreed to in 1972 in order to end the series of large legislated increases.[36] The other was shoring up employer pensions. In the words of Senator Javits:

> Besides establishing security in retirement for the U.S. worker, ERISA also benefits the economy by holding down Social Security taxes. In order to keep the Social Security system viable, these taxes have been increased to the point where employers and workers are now paying the government more than 12 percent of the wage package for Social Security taxes. If there were no ERISA, no insured private pension plans, we would have to pay about 20 percent of our income to the government to provide an adequate income for retired persons. If we allow the government to support the system of retirement benefits to such a degree, the state will become too large a factor in our lives.[37]

The Americans with Disabilities Act looked attractive because it promised to reduce the number of handicapped people receiving income support and medical care from the government. To compensate for the benefits extended to families who paid for child care, Republicans championed the Child Tax Credit. This way, more parents could afford to care for their children at home, and the need for publicly subsidized day care centers might diminish. Ideally, many Republicans would have preferred to eliminate existing programs, reduce benefits, or restrict eligibility. When they could not eliminate, or could not do enough reducing and restricting, they created programs that would limit the future growth of traditional social insurance and grant programs.

At bottom, Republicans have been engaged in what Jacob Hacker and other scholars refer to as institutional "layering."[38] Because institutions are remarkably durable, replacing them is often harder than building on top of them. In the United States, new layers of social policy have been added on top of old layers, in part to keep those old layers from growing. Republicans have thus helped give the American welfare state its distinctive shape. With some exceptions, the general pattern for the twentieth century appears to be new layers of social regulation, tax expenditures, and insurance stacked on top of old layers of social insurance and grants (see table 3.1). Important regulations on company pensions and government-backed pension insurance were approved years after Social Security and means-tested retirement pensions were created. Regulations designed to foster greater employment of the disabled appeared years after disability insurance and grants for vocational rehabilitation.

The significance of layering helps explain why Republicans were more supportive of ERISA and the ADA than another piece of social regulation from this era, the Family and Medical Leave Act (FMLA) of 1993.[39] This Act provides for twelve weeks of unpaid leave for workers who want to care for a new child or sick relative. Enactment of the FMLA followed the more familiar pattern of liberal Democrats and interest groups squaring off against conservative Democrats, Republicans, and business interests. To lessen opposition, advocates gradually reduced the numbers of weeks of leave that workers could take and increased the number of small businesses that were exempted from coverage, making the FMLA far less comprehensive than its counterparts in Europe. Nevertheless, President George Bush vetoed family leave bills in 1990 and 1992. The second time he did so, Democratic presidential candidate Bill Clinton criticized Bush for making " 'a bad mistake' and repeated his support for 'a law that would support family values.' "[40] The FMLA did not become law until Democrats regained control of government with the election of President Clinton. Unlike the Americans with Disabilities Act, which Bush and many other Republicans supported, family leave regulations did not have clear potential to reduce social spending elsewhere. It was hard to argue that giving people unpaid leave would reduce spending on welfare or unemployment, and the ultimate benefits of improving the bond between parent and child were too speculative and distant. If anything, opponents feared that family leave would open the door to other regulations on business such as mandatory health insurance.[41]

To the question posed at the end of chapter 1, "Is the strange shape of the American welfare state due to national values or institutional fragmentation?" we can now offer an alternative possibility—party politics. As party polarization and divided government became the norm in the late twentieth century, Democrats and Republicans embraced less traditional tools of social welfare. Republican officials moved to the right between the 1960s and the 1990s, leaving new social insurance and grant programs increasingly outside their zone of acceptable outcomes. Policies that had previously generated little support, such as privatization of Social Security, moved into the mainstream of the GOP zone. It became harder and harder for Republicans to find common ground with Democrats, whose concurrent shift to the left only helped to solidify their commitment to the more traditional tools of social policy. Often at odds over building up or tearing down the American welfare state, the two parties decided to add new rooms in different architectural styles.

They did not build in just any direction. Two of the programs discussed in this chapter, ERISA and the ADA, were designed specifically for wage workers. In the first case more workers would be rewarded with viable pensions, and in the second more of the handicapped would find it easier to become employed. The third program, the CTC, was aimed at families whose parents stayed home to care for their children. Republicans may have worked to defeat the Clinton health plan and reduce the welfare rolls, but they were not averse to using government to promote certain policy objectives and favor certain groups. It certainly did not hurt politically that each of these groups was large, numbering in the millions, and geographically dispersed across the nation. It was no coincidence that so many beneficiaries were middle- and even upper-middle class, a point that I will return to toward the end of the book.

The immediate benefits conferred on favored groups were important because the other benefits of layering—limiting the growth of less favored programs—may not appear for many years. Even when they do, the connection between slower growth in traditional social programs and the creation of nontraditional programs may be too indirect for voters to appreciate. Layering is not always conducive to the credit claiming that elected officials cherish. As a result, Republicans chose to layer in ways that could generate more tangible and immediate benefits to large numbers of potential voters. They tried to reconcile their policy goals with their electoral needs.

At one point in the hit animated movie *Shrek*, the title character tries to explain that ogres are more complicated than they appear. Ogres have layers. His companion, a donkey who cannot stop talking, is confused. Does Shrek mean that ogres are like onions that stink and make you cry? Or are ogres like cakes? Or parfaits? (After all, everybody loves parfaits.) Shrek quickly grows frustrated with the food analogies but cannot articulate what he means by layers. He has my sympathy. At this point in the book, I cannot say much more about the layers of the American welfare state other than to note their existence and to show that both political parties have added layers. Later on we will see why policy makers might choose to add certain layers at certain times in American history, and how these layers affect our collective ability to fight poverty and inequality.

CHAPTER 5

Programs for the Poor Are Not Always Poor Programs

THIS CHAPTER EXTENDS THE DISCUSSION of overlooked possibilities. Scholars who believe that the American welfare state has two distinct tiers portray the lower tier as the home of politically marginal programs like welfare. The upper tier, anchored by Social Security, has all the advantages. Nevertheless, as noted in chapter 2, spending in the lower tier increased faster than spending in the upper tier between 1980 and 2000. The main reason was the very rapid expansion of two means-tested programs, Medicaid and the Earned Income Tax Credit (EITC). Our sense of political possibilities is too limited if we think that all means-tested social programs must be political orphans. Some of these programs have been treated like favorite sons, and the main purpose of this chapter is to figure out why. By comparing Medicaid and the EITC to each other and contrasting them to less fortunate means-tested programs, I hope to draw out some general lessons about political viability. Combined with the enactment of new social programs, discussed earlier in the book, the expansion of existing programs shows that the last decades of the twentieth century were not strictly an era of austerity and retrenchment.

There were indeed cutbacks, most of them affecting means-tested programs. The most dramatic episodes occurred in 1981 and 1996. As part of a drive to cut domestic spending, elected officials reduced or eliminated a number of means-tested social programs in 1981. Despite accounting for less than 15 percent of the national budget, these programs represented 70 percent of the total cuts. Officials removed close to half a million families from Aid to Families with Dependent Children (AFDC, aka welfare) through tighter eligibility requirements. As a result, the number of poor families eligible for Medicaid dropped as well. An additional 300,000 AFDC families saw their monthly benefits cut substantially. Approximately one million families lost Food Stamp benefits. The budgets for subsidized school lunches, social services, and job training were all cut. In terms of dollars, the biggest loser was subsidized housing for the poor. The public service employment program, providing hundreds of thousands of jobs for low-income workers, was terminated. After decades of expansion, the American welfare state experienced its first serious retrenchment in 1981.[1]

Social insurance programs, which cost far more than everything targeted at the poor, were largely spared the budgetary ax. Although extended unemployment benefits were cut back, core programs including Social Security and Medicare were simply trimmed. By 1984 these small changes in eligibility and benefits had reduced Social Security spending 1.5 percent, compared to the 16 percent cut in AFDC and the 19 percent cut in Food Stamps. Spending on Medicare was reduced by half as much as spending on Medicaid.[2]

The political context of 1981 fits the traditional two-tiered model quite nicely. One tier has friends in high places and the other does not. When Republicans led the assault on means-tested programs in 1981, plenty of Democrats joined them. The main groups protesting against these cuts were professional associations of social workers—not exactly on the short list of America's power elite. Politics in the upper tier were much different. After the Reagan administration proposed major reductions in Social Security benefits for early retirees, an immediate backlash from senior citizens ensued. Elderly constituents inundated members of Congress with angry letters and phone calls, and many letters protesting the cuts appeared on the editorial pages of local and national newspapers. Congressional Republicans quickly disavowed the idea, and the White House backed off. Democrats were still able to use this episode effectively in the 1982 congressional elections, and members of both political parties came away convinced that Social Security was the deadly "third rail" of American politics.[3]

In light of these developments, it is no wonder that prominent analysts of American politics embraced the old saying that "programs for the poor are poor programs."[4] From this perspective, programs such as welfare and Food Stamps are not "poor" in the sense of inefficient or ineffective. They are politically vulnerable. They never get a fair chance to fight poverty. Anyone who wants to design politically sustainable social policies should model them after programs in the upper tier. Writing in the mid-1980s, Hugh Heclo declared that

> the poverty-line poor are a nonexistent political constituency in an institutional system designed to reflect constituency pressures outside and organizational pressures within the federal government. Without the protective coloration of a larger program agenda that—as with Social Security—embraces the felt needs of many Americans, antipoverty efforts are likely to remain a political afterthought.[5]

A few years later, Theda Skocpol analyzed a variety of social policies in the nineteenth and twentieth centuries and came to a similar conclusion:

> U.S. history speaks loud and clear to those who would do more now to help the poor through public social policies. Rather than devising new programs

narrowly focused on low-income people or the urban poor, and rather than seeking to reform or expand aid to families with dependent children and other means-tested public assistance programs, policymakers should work toward displacing welfare with new policies that could address the needs of less privileged Americans along with those of the middle class and the stable working class.[6]

Looking back at the 1960s, Jill Quadagno argued that

the War on Poverty initiated ambitious programs to improve communities, train workers, and increase housing for the poor. But because these programs also promoted racial equality, they created a backlash against the welfare state. Proposals for child care and welfare reform also failed because they became entangled in racial issues. These outcomes suggest that targeting, whether by income or by race, is an ineffectual strategy for expanding the welfare state.[7]

These were not fringe opinions. All three of these scholars have won prestigious fellowships and major book prizes. Skocpol has served as president of the American Political Science Association and Quadagno as president of the American Sociological Association.

The passage of welfare reform in 1996 gave added credibility to this view. For the first time, a U.S. social program lost its entitlement status. TANF (Temporary Assistance for Needy Families), a block grant, replaced the old AFDC program. Instead of paying for whatever number of families met states' eligibility criteria, the national government would allocate a fixed sum of money each year. If welfare rolls went up, as they usually did in recessions, states would have to choose between cutting benefits, cutting off recipients, or raising additional revenues. The TANF program featured new time limits on recipients and greater work requirements. It also gave states the options of excluding teenage mothers or denying additional benefits to current welfare mothers who had additional children (the so-called family cap). Along with a booming economy and changes to the EITC, these changes in welfare law were a big reason why welfare rolls dropped dramatically. By 2001 there were only 5.3 million TANF recipients, compared to 12.2 million AFDC recipients in 1996. Such a decline was unprecedented in U.S. history.[8]

Welfare was not the only means-tested social program to be "reformed" in 1996. Officials cut about $50 billion from Food Stamps and Supplemental Security Income (SSI), spread over five years. The main change involved declaring almost all legal immigrants ineligible for benefits unless they were naturalized citizens.[9] President Clinton signed the Personal Responsibility and Work Opportunity Reconciliation Act into law in August of 1996, less than a year after he had staunchly and successfully defended Medicare against cuts, and at about the same time that he was defending

Social Security against the more radical forms of "privatization." It is hard to imagine a starker contrast between the two tiers of the American welfare state.

Medicaid and the Earned Income Tax Credit, however, are huge exceptions to this pattern. Policy makers expanded coverage and benefits for both of these programs during the "retrenchment" era, not just once but several times. Officials increased spending on these programs even when passing deficit reduction measures. As we shall see, the politics of Medicaid and the EITC were not identical. One obvious difference involved the main interest groups pushing for expansion. The Children's Defense Fund has been widely credited with helping to extend Medicaid coverage; other notable advocates included associations of governors and of health providers. The Center on Budget and Policy Priorities, on the other hand, was the preeminent advocate for the EITC.[10] Nevertheless, there were interesting similarities between the two programs.

One key lesson we can draw from the exceptional growth of Medicaid and the EITC appears to be that "programs for the poor" cover a large range of individuals, some of whom are considered to be more deserving than others of public support. Social policies aimed at more deserving groups, such as children (Medicaid) and the working poor (EITC), have been capable of winning bipartisan support, resisting retrenchment, and expanding in recent decades.[11] Social policies helping nonworking adults and recent immigrants have been more susceptible to attack. Another lesson concerns issue definition and visibility. If policy makers were debating domestic spending cuts (1981) or welfare reform (1996), then means-tested programs were the center of attention and fared badly. If, on the other hand, the debate was over issues such as tax reform or deficit reduction, then it was possible to expand public assistance while officials' attention was focused elsewhere. In some cases there were literally no separate votes, hearings, or debates on legislated changes to Medicaid and the EITC. When it comes to means-tested social programs, less visibility has meant less vulnerability.[12]

MEDICAID EXPANSION

Before explaining why Medicaid and the EITC were so special, let me briefly describe their expansion. National and state governments combined to spend about $25 billion on Medicaid in 1980. By 2000, total Medicaid spending was a little over $200 billion. Adjusted for inflation, spending on Medicaid quadrupled in two decades. That was a remarkable change, making Medicaid one of the fastest-growing programs in all of government. Between 1980 and 2000, Medicaid's share of the nation's means-tested social spending increased from one-quarter to one-half. Medicaid is the largest social program by far in the traditional lower tier of the American welfare state.[13]

The sources of Medicaid's growth are varied and complicated, and sorting them out properly could take an entire book.[14] Medicaid spending went up partly because the mix of patients changed; the blind and other people with disabilities make up a greater share of the Medicaid population than they did twenty-five years ago, and these patients are much more expensive to treat than welfare families. Spending went up because medical costs generally have increased faster than the overall rate of inflation. Spending went up because of greater life expectancy, which meant longer stays in nursing homes for Medicaid's elderly patients. Much of this growth happened without any deliberate action by public officials. My interest is in understanding how and why legislators chose to expand Medicaid.[15] Many of those changes affected pregnant women and children.

The main result was to make it easier for poor mothers and children to qualify for Medicaid, even if they did not qualify for welfare.[16] The decoupling of the two programs was, in the words of one state Medicaid director, "a revolutionary step."[17] Among other things, it meant that after welfare reform in 1996, poor children who did not qualify for TANF could still get Medicaid. The first notable change to Medicaid, enacted in 1984 (table 5.1), extended coverage to pregnant women who would be eligible for AFDC if their child were already born, and to children age five and under whose family met the financial tests for AFDC but did not qualify for other reasons (e.g., family composition). Coverage was extended the following year to all pregnant women who met the financial tests for AFDC but did not otherwise qualify.

In 1986 the national government gave states the option to extend coverage to pregnant women and children up to the age of five if their family income was above their state's AFDC threshold and below the federal poverty line. This was potentially a huge change, given that AFDC did not serve many poor families. For example, the poverty line for a family of three in 1985 was $8,573, or $714 per month. In the average state, a family of three was ineligible for welfare if its monthly income was above $401. In a dozen states the AFDC threshold was less than half the poverty line. Thus it was quite possible to be poor, really poor, but too rich for welfare and therefore too rich for Medicaid.[18]

Starting in 1987, coverage for children under the age of seven was phased in as long as their family income was below the state AFDC threshold (an extension of the 1984 reforms). States could also exercise the option to offer Medicaid to all children under the age of eight who lived below the federal poverty line (an extension of the 1986 reforms). The same offer applied to all pregnant women and infants with a family in-

TABLE 5.1
Chronology of Medicaid and EITC Expansion

	Medicaid	EITC
1984	Expand coverage of pregnant women; expand coverage for all children age 5 and younger who meet income test but not other eligibility rules.	
1985	Expand coverage of pregnant women who meet income test but not other eligibility rules.	
1986	State option to cover pregnant women and children age 5 and under with family incomes up to 100% of federal poverty line (FPL).	Eligibility extended to more of the near poor; benefits increased; credit indexed for inflation.
1987	Expand coverage to all children age 7 and under who meet income test but not other eligibility rules; state option to cover all children under age 8 who live below 100% of FPL, and all pregnant women and infants up to 185% of FPL.	
1988	Expand coverage to all pregnant women and infants up to 100% of FPL.	
1989	Expand coverage to all pregnant women and children up to age 6 up to 133% of FPL.	
1990	Expand coverage of all children under age 18 with family income below 100% of FPL (phased in over 12 years).	Eligibility extended to more of the near poor; benefits adjusted for family size and increased.
1993		Eligibility extended to workers without children and more of the near poor; benefits increased.

come below 185 percent of the federal poverty line. The Medicare Catastrophic Coverage Act of 1988 mandated what had previously been optional. States had to offer Medicaid to all pregnant women and infants living in poverty, even if their family income was above the AFDC threshold. Although much of that Act affecting Medicare was later repealed, the changes to Medicaid remained on the books. The Family Support Act of 1988 required states to offer Medicaid for one year to families who earned enough money to leave AFDC. The next year, mandatory coverage was extended to all pregnant women and all children under the age of six with a family income up to 133 percent of the federal poverty line. Beginning in 1990, Medicaid was gradually extended to all children under the age of eighteen whose family income was below the federal poverty line.

Taken together, policy changes made between 1984 and 1990 were the largest expansion of coverage since Medicaid originated in 1965. Medicaid paid for an estimated 17 percent of all births in the United States in 1985 and almost 45 percent in 1991. In 1980, 9 million children received medical care through Medicaid; by 1995 the figure was over 16 million, and by 2000 it was up to 19 million.[19] On paper, the United States offered health insurance to every poor pregnant woman and every poor child in the nation, and to many women and children who lived just above the poverty line. Poor children joined the elderly as the two most favored groups when it came to public health insurance.

These gains were seriously threatened when Republicans took control of Congress after the 1994 elections. One of their first priorities was reducing government spending, and they proposed major reductions in the growth of Medicare and a new block grant structure for Medicaid in their first budget. To many members of the medical and social welfare communities, as well as many Democratic officials, a Medicaid block grant would inevitably lead to cutbacks. It would allow the national government to reduce its financial support and state governments to tighten up on eligibility and benefits. A number of interest groups pressured the Clinton administration to oppose the block grant proposal, and Clinton cited Medicaid as one of the main reasons for his veto of the Republicans' budget in December of 1995. The final budget signed by Clinton did not convert Medicaid into a block grant. Republicans then tried to couple changes to Medicaid with welfare reform, and Clinton again insisted successfully that Medicaid be left alone.[20]

EITC EXPANSION

The Earned Income Tax Credit followed a somewhat different path from Medicaid, with equally impressive results. The process took longer and affected both eligibility and benefits (table 5.1).[21] Because the EITC has not received as much attention as welfare or Medicaid, it may help to summarize how the program works. Almost all recipients claim the EITC when filing their annual tax return. The credit reduces the amount of income tax owed and in most cases produces a tax refund.[22] The value of the credit depends on the amount of earned income. For a family with two kids in 2003, the credit was worth 40 cents for every dollar earned up to $10,510 (the phase-in range), and a maximum of $4,204 for incomes between $10,510 and $14,730. It then gradually declined in value for incomes up to $34,692 (the phase-out range). If this family with two kids earned $8,000, their EITC for 2003 would have been worth $3,200. If they earned $25,000, their EITC would have been worth a little over $2,000. In 2003, the EITC reduced the income tax of the average eligible family to zero and generated a refund check of $1,600.[23]

The EITC started small in 1975. The maximum credit was originally $400, and the phase-out range ended at incomes of $8,000. Small increases in eligibility and benefits occurred in 1978 and 1984. Despite these changes, the real value of the average EITC benefit declined between 1975 and 1985. The program initially served people below and slightly above the poverty line. By the early 1980s, the near poor and some of the poor were no longer eligible because the upper end of the phase-out range had not kept pace with inflation. The first major episode of expansion happened in 1986 when officials expanded eligibility, increased benefits, and indexed the credit for inflation. The impact of the 1986 reforms was considerable. Between 1985 and 1990, the number of families receiving the EITC grew from 7.4 million to 12.5 million, the average benefit more than doubled, and the maximum benefit increased from $550 to $953. The total cost of the program more than tripled.

Congress expanded the EITC in 1990, and in just three years the total cost of the EITC doubled again. This was due to a modest increase in eligibility, the first-ever adjustments for family size, and a significant increase in benefits per family.[24] By 1993 the maximum benefit was over $1,500. The last major expansion occurred in 1993. For the first time, individuals without children were eligible. Benefits were increased above and beyond inflation, and the income range for eligibility was likewise expanded. One year later, the number of recipient families had gone up 25 percent and the total cost of the program had increased by 35 percent. By 2000 a family of four with two children could receive the EITC even if its income was 175 percent of the poverty line.

Over the course of the 1990s, the number of EITC families grew from 12.5 million to 19.3 million. The real value of the average credit more than doubled. The total cost of the EITC, expressed in constant 2000 dollars, grew from just under $10 billion in 1990 to over $32 billion in 2000. In the process, the EITC passed welfare and Food Stamps in size. No other U.S. social program grew faster at the end of the twentieth century than the Earned Income Tax Credit.

Like Medicaid, the EITC faced threats in the mid-1990s. Troubled by the program's rapid growth, and by evidence that some families were receiving more money than they should, a number of congressional Republicans attacked the EITC. The biggest challenge emerged in the Senate, which approved a seven-year, $43 billion cut to the EITC in 1995 as part of the overall budget. Republicans also tried to scale back the EITC in 1997 in order to free up monies to pay for other tax cuts they favored. In the first instance, President Clinton vetoed the budget and singled out cuts to the EITC as one of the main reasons. In the second, Clinton signaled his opposition and Republicans removed the EITC from the tax bill before sending it to the president. Very small cuts to the EITC were adopted as part of the 1996 welfare reform bill, but they did little to slow the program's growth. Congressional Republicans tried to cut the EITC again in 1999 until Texas governor George W. Bush, the leading Republican presidential candidate, told the media: "I don't think they ought to balance their budget on the backs of the poor." The historic tax cuts of 2001 included a small increase to the EITC.[25]

Seeking Explanations

The first question we need to ask is what Medicaid and the Earned Income Tax Credit had in common that might explain their remarkable development. We can rule out certain features of policy design. Success was not a matter of finding a unique policy tool: Medicaid is a grant, and the EITC is a tax expenditure. The specific form of benefits did not matter, either. Some observers have suggested that when it comes to helping the poor, in-kind benefits (e.g., job training, housing) are more likely to gain support because policy makers do not trust the poor to spend wisely any cash they receive from the government.[26] Medicaid provides medical services to the poor, but the EITC offers income support that can be spent any way recipients want. Others have argued that means-tested programs can be sheltered from cutbacks if powerful third-party service providers offer support.[27] Medicaid does benefit from the support of doctors and hospitals that are paid by the government to treat Medicaid patients. In contrast, the EITC goes directly to individuals and families.

We can rule out some institutional factors as well. The EITC is a truly national program, whereas Medicaid relies on national and state governments for financing and administration. At the national level, Medicaid is administered by the Department of Health and Human Services. The EITC, like all tax expenditures, is run by the Treasury Department.

Divided government is a more attractive explanation. All the legislated changes to Medicaid and two of the three major changes to the EITC were enacted with Republicans in the White House and Democrats partly or wholly in control of Congress. Perhaps when neither party controls government, both parties have an incentive to expand social programs in order to win votes from the poor and gain unified control. Here is where it pays to examine some of the more vulnerable means-tested programs. We should look not only at what Medicaid and the EITC had in common but also at what they had that other social programs did not. Unfortunately for this explanation, the two most important episodes of welfare state retrenchment, in 1981 and 1996, also occurred under divided government.

Focusing on the legislative process brings us closer to the answer. In both cases, the key provisions were tucked away in massive, complicated bills.[28] All the changes to Medicaid and the EITC were dwarfed by other taxing or spending items. The first important changes to Medicaid were buried deep in the Deficit Reduction Act of 1984. Subsequent changes in 1985, 1986, 1987, 1989, and 1990 were embedded in omnibus budget reconciliation acts. The first major expansion of the EITC was a small part of the Tax Reform Act of 1986, which was the biggest overhaul of the tax code in decades. The other two major increases, in 1990 and 1993, were also part of omnibus budget acts.

Going this route offered several advantages. Few legislators read, much less understood, every single item in such bills. The 1990 Budget Act, for example, was almost five hundred pages of small print. It touched on everything from the Rural Electrification and Telephone Revolving Fund to a national aviation noise policy. To find the relevant language about Medicaid and low-income children, one would have to locate Title IV, Subtitle B, Part 2, Sections 4601–4605 of the Act. In the words of Hall of Fame pitcher Walter Johnson, who was famous for his fastball: "you can't hit what you can't see."

A related advantage was the attention drawn to other parts of these comprehensive bills. The tax reform debate in 1986 focused far more on changes to tax rates and on tax loopholes for business than on the Earned Income Tax Credit. Medicaid expansion in 1988 was overshadowed by expansion of Medicare. The budget debate in 1990 turned more on how much deficit reduction officials could agree on and whether President George Bush would break his "no new taxes" promise. The 1993 budget debate revolved around the particular mix of tax increases and spending cuts used to reduce the deficit, a controversial new energy tax, and President Clinton's efforts to win passage without a single Republican supporter in Congress.[29]

Working with an omnibus bill gave supporters some bargaining power. Once President Reagan and then President Bush began accepting tax increases to rein in the deficit, they started to lose support among the more conservative members of their own party. They needed to win over some Democrats to pass their budgets, and one method was to add "sweeteners" like Medicaid expansion.[30] In a similar fashion, policy makers expanded the EITC to make the overall distribution of winners and losers in tax reform or the budget look more progressive (or less regressive). Someone wanting a new or bigger tax break for business might have to support the EITC.[31] A stand-alone bill expanding either program would have made such trades more difficult.[32]

Finally, working with an omnibus reconciliation bill was attractive because Congress considers such measures under special rules. Compared to traditional legislation, there is less time for debate, and there are fewer opportunities for amendments. Legislators therefore have a harder time modifying or deleting any provision they oppose. For Medicaid's supporters, this was an important lesson from 1981. "We learned how to turn Reagan's legislative ploy back on him," said Sara Rosenbaum, a senior official at the Children's Defense Fund during the 1980s. "Just as he used the reconciliation process to advance his agenda cutting social programs, people in Congress learned how to use that process to expand and improve social programs."[33] Even if you saw Medicaid expansion coming and wanted to hit it, you would have had a hard time connecting.

The low profile of both programs means that we should not expect national elections or public opinion to have played a major role. Few people outside the nation's capital were aware of what was happening to Medicaid or the EITC. The key actors were inside the Beltway, and both programs owed much of their success to support from government officials and interest groups.

Representative Henry Waxman (D-CA) was the prime force behind expansion of Medicaid. A stronger champion would be hard to imagine. Waxman was a classic New Deal Democrat who had been raised to believe in government's ability, and positive duty, to help ordinary people. He came to Congress in 1974 and was chairman of the health subcommittee of the House Energy and Commerce (then called the Interstate and Foreign Commerce) Committee from 1979 to 1994. In that position, Waxman had jurisdiction over Medicaid and used his power to expand the program. "In the absence of national health insurance," he told one interviewer, "we needed to do more for the poorest of the poor." One Republican staffer who served on the same subcommittee was clearly impressed with Waxman's commitment: "A lot of legislators just kind of nodded off when it came to Medicaid because they didn't understand it or there wasn't a lot of political capital to be gained in helping poor people. . . . But Henry was a bulldog on this. He was in there for the long haul. He struck me as someone who would be happy spending his whole life protecting the health of moms and kids."[34] Yet commitment alone is seldom enough in politics. Waxman also benefited from a good working relationship with Rep. John Dingell (D-MI), the powerful chair of the entire House committee; from the ability to distribute thousands of dollars of campaign contributions to fellow Democrats in the House and Senate; from a talent for forging partnerships with Republicans in both houses of Congress; and from a well-respected staff.

Moreover, Waxman was a gifted strategist. He realized early on how to use the reconciliation process to facilitate Medicaid expansion. He knew that giving states the option to adopt certain policy changes would be difficult for Republicans to oppose. And he figured out how to spread out the costs of expansion so that they never looked large. The changes to Medicaid frequently started small and did not kick in fully until years later. Provisions enacted in 1990, for instance, were phased in through 2002. Around Washington, this technique became known as "the Waxman wedge."[35]

During the 1980s and 1990s, congressional support for the Earned Income Tax Credit was centered in the House Ways and Means Committee. Early advocates included Rep. Charles Rangel (D-NY) and staff member Wendell Primus. The main lesson they took away from 1981 was that means-tested social spending was not going to increase in the foreseeable future. Instead, they saw their job as finding ways to lower taxes for the poor and near poor. The EITC was ideally designed to accomplish that objective. No one official stood out as the EITC's champion the way Waxman did with Medicaid. At various times Eugene Steuerle (a Treasury official in the Reagan administration), Rep. Thomas Petri (R-WI), leaders of the centrist Democratic Leadership Council, and President Clinton were important proponents of a larger tax credit.[36]

That said, something is not quite right about this explanation. If all it takes to expand means-tested social programs is a big reconciliation bill and a few friends in high places, why didn't more programs grow as fast as Medicaid and the EITC? As formulas for success go, this one does not seem very complicated or exclusive. The missing ingredient, I argue, is that advocates worked very hard to distance Medicaid and the EITC from welfare. They targeted aid at wage earners and children rather than non-working adults. Proponents consciously and repeatedly portrayed their efforts as something different—a public health initiative, family policy, tax fairness, anything except welfare. When they framed the issue in different ways, they generated more friends in high places.

Many advocates considered Medicaid expansion, for instance, to be an important step in reducing infant mortality and low-weight births. The latter issue steadily gained prominence in the late 1970s and early 1980s. Milestones included a 1979 report by the surgeon general, hearings held by the newly created House Select Committee on Children, Youth and Families, and reports issued by the Institute of Medicine, the Children's Defense Fund, and other advocacy groups and foundations. These studies showed that the United States was lagging behind other nations in infant mortality, and that progress was slowing. In 1987, "more than a quarter . . . of all women of childbearing age had no insurance for prenatal care."[37] Some of the worst problems were in the South. In 1985 the Southern Governors Association "recommended that states have the option to provide Medicaid to pregnant women and children with family incomes below the federal poverty level" in order to improve the health of infants and children.[38] The National Governors Association endorsed that recommendation, even though it entailed greater spending by state governments.[39] At about the same time, groups representing the medical community—the American Academy of Pediatrics, the American Public Health Association, the National Association of Children's Hospitals and Related Institutions—became vocal supporters.

Medicaid expansion always had a certain moral appeal because the chief beneficiaries were infants and young children. Now it had strong practical appeal, for studies showed that babies who failed to receive good prenatal care were likely to require more expensive care later in life. Medicaid for pregnant mothers and children was an investment, not expense. Conservative legislators such as Rep. Thomas Bliley (R-VA) and Senator Strom Thurmond (R-SC) joined well-known liberals like Waxman in pushing for Medicaid expansion. Toward the end of the 1980s, business groups came on board using a variant of the investment rationale. "Poor children are not a natural constituency of ours," admitted a U.S. Chamber of Commerce official. "But it is important to the business community to have a healthy, productive work force. Expansion of Medicaid to cover additional poor children will produce a better work force. Early preventive care for children will reduce the incidence of chronic disabling conditions among workers in later years."[40]

From another perspective, expanding Medicaid was antiabortion policy. Better medical care for poor pregnant mothers might increase the number of babies carried to term. Thus the United States Catholic Conference and some conservative legislators (e.g., Republican Henry Hyde of Illinois) became advocates.[41]

For others, expanding Medicaid was a good alternative to national health insurance. After President Carter's plans for national health insurance failed in the late 1970s and the 1980 elections ushered so many Republicans into national office, many liberal advocacy groups decided that expanding Medicaid coverage was the next best thing. They would first try to establish universal coverage for poor children and then seek coverage for all children and all adults. Several years later, when Democrats started calling for mandates on all employers to offer health benefits to their workers, a number of business groups embraced Medicaid expansion as a defensive maneuver. "If we don't find a way to provide coverage for the nation's 31 million uninsured," avowed a Travelers Corporation insurance executive, "the Federal Government may move to adopt some foolish, ill-advised, ill-conceived national insurance strategy."[42] Expanding Medicaid had some of the same appeal as ERISA, the Americans with Disabilities Act, and the Child Tax Credit—as a way to forestall growth in other parts of government. Thus was born the Children's Medicaid Coalition, combining the efforts of the Children's Defense Fund, the American Medical Association, the National Association of Manufacturers, the Health Insurance Association of America, and several other groups. Ironically, some members of the coalition thought that national health insurance was unattainable while others thought it was imminent.

From the beginning, proponents depicted the EITC as the antithesis of welfare.[43] Instead of guaranteeing poor families a certain income, whether or not the parent(s) worked, the government would target benefits at families with wage income. The EITC would create an incentive for poor families to move off welfare and would reduce the numbers of families who became so poor that they needed welfare in the first place. The EITC would reinforce the nation's work ethic, not undermine it. This was the main reason that Senator Russell Long (D-LA), a longtime and often harsh critic of welfare, was the program's original advocate. The first expansion, in 1978, was rooted in President Carter's ambitious (but ultimately unrealized) plans for welfare reform. "The existing welfare system, Carter declared in 1977, was 'anti-work and anti-family.' "[44] Before the Tax Reform Act of 1986 became law, EITC expansion was part of welfare reform bills circulating in Congress. When the EITC came under attack in the mid-1990s, President Clinton vigorously defended the program because it was so integral to his vision of "ending welfare as we know it."

The EITC was not only the opposite of welfare. It also gained support for its ability to restore fairness to the tax code. At the same time that President Reagan cut spending on the poor, he offered sizable tax cuts to upper-income individuals and corporations. Combined with recession, Reagan's fiscal policies contributed to higher rates of poverty and inequality in the early 1980s. Many Democrats concluded that Republicans were vulnerable on the fairness issue and that tax reform was the right way to exploit that weakness. They persuaded a variety of antipoverty groups, notably the Center on Budget and Policy Priorities, to push for a larger EITC. Their efforts bore fruit when the historic Tax Reform Act passed in 1986. That Act removed several million low-income individuals from the income tax rolls, making it one of the biggest antipoverty measures in U.S. history. One of the key ingredients was a sizable increase in the number of families eligible for the EITC and in the benefits they could receive.

Like Medicaid, which was seen as an alternative to national health insurance, a larger EITC was sometimes embraced as an alternative to policies that someone disliked. Moderate and conservative Democrats, hoping to reinvent their party in the 1980s, promoted the EITC as a superior alternative to the party's old tools of direct spending and regulation. If you want to "make work pay," they argued, don't raise the minimum wage; increase the EITC. If you want to help working parents afford child care, don't spend more on subsidized day care centers; increase the EITC. These Democrats wanted to sustain their party's long-standing concern with poverty and the working class, yet find a tool that entailed less bureaucracy and more choice (and whose costs were less visible).[45] The EITC fit the bill perfectly. A number of congressional Republicans and business groups also preferred a larger EITC to a higher minimum wage or more child care spending, and by the late 1980s the Earned Income Tax Credit enjoyed broad support. Presidents as different as Ronald Reagan and Bill Clinton have praised the EITC and pushed for its expansion, as have interest groups as far apart as the Chamber of Commerce and Bread for the World. Despite their many differences, all would likely agree with Clinton's well-known declaration that "people who work hard and play by the rules shouldn't be poor."

CONCLUSION

Many people believe that policies targeted at the poor are ripe for attack. Look at 1981. Look at 1996. The poor lack the political resources needed to be an effective force in U.S. politics, and they don't have enough powerful friends working on their behalf. The smarter strategy, politically, is to work for large, inclusive social programs that unite the poor with the middle classes—national health insurance, universal family allowances, and the like. That way, the interests of weak and strong groups are aligned, and they can work together to defend and expand their benefits.

Clearly, I have some doubts about this argument. Inclusive social programs might have greater moral appeal than targeted programs, based on considerations of equal treatment and social solidarity. Inclusive social programs might have greater technical appeal because of their lower administrative costs. But greater political appeal? Not lately. Evidence from recent decades indicates no significant difference in the political fortunes of upper-tier versus lower-tier social programs. In both tiers, one can find notable examples of political success and political failure. Prescription drug benefits for Medicare were added (1988), repealed (1989), and added again (2003).[46] National health insurance failed (1993–94). Welfare and Food Stamps were periodically retrenched (1981, 1996); Medicaid and the Earned Income Tax Credit were repeatedly expanded (1984–93). Between 1980 and 2000, annual spending grew by 4 percent in the upper tier and 5 percent in the lower tier. I am certainly not claiming that means-tested social programs are more viable than broader social insurance programs. The usual distinction between tiers just doesn't strike me as very useful in identifying winners and losers.

These developments should offer some consolation to fans of activist government. During the George W. Bush administration, several rounds of tax cuts helped transform an historic budget surplus into a massive deficit. Any thoughts of new, inclusive social programs (e.g., national health insurance) now seemed like pipe dreams. On the other hand, maybe there was and is room for expansion of existing programs, even those targeted at the poor. The practical lessons learned from Medicaid and the EITC are to work for incremental changes, avoid the spotlight, distinguish the policy in question from traditional welfare, and portray the benefits of expansion in different ways to different audiences.

Before declaring this The Formula for building sustainable means-tested programs, let me offer two caveats. As some readers may know, Medicaid's troubles did not end when President Clinton thwarted the plans of congressional conservatives. The program's rapid growth remained a source of concern, particularly when the economic slowdown at the start of the twenty-first century increased the Medicaid rolls. While few people have suggested dropping the pregnant mothers and children who were added to the program in recent decades, officials have found other ways to cut spending. A number of states have increased co-payments and deductibles charged to their Medicaid patients. Other states have taken aim at optional medical services by, for example, eliminating dental care for adults or lowering the number of drug prescriptions that can be filled each month. The National Governors Association and the National Conference of State Legislatures recently asked national officials for the authority to create different benefit packages for different groups within Medicaid. Given states' overriding concern with Medicaid's cost, it seems safe to predict that some groups will receive less coverage than they do now. In short, historic gains for some people in the Medicaid program may be balanced out by losses imposed later on others.[47]

Second, I am not sure that the similarities between Medicaid and the Earned Income Tax Credit were truly decisive. In previously published research, I argued that party competition played an important role in the expansion of the EITC. Prominent Democrats and Republicans used the EITC to attract support from the working poor.[48] Given how closely divided the nation was politically, how large this group of voters was, and how evenly they cast their votes for the two parties in the 1980s, competition made sense. Some juicy quotations from party officials seemed to confirm this strategy, and I still believe it was important for that program. But no one pushed for Medicaid expansion in order to win the votes of poor children and pregnant women. So the politics of the two programs may be more different than alike, and we may have two formulas for success, not one. I have the political scientist's urge to generalize when what may be needed is the historian's appreciation of the unique.[49]

One way to determine the significance of the similarities between the two programs would be to examine additional examples. Head Start and job training would be interesting cases, for they seem to have many of the same positive characteristics as Medicaid and the EITC. One serves young children, and the other tries to give adults the skills needed to get off welfare and hold down a paying job. What's not to like? There must be something, because neither has enjoyed anything like the popularity or growth of Medicaid and the EITC. I end with the hope that some readers might be intrigued enough to pursue these questions further. What should be clear for now is that some of the leading programs for the poor have definitely not been poor programs.

CHAPTER 6

Shaq Is Still Pretty Tall

PUBLIC SUPPORT FOR THE AMERICAN WELFARE STATE

> The State plays a more limited role in America than
> elsewhere because Americans, more than other people, want
> it to play a limited role.[1]
> *—Anthony King* (1973)

> Cross-national polls continue to reveal that Americans are
> less favorable toward an active role for government in the
> economy and to large welfare programs than the citizens of
> Canada and European countries.[2]
> *—Seymour Martin Lipset* (1996)

MY ARGUMENT THROUGHOUT HAS BEEN that the American welfare state is more extensive and more vibrant than commonly believed. Although U.S. social insurance programs may be lacking relative to those in Europe, other policy tools such as tax expenditures, loans and loan guarantees, and social regulation are comparatively well developed (chapter 1). Democrats and Republicans have agreed to use these other tools at the same time they were clashing over national health insurance and cuts to traditional forms of social spending (chapters 3–5). Why is that? I hypothesized that some Republicans acted strategically when pushing for laws such as ERISA or the Americans with Disabilities Act, hoping to keep established spending programs in check. Still, one might wonder why Republicans didn't choose instead to devote all of their energies to cutting, block-granting, and privatizing. After all, what is the point of becoming a more cohesive and more conservative party if you can't wage all-out war on the welfare state? The same basic question arises in connection with Republicans' willingness to increase some types of aid to the poor and near poor (chapter 5).

This chapter examines one factor that connects these different puzzles—public opinion. It is by no means the only explanation, and it may not even be the most important. Nevertheless, a closer look at public opinion does shed light on much that we have seen so far. Public opinion will not help us understand specific questions such as why Congress dropped the Chapman amendment from the Americans with Disabilities

Act, or how legislators decided that Medicaid should be available to pregnant women and young children with a family income up to 133 percent of the poverty line, rather than 150 percent. Past studies of social policy making have rarely found public opinion to be important at this level of detail.[3] For one thing, very few citizens have that much factual knowledge about politics.[4] Interest groups and public officials are more likely to work out the particulars of eligibility criteria, financing mechanisms, and benefit formulas. Scholars have found that at a more general level—whether government should address a given problem, whether its involvement should be increased or decreased—public opinion does influence public policy. Important effects persist even when other political and economic influences are examined.[5] Unless a democracy is truly crippled, the views of its citizens ought to have some bearing on public policy.

Linking the general contours of social policy to public opinion is fairly common. The usual approach is to portray public opinion as a drag on the American welfare state. Some of the same authors who refer to the American welfare state as a laggard (chapter 1) attribute that fact to the nation's distinctive values. The quotations at the outset of this chapter, by two eminent political scientists, capture the heart of this argument. Support for the welfare state is lower in the United States than in other countries. Compared to Austria, Germany, Italy, and the United Kingdom, one study found that "America has been generally less supportive of principles underlying the welfare state and less eager to expand its scope."[6] Another comparison involving a larger number of welfare states noted that "the differences are large and they do strengthen the case for the ideological distinctiveness of the United States."[7] "In general," notes Everett Carll Ladd, a veteran analyst of public opinion, "recent surveys show the U.S. public consistently less inclined than citizens of most other industrial nations to turn to government for various guarantees and assistance."[8] As a result, the American welfare state developed later and stayed smaller.

All this seems to make good sense. Americans are known for believing strongly in individualism, liberty, equality of opportunity, and limited government.[9] These values have deep roots. The first immigrants in the seventeenth century included many religious dissidents who were fleeing government persecution. They came to a place where class lines had not been hardened by centuries of feudalism. After breaking away from England in the 1770s, American leaders made their new national government as weak as possible by creating a loose confederation of individual states. After this arrangement proved unsatisfactory, they increased the authority of the national government and instituted a number of checks and balances to prevent the new government from growing too powerful. The basic structure has remained fragmented for over two hundred years.

Subsequent waves of immigration in the nineteenth and twentieth centuries reinforced the nation's core values. Most immigrants came to the United States precisely because of its individualism and limited government. The people who remained in Europe presumably had a greater tolerance of big government and a greater commitment to their group—be it their class, ethnicity, region, or some other social division—than those who emigrated. From these different sets of values emerged different kinds of welfare states, one smaller than the other.[10]

A full-fledged test of this argument is beyond the scope of this chapter. It may be true that ordinary Americans in the 1880s, 1920s, or 1950s wanted less government than their counterparts in Canada and Europe. My focus is on ordinary Americans at the end of the twentieth century. As we shall see, they do not sound like staunch advocates of limited government. While Americans may not be quite as enthralled with their welfare state as people in other wealthy democracies, the level of support in the United States is often impressive. It helps explain why elected officials from both parties have looked for opportunities to create new social programs and expand existing ones. In addition, the combination of what Americans want government to do and what Americans trust government to do helps explain how elected officials choose among different tools of social policy.

CROSS-NATIONAL COMPARISONS

Of all the ways one might analyze national values, probably the most common among social scientists is the public opinion poll. Despite their ubiquity, polls have their drawbacks. Variations in question wording and sequence can have a significant impact on the responses, a fact that poll sponsors can exploit to serve their policy or partisan goals. If advocates want to demonstrate support for privatizing Social Security, they can structure a question or series of questions so that many people will find this option attractive. Good cross-national polls face the additional problem of cost. It is very expensive to contact thousands of individuals in many different countries. This is one reason that some of the best studies of public opinion and the welfare state have relied on comparisons among a small number of countries, or on similar but not identical questions asked at similar but not identical points in time.[11] Ideally, we want poll results from reputable, unbiased organizations that administer surveys in identical form in many countries.

Fortunately, the International Social Survey Program (ISSP) fits the bill. The ISSP is a consortium of polling organizations in over two dozen countries.[12] The U.S. representative to the ISSP is the National Opinion Research Center at the University of Chicago, which for years has conducted the General Social Survey (GSS) and many other surveys. Since the mid-1980s, the ISSP has sponsored cross-national surveys about topics such as gender roles, religion, and the environment. Its most relevant survey for our purposes is called the Role of Government survey, which was completed in 1996.* Over 35,000 individuals in twenty-four nations responded to this survey, making it one of the largest of its kind. Over 1,300 Americans completed the survey as a supplement to the 1996 General Social Survey. Anywhere from 1,000 to 3,000 people in each of the other nations completed the Role of Government survey. The sample size in each country is large enough to make us quite confident of the results.

Most of the countries included in the 1996 survey will be excluded here. To be consistent with previous studies of welfare states, I will focus on comparisons between the United States and other affluent democracies. This leaves out countries such as Bulgaria, Cyprus, and the Philippines that were part of the 1996 survey.[13] To keep from overwhelming readers with data, I will compare American attitudes toward social policy with attitudes in six other countries. These countries represent the three kinds of welfare states identified by Gosta Esping-Andersen in his widely used typology. Two of these countries, Canada and Great Britain, are classified as liberal welfare states "in which means-tested assistance, modest universal transfers, or modest social-insurance plans predominate."[14] The United States is considered to be more "liberal" than either of these countries, and thus less generous.† Germany and Italy represent the corporatist welfare states typically found in continental Europe. Sweden and Norway exemplify the social democratic welfare states; they are the biggest spenders and the most committed to universalistic policies. If differences in public opinion parallel differences in social policies, then support for a large government role should be lowest in the United States, followed by Canada and Britain. Sweden and Norway should be at the other end of the spectrum with the highest levels of support. Germany and Italy should fall somewhere in the middle.

In some respects, Americans do want less government. Most Americans do not want government to control prices in order to boost the economy. Most Europeans do. Most Americans do not want government-run electric utilities. Most Europeans do. Neither of these issues, however, is exactly central to social policy. The most pertinent question is what Ameri-

---

* The next Role of Government survey is planned for 2006, which means that the results may not be available until 2008 (or later).

† "Liberal" here refers to the classical liberalism of Adam Smith and John Stuart Mill, in which individual liberty and limited government are valued highly.

TABLE 6.1
U.S. Public Opinion in Comparative Perspective

	U.S.	Canada	U.K.	Germany	Italy	Sweden	Norway	7-nation average
Government responsibilities								
Health care for the sick	84.6%	94.1%	98.6%	97.4%	98.7%	96.2%	99.2%	95.5%
Decent standard of living for the old	86.7	90.1	98.2	96.8	98.0	97.7	99.1	95.2
Financial help for low-income college students	85.3	85.4	90.1	89.4	94.2	79.1	79.3	86.1
Decent housing for those who can't afford it	67.0	72.1	88.6	82.2	88.1	81.8	74.1	79.1
Decent standard of living for the unemployed	47.7	65.5	78.7	84.1	75.0	80.3	92.7	74.9
Run hospitals	26.2	74.4	88.9	70.5	49.6	93.8	91.8	70.7
Reduce income gap between rich and poor	48.0	50.5	67.7	69.4	75.4	70.6	73.3	65.0
Jobs for all who want them	39.4	36.5	69.4	80.2	76.6	65.1	80.8	64.0
Govt spending priorities								
Health								
more	67.6	55.5	91.5	59.4	76.8	76.6	85.3	73.2
less	6.7	6.5	0.4	5.4	4.9	1.0	1.3	3.7
Education								
more	77.3	66.3	84.5	54.0	70.9	58.8	51.0	66.1
less	5.3	4.3	0.9	5.2	5.1	2.7	4.3	4.0
Old age pensions								
more	50.8	29.3	80.0	49.3	67.8	56.9	57.0	55.9
less	10.0	10.6	0.8	4.1	7.4	2.5	1.6	5.3
Unemployment benefits								
more	28.3	16.6	35.9	37.6	48.6	42.7	19.7	32.8
less	21.6	31.0	20.2	13.9	21.2	14.9	19.3	20.3

cans and Europeans think about classic social welfare programs: old age pensions, health care, unemployment benefits, and the like.

Answers to these kinds of questions appear in table 6.1. The first questions entail judgments about the proper role of government. Pollsters asked individuals whether they thought that certain policy objectives (e.g., providing a decent standard of living for the elderly, reducing the income gap between rich and poor) were the responsibility of government. The figures reported in the table reflect agreement, meaning the

TABLE 6.1 (cont'd)

	U.S.	Canada	U.K.	Germany	Italy	Sweden	Norway	7-nation average
Spend more on social services or	59.9	38.7	72.6	40.5	38.7	44.0	59.3	50.5
Reduce taxes	40.1	61.3	27.4	59.5	61.3	56.0	40.7	49.5
Spend same, even if debt and deficit stay same or	63.1	44.3	na	na	54.1	na	na	na
Cut spending to lower debt and deficit	36.9	55.7	na	na	45.9	na	na	na

Source: International Social Survey Program, Role of Government III data set (1996), available at http://www.issp.org.

Note: For government responsibility, the figures represent the percentage who agreed that each function was "definitely" or "probably" a governmental responsibility. For spending, the figures for "more" represent the percentage agreeing that government should spend "much more" or "more," and the figures for "less" represent the percentage agreeing that government should spend "less" or "much less." The figures for Germany equal the sum of East and West Germany, which are reported separately by the ISSP for purposes of comparison with previous surveys. In some cases, answers are not available (na), usually because the question was not asked in that country.

sum of those who said that a given objective definitely was or probably was government's responsibility.

Americans' views about their welfare state are exceptional in certain ways. On most of the government responsibility questions, public support in the United States is lower than in any of the other nations. The best American finish is fifth place (financial help for low-income college students); most of the time the United States comes in last. Compared to the British, who are supposed to share many of the same values, Americans are less likely to favor guaranteed jobs, government-run hospitals, or a decent standard of living for the unemployed. The gaps between the United States and the two Scandinavian countries on these questions are even larger.

On the other hand, there are some striking similarities. The rank order of priorities across the seven nations is fairly consistent. In all these nations, including the United States, health care for the sick and a decent standard of living for the elderly are at the top of the list. Reducing income inequality and providing jobs for all who want them are lower priorities. Moreover, in several cases, the United States does not finish last by much. In Canada and Europe, 90 to 99 percent of the people want government to provide a decent standard of living for the elderly. In the United States,

87 percent want the same thing. Almost everyone wants government to provide health care for the sick, including 85 percent of Americans. Even on the housing question, two-thirds of Americans agree that government has a responsibility.

The second group of questions in table 6.1 indicates spending priorities. These are conceptually distinct from the questions about government responsibility. One might believe that government ought to take care of the elderly, yet feel that the current policies are too generous and ought to be cut. Typically, pollsters asked respondents whether government should spend much more, more, about the same, less, or much less on a particular policy. Those who wanted to spend much more or more are grouped together in the table, as are those who wanted to spend less or much less.

Americans were more likely than people in other nations to support spending cuts in general. That is what the conventional wisdom would predict. When asked about specific programs, however, Americans' willingness to cut dropped substantially. Indeed, they were more likely to favor spending increases, and often by a large margin. More than three-quarters of Americans favored greater government spending on education, a higher percentage than in any other nation except the United Kingdom. Two-thirds favored more government spending on health, which put the United States ahead of Canada and Germany. One-half of Americans wanted more spending on retirement pensions, which put the United States in front of Canada and close to Germany, Sweden, and Norway. No more than 10 percent of Americans wanted to spend less on any of these policies.[15]

One might worry that these figures overstate the real level of support. Ask most people whether they want more or less of something, and naturally they will say more. If this were true, then we should see strong support for more spending across the board, and we do not. Americans did not want more of everything. Only about a quarter of Americans wanted to spend more on unemployment benefits. Interestingly, when asked about the military and defense (not reported in table 6.1), only one-fifth of Americans wanted to spend more; one-third wanted to spend less. In contrast, "spend more" outnumbers "spend less" in all four of the social-spending questions. The story in Canada and Europe is the same—considerably less support for unemployment benefits than other types of social spending. There were actually more Americans who wanted to increase these benefits than there were like-minded Canadians or Norwegians.

A stronger test comes when we examine questions posing explicit trade-offs. Would people prefer their government to spend more on social programs or reduce taxes? In the United States, the home of limited government, 60 percent favored more social spending in 1996 (table 6.1). A majority of Canadians, Germans, Italians, and Swedes opted for lower taxes. Do people want government to keep spending, even if it means sustaining deficits and debt? Almost two-thirds of Americans agreed, which exceeded the number of Canadians or Italians in agreement.[16]

By now it seems clear that Americans do not view the welfare state with fear or loathing. They embrace their welfare state, or at least major parts of it. Americans overwhelmingly believe that government should take care of the old and the sick, and that government should spend as much or more on these objectives as it does already. Their views are entirely consistent with a welfare state in which Social Security, Medicare, and Medicaid are far and away the largest pieces, and among the fastest growing (chapter 2). In contrast, Americans are divided on what to do about unemployment, which helps explain why unemployment benefits lack the uniformity and generosity of Social Security or Medicare. Most Americans do not want government-run hospitals, and sure enough, calls for a British-style National Health Service are almost unheard of in the United States.[17]

Conceivably, general public opinion is the wrong thing to compare. Analysts have found that opinions on a given issue can vary substantially among subgroups within a population, making the aggregate numbers somewhat misleading. Depending on the issue, wide differences may appear along gender, racial, religious, regional, educational, or income lines.[18] We might expect public officials, especially those who are elected, to listen most closely to the opinions of people who vote regularly, make campaign contributions, or keep up with current events. Such people might be considered the "attentive public" and have influence greater than their numbers would predict.[19] Claims about American exceptionalism might be more credible if we could show that some influential minority was less enamored of the welfare state than the average citizen was.

To test this possibility, I examined the views of three kinds of attentive publics in the 1996 Role of Government survey: college graduates, the rich, and voters.[20] Although their support for government's role in social policy was less than the national average, the differences were generally small. For example, in the question about government responsibility for the elderly, support ran between 78 and 87 percent among the three groups, compared to 87 percent nationwide. The pattern was almost identical for government responsibility toward the sick. On the housing question, 63 to 65 percent of these groups agreed, compared to the national average of 67 percent. Spending more on health won support from 60 to 65 percent of all three groups versus 68 percent of the total. The biggest drop-off in support came from college graduates answering some of the spending questions. Even then, the views of voters and the rich toward social spending were very close to the national average.[21] If politicians listen closely to what the more influential citizens say, they will not hear a message much different from what ordinary Americans are saying.[22]

COMPARISONS OVER TIME

Some readers may worry that I am placing too much emphasis on a single survey. Perhaps Americans were in an exceptionally good mood in 1996. The Cold War was over, and no terrorists were crashing commercial jets into American skyscrapers. The economy was strong and the deficit was shrinking. No one outside the White House had heard of Monica Lewinsky. Perhaps Americans' views about what government could do and should do were unusually grand. Although cross-national data as good as the most recent Role of Government survey are lacking, we can examine additional polls from the United States to determine if 1996 was an aberration.

The Pew Research Center for the People and the Press has repeatedly asked questions about government responsibility. Between 1987 and 2003, on average, two-thirds of Americans said that "it is the responsibility of the government to take care of people who can't take care of themselves." During this period two-thirds also agreed that "the government should guarantee every citizen enough to eat and a place to sleep." In both cases the figures dropped a bit in the early 1990s, then recovered.[23] Recent wars on terrorism and Iraq have not dampened the public's support for social programs. Many Americans in 2005 felt that Social Security (88%), Medicare (83%), and Medicaid (74%) were very important, more so than defense and military spending (57%) or foreign aid (20%).[24]

Since the early 1970s, the General Social Survey (GSS) has recorded Americans' views of national spending priorities.[25] Typically, pollsters ask people whether current spending on a particular problem or program is too little, about right, or too much. For each question we can calculate a *net spending score*, which is the percent of people saying "too little" minus the percent saying "too much." Negative net scores indicate opposition to more spending, and positive scores indicate support. The scores can range from −100 to +100. The net spending score for Social Security was +43 in 1996. During the 1980s, the Social Security scores were closer to +50. The net spending score for health was +56 in 1996; it averaged over +60 for the previous ten years. The net spending score for education was +68 in 1996, making it one of citizens' top priorities; this score was about the same as the average for the previous decade.

The GSS also includes questions about spending priorities that have not been part of the Role of Government survey, and which reinforce some of the general points made here and in previous chapters. The responses show support for other parts of the welfare state, such as assistance to the poor (+37 in 1996). They show that support for the lower tier can be just as great as for the upper tier. In every single survey taken between 1984 and 1994, the net support scores were higher for assistance to the poor than for Social Security. Finally, the responses show that Americans do not mindlessly call for more spending across the board. The net support scores for welfare were consistently negative between the 1970s and the 1990s, at times dropping below −40. Americans also felt that too much was being spent on space exploration, foreign aid, and assistance to big cities. Net support for assistance to blacks hovered around zero during the 1980s and 1990s.

Many observers have sensed a "right turn" in American politics, starting with the election of President Reagan in 1980 and solidified by Republicans' takeover of Congress in 1994. In some cases, support for social spending was lower in the mid-1990s than in the 1980s. More recent polls, however, show that public support has rebounded. The net spending score for Social Security increased from +43 in 1996 to +54 in 2002, and similar gains were registered for health (from +56 to +69). There have been tremendous gains for assistance to the poor (from +37 to +59).[26] Moreover, many people feel that officials in Washington are not paying nearly enough attention to social problems. The Pew Research Center for the People and the Press found that 75 percent of Americans in 1997 thought government should make access to affordable health care a high priority, but only 15 percent thought government had done so. Seventy-two percent thought that a decent standard of the living for the elderly should be a high government priority, but only 17 percent thought it actually was. Sixty-five percent thought that reducing poverty should be a high priority, but only 16 percent thought it was. The right turn, which was never big to begin with—more Americans still said too little was being spent on key parts of the welfare state, compared to those who said too much—seems to have given way to a left turn when it comes to social policy.[27] Overall, these figures show that Americans' answers in 1996 were pretty typical of their views during the last decades of the twentieth century.

Republicans and Democrats

Looking at the poll numbers, we can see why Republican officials would have felt pressure to create and expand social programs in recent decades (chapters 4 and 5). Ordinary Americans have wanted government to do more, not less, in many realms of social policy. Of course, Republican officials might have cared a lot more about what ordinary Republicans wanted than what ordinary Americans wanted. But that distinction does not turn out to make much of a difference. Figure 6.1 presents the net support scores for a variety of social policies, broken down by the party identification of respondents. The first set of numbers (concerning government responsibility) comes from the 1996 Role of Government survey. The second set (spending numbers) is based on pooled data from the General Social Survey, with some pools larger than others depending on when the GSS started and stopped asking a given question.

Not surprisingly, strong Democrats voice the greatest support for social policies, strong Republicans the least, with independents squarely in between. Note, however, how strong support is among Republicans. Republicans definitely believe that government should care for the old and the sick. More Republicans want to increase spending on Social Security than decrease spending (+38). The same goes for spending on health (+47), education (+46), assistance to the poor (+35), and assistance for child care (+39). Remarkably, even strong Republicans follow this pattern. In short, very few ordinary Republicans say they want government to spend less; they want government to spend the same or more. The main exceptions are welfare, which both Democrats and Republicans view negatively, and unemployment benefits, which is about the only place where Democrats and Republicans genuinely disagree. Neither of these latter policies accounts for much social spending. On the big-ticket items, Democrats and Republicans want to preserve and often expand the government's role.[28]

By unpooling the spending data and examining the end points, we can determine whether support among Republicans has been growing or declining. In 1984 the net support score for Social Security among strong Republicans was +14. By 2002 it was +35. During this same period, strong Republicans' support for health spending increased from +12 to +51. Their support for educational spending increased slightly and for assistance to the poor was virtually unchanged. Thus, while Republican legislators became more conservative in the 1980s and 1990s, ordinary Republicans remained strongly committed to major parts of the American welfare state.[29]

If Republican officials wanted to heed the views of their closest supporters, then they should have cut back on unemployment benefits and welfare but increased assistance to the poor.[30] Lo and behold, Republicans reduced unemployment and AFDC benefits in 1981, stripped welfare of its entitlement status in 1996, and implemented shorter time limits on welfare recipients that same year. A number of Republicans also cooperated in the expansion of the Earned Income Tax Credit and Medicaid between the mid-1980s and mid-1990s. If Democratic officials paid attention to their supporters, then they too would have pushed to cut welfare while increasing the EITC and Medicaid (chapter 5). All this makes public opinion pretty consistent with recent milestones in social policy.

The trickier task for Republican officials was acting on their conservative impulse to cut other parts of the welfare state while respecting public demands for more spending on social policy. One strategy for resolving

Government Responsibility

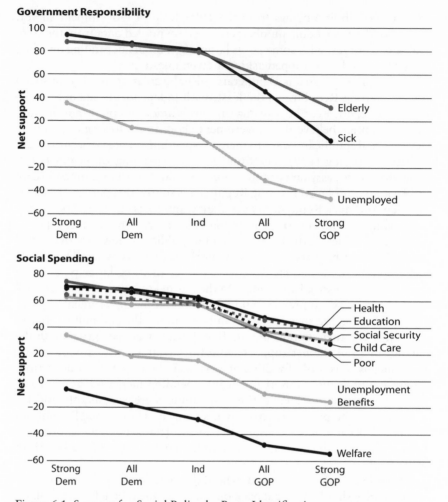

Figure 6.1 Support for Social Policy by Party Identification.
Note: Figures for government responsibility date from 1996. Figures for social spending are pooled depending on data availability: poor (1984–2002), health (1974–2002); child care (2000–2002); education (1974–2002); social Security (1984–2002); unemployment benefits (1985–96); and welfare (1974–2002).

Sources: International Social Survey Program, *Role of Government III* data set (government responsibility); General Social Survey 1972–2002 cumulative data file (social spending).

these seemingly incompatible objectives was creating new social programs that might curb the growth of existing social programs—hence Republican support for ERISA, the Americans with Disabilities Act, and the Child Tax Credit, but not the Family and Medical Leave Act (chapter 4). This was by no means the only strategy. Some Republican officials, aided by conservative think tanks and interest groups, also tried to change public opinion by undermining confidence in existing programs such as Social Security and Medicare and by promoting private-sector alternatives such as Individual Retirement Accounts and Medical Savings Accounts.[31] Those efforts would take years to bear fruit, and success was by no means guaranteed. In the meantime, Republicans added new layers of social programs in order to satisfy voters and slow down the growth of existing layers.

To recap: The American welfare state is supposed to be relatively small, and Americans are supposed to like it that way. It may even be small because Americans like it that way. I argued earlier that the contemporary American welfare state is comparable in size to many European welfare states, and I have argued in this chapter that American attitudes are currently not much different from attitudes in Europe and Canada, either. U.S. public opinion and social policy are congruent, but at a higher level of support and government involvement than the conventional wisdom claims. If we think in terms of a sports analogy, the American basketball player Shaquille O'Neal (7'1") is indeed shorter than China's Yao Ming (7'6"). Shaq is still pretty tall. While public support for the welfare state may be greater in Europe, it is broad and deep in the United States. There may have been a time when Americans were deeply ambivalent about their welfare state. That time has passed.[32]

PUBLIC OPINION AND POLICY TOOLS

Although the size of the American welfare state is not especially distinctive, the composition is. The United States relies less on social insurance and more on other policy tools than many other affluent democracies. As a result, we might ask if and how public opinion contributes to the unusual mix of social policy tools employed in the United States. This question cannot be answered conclusively, in part because polling organizations seldom ask Americans about different policy tools. Cross-national surveys on the subject are, to my knowledge, quite rare. My provisional answer is based on circumstantial evidence and a certain measure of plausibility. It highlights the mixed signals sent by citizens who feel that government is too powerful and cannot be trusted, and yet who want government to do more to help the elderly, the sick, the poor, and children. Faced with seemingly contradictory demands, many policy makers look for ways to expand government's role without seeming to expand government. They turn to tax expenditures, which rely on existing bureaucracies and have the wonderful quality of appearing to do more while taxing less. They issue loan guarantees to help individuals qualify for loans from private lenders. They may even turn to social regulations, for which costs are harder to quantify than for social insurance or grants, and which spread responsibility for addressing social problems among individuals, corporations, and governments.

The prolonged decline of trust in government has generated considerable scrutiny in the media and among academics. I am less interested in explaining this decline than in understanding the implications for policy making. The basic pattern is familiar. In the early 1960s, about three-quarters of Americans trusted the national government to do the right thing most of the time or just about always. By 1980 only one-quarter of Americans had that much faith in government. Over half of Americans in the 1960s thought that government was run for the benefit of all rather than a few big interests. Fewer than a quarter of Americans felt the same way in 1980. The number of Americans who felt that the national government was growing too powerful increased as well. Trust rebounded a bit in the 1980s but fell again in the early 1990s. The historic low point was 1994, when barely 20 percent of Americans trusted the national government to do the right thing. Since then, trust has grown substantially. Over half of Americans said they trusted the government in 2002. Although some of that increase might be attributable to a "rally round the flag" effect after the terrorist attacks of September 11, 2001, general trust in government was already up to 44 percent by 2000. Nevertheless, trust has not returned to levels reached in the heyday of Presidents Kennedy and Johnson.[33]

For the last decades of the twentieth century, then, we have two trends. Public support for social policy fluctuated a little but was generally quite strong. Public trust in government started high, declined for almost three decades, then recovered some of the lost ground. Policy makers faced strong demands for government involvement in social welfare from citizens who were losing faith in government and thought officials already had too much power.[34] This was an unenviable position but not an impossible one. To see how policy makers worked through this dilemma, we might revisit our chronology of the American welfare state (table 3.1). When trust in government was high, as it was in the early and mid-1960s, policy makers turned to the traditional tools of social policy: social insurance and grants. The major achievements of the Great Society were health insurance for the elderly (Medicare) and a number of means-tested grants including Medicaid, Food Stamps, and Head Start. The recent adoption of Medicare part D, covering prescription drugs, also fits this pattern. It passed in 2003, right after trust in government surpassed 50 percent for the first time in decades.

When trust was low or declining, policy makers found it difficult to enact new social insurance or grant programs. Calls for national health insurance, guaranteed incomes for the poor, and major jobs programs went nowhere between the late 1960s and the mid-1990s. The Medicare Catastrophic Coverage Act of 1988 might have stood as a notable exception, but it was quickly repealed.[35] The more indirect tools of social welfare have not needed as much trust to become law. Legislators enacted ERISA (1974)—a historic combination of new social regulations, insurance, and tax expenditure—after trust in government had declined to half of what it had been during the Great Society. The Earned Income Tax Credit passed one year after ERISA. Officials created a number of social regulations between the mid-1980s and the mid-1990s designed to help the sick and the disabled, most notably the Americans with Disabilities Act. The basic reason why these tools fare better when trust is low is that government is forced to share responsibility with individuals, businesses, and nonprofit organizations for achieving social policy objectives.[36]

By itself, trust in government does not determine which policy tools succeed or fail. A lack of trust needs to be exploited, as opponents of the Clinton health plan did effectively from 1993 to 1994. Rep. Dick Armey (R-TX) published an infamous critique in the *Wall Street Journal*, accompanied by an incredibly complicated (and misleading) chart of all the government bureaucracies that might be created by the Clinton plan. A bumper sticker from that time declared, "National Health Care? The compassion of the IRS! The efficiency of the post office! All at Pentagon prices!"[37] Such arguments resonated with many people because they were already so skeptical of government. Nor is trust in government likely to be the only contextual factor that matters. Party control of government seems to affect which tools are selected (chapter 3), and the two factors may well be interrelated.

By the end of the twentieth century, trust in government had recovered to the point where Americans did not have strong preferences for one policy tool over another. They just wanted government to do something about a number of pressing social issues. In 2000, for example, the Kaiser Family Foundation asked a national sample of adults what policies they would support to extend health insurance coverage. Over three-quarters (78%) agreed with expanding means-tested programs such as Medicaid. Over three-quarters (77%) said they would support new laws compelling employers to offer health insurance to their workers. Almost three-quarters (74%) favored tax deductions and tax credits for individuals who bought private health insurance. Two-thirds (67%) wanted to expand

Medicare. When forced to choose the one best option, 21 percent of respondents opted to expand Medicaid, 21 percent chose new regulations on business, 20 percent chose tax incentives, and 14 percent wanted to expand Medicare. Another recent poll, concerning long-term care for the elderly and disabled, found that 92 percent of people endorsed government-financed long-term care insurance, and 92 percent also endorsed tax breaks for family members who provide unpaid care to their elderly or disabled relatives.[38] If I am right about trust and tools, then policy makers currently have a wider range of politically feasible choices than they have had in a long time.

Compared to Europeans, Americans offer less support for the most direct, most visible forms of government involvement in social policy. Attitudes toward government-run hospitals and government jobs programs offer clear evidence of this gap (table 6.1). That part of American exceptionalism remains intact. Public officials, however, can use other policy tools to enhance social welfare, and the United States seems perfectly capable of deploying these tools to address social problems. Officials feel pressure to act because so many Americans have accepted the welfare state and want to expand it. Depending partly on trust in government, some tools may be more or less attractive at different points in time. For those who want to expand government's role, the practical lesson may be to match the tool to the times. The failure of initiatives like the Clinton health plan may tell us less about the public's views on health policy than the public's views toward government.[39]

CHAPTER 7

The World According to AARP

SO FAR IN PART 2 WE HAVE SEEN that political parties, means-testing, and public opinion are not as big obstacles to social policy as commonly believed. A skeptic might concede that more children are now covered by Medicaid, and that the Earned Income Tax Credit and Child Tax Credit give us something like European-style family allowances, but insist that the basic roster of winners and losers in this country has not changed. The real story is still how U.S. social policy favors the elderly. As noted in chapter 2, most social spending is designed to provide senior citizens with pension income, medical care, and long-term care (usually in nursing homes). More money is spent on Social Security than the combined budgets of the Departments of Agriculture, Commerce, Energy, Interior, Justice, State, Transportation, and Veterans Affairs, as well as NASA and the Environmental Protection Agency. Basically, the top priorities of the national government are protecting the country from attack, taking care of old folks, and paying interest on the debt.

If anything, these trends are becoming more pronounced. The main spending initiatives of the George W. Bush administration have been greater funding for "homeland security" and a new prescription drug benefit attached to Medicare. Prescription drug coverage was an important issue during the 2000 presidential campaign, and it remained a high priority within official circles despite significant increases in defense spending and mounting deficits. The willingness of conservatives in the White House and Congress to endorse a drug plan costing hundreds of billions of dollars was astonishing. Even without this new benefit, a large cohort of baby boomers approaching retirement all but guarantees that government spending on the elderly will continue to increase.[1]

Fifty years ago, the elderly were worse off than the rest of the population. Not any more. Practically all the elderly now have health insurance. Twenty-five percent of young adults and 30 percent of the poor do not. A smaller fraction of the elderly than of the nonelderly reports having trouble paying their rent or mortgage. The chances that an elderly household experiences what the Agriculture Department calls "food insecurity with hunger" are less than half the national average. The poverty rate among the elderly is half that of young children.[2]

A number of critics now contend that the pendulum has swung too far in favor of older Americans. Lawrence Kotlikoff, an economist who writes frequently about entitlement programs, argues that the "intergenerational transfer represented by Social Security and Medicare 'has now gone way beyond what could be rationalized as an antipoverty program. What we are dealing with now is the expropriation of billions of dollars every year from young workers to finance the ever-rising consumption by greedy geezers.'"[3] Pete Peterson, head of the Concord Coalition and a former official in the Nixon administration, believes that elected officials have essentially declared war on future generations by promising to spend so much on Social Security and Medicare. Federal Reserve Board chairman Alan Greenspan has warned Congress about the dangers of continued growth in spending on the elderly.[4] Recent titles such as *The Coming Generational Storm* and *Young v. Old: Generational Combat in the 21st Century* portray a zero-sum struggle between generations.[5]

How older Americans came to occupy such a privileged position is no mystery. Two decades ago, the noted demographer Samuel Preston argued that "in a modern democracy, public decisions are obviously influenced by the power of special interest groups, and that power in turn is a function of the size of the groups, the wealth of the groups, and the degree to which that size and that wealth can be mobilized for concerted action. In all of these areas, interests of the elderly have gained relative to those of children."[6] Recent critics seem to agree. From their perspective, the growth in spending on programs for the elderly indicates what powerful groups can extract from government. Senior citizens are represented by the single largest interest group in the country, AARP (formerly the American Association of Retired Persons), and they are quite active in elections and campaigns.* If older Americans have a lot of political clout, and they benefit a lot from social spending, then it seems only logical to conclude that the elderly have shaped social policy to serve their own needs.

The main purpose of this chapter is to challenge the idea that the elderly dominate social policy making. Yes, AARP is enormous. That does not necessarily make it a powerful influence on social policy. Yes, voter turnout among the elderly is high. That does not mean the elderly make government do things that other groups do not want done. The bottom line is that the political power of the elderly in the United States has been overstated. Helping the elderly is something that everyone, young and old, agrees on. The American welfare state is built on a fairly broad generational consensus about who should be helped, and how much. I realize how far-fetched this argument will sound to some readers and therefore

---

* The organization dropped explicit reference to retired persons in the late 1990s in part because so many of its members were under the age of sixty-five and not retired. Currently, individuals can join AARP at age fifty.

marshal evidence about interest groups, voting, and public opinion across several decades in order to make my case.

AARP

In recent years, *Fortune* magazine has asked hundreds of Washington power brokers—lobbyists, congressional staff, and elected officials—to identify the most powerful interest groups in America. AARP has ranked at or near the top of the list every time, alongside such powerhouses as the National Rifle Association and the National Federation of Independent Business.[7] AARP's reputation has spread far and wide. Stories in the media have referred to the "legendary power of the AARP," calling it "one of the most powerful advocacy groups of any kind in the nation" and the "800-pound gorilla of senior lobbyists."[8] Jeffrey Birnbaum, a respected journalist who writes often about interest groups and lobbying, has named AARP "the most potent force in American politics" and identified AARP's leader as "Washington's Second Most Powerful Man."[9] Other accounts have been more critical, referring to AARP as "the enforcer of an insatiable and all but invincible gray lobby."[10] Humorist Dave Barry is exaggerating the conventional wisdom only a little when he writes:

> AARP is a large and powerful organization, similar to the Mafia but more concerned about dietary fiber. AARP is greatly feared in Washington, D.C. because of the fierce way it lobbies for issues of concern to senior citizens, such as Social Security, Medicare, and the constitutional right to drive without any clue where the actual road is.
>
> Whenever Congress is considering legislation that in any way affects these programs, AARP sends trained commando squadrons of elderly people to visit the congresspersons who disagree with the official AARP position. If these congresspersons do not change their minds, their bodies are later found bound hand and foot with support stockings, their skin covered with ugly round welts from being viciously jabbed with cane tips.[11]

There are plenty of reasons to think of AARP as all-powerful. It claims 35 million members, making it the largest organized group in the United States after the Roman Catholic Church. With revenues of $770 million in 2003, AARP looks like a member of the Fortune 1000.[12] It is well designed to apply pressure at every level of government. The organization has an imposing headquarters building in Washington, DC, offices in many states, and thousands of local chapters across the country. The flagship publication, *AARP: The Magazine* (formerly *Modern Maturity*), reaches more homes than any other magazine in the country—more than

Reader's Digest or *TV Guide*, and far more than *Time* or *Newsweek*. It gives AARP's leaders an important vehicle for communicating with rank-and-file members. The organization does so much business through the mail that it even has its own zip code.

Among interest groups trying to influence social policy, AARP is a giant. There is no comparable group advocating for children. While organizations such as the Children's Defense Fund and the Center on Budget and Policy Priorities work on behalf of programs such as Head Start and Food Stamps, they do not have millions of dues-paying members. Their main resources—expertise, information, and moral suasion—are not usually considered to be as powerful as money and votes. Groups claiming to speak for young adults (e.g., Third Millennium) are media savvy but have very few members. Labor unions represent a small fraction of the U.S. labor force. Union leaders have devoted considerable energy to winning benefits for their members via collective bargaining agreements with employers, rather than winning benefits for all workers or all families via government. About the only groups comparable to AARP in size and power are the Chamber of Commerce and the National Federation of Independent Business, which consistently push for smaller government, and the American Medical Association (AMA).[13]

I am not so intent on debunking the conventional wisdom that I will portray AARP as a political weakling. That would be foolish. But I do think its power needs to be qualified in a couple of important ways. First, AARP is a relative newcomer to politics. It had little influence in the creation or expansion of the American welfare state for much of the twentieth century. One crucial reason was timing: the organization was established in 1958. Unless one subscribes to some strange notion of cause and effect, there is no way to credit AARP with the enactment of Old Age Insurance (now called Social Security) or the means-tested Old Age Assistance (now part of SSI) programs in 1935. There is no way to credit AARP with the addition of survivors insurance in 1939 or disability insurance in 1956. AARP did not exist when policy makers extended Social Security to cover many agricultural and domestic workers in 1950, which effectively brought many women and racial minorities into the system. Martha Derthick's definitive history of Social Security from the 1930s to the 1970s contains but one brief mention of AARP.[14]

Even after its founding, the organization made politics a secondary concern for a number of years. AARP's main objective was selling life insurance policies and other services to seniors. The group's first headquarters was Long Beach, California, not Washington, D.C.[15] According to Theda Skocpol, AARP was "virtually irrelevant to the public policy breakthroughs of the 1960s and 1970s."[16] For example, its vision of health reform bore little resemblance to the legislation creating Medicare and

Medicaid in 1965, and it was far less visible than the American Medical Association or organized labor.[17] The group played almost no role in passing the Older Americans Act (1965), which created a range of social services for the elderly. The same was true of major benefit increases to Social Security in the years from 1968 to 1973, increases that helped move millions of elderly citizens out of poverty and keep them out (because benefits were subsequently indexed for inflation). Thus, AARP had practically no influence on any of the major policy decisions that created and expanded Social Security, the nation's largest social program, during the twentieth century. The one policy issue AARP initially cared most about was repealing the mandatory retirement age, and it took nearly twenty years of lobbying to register a partial victory in Congress.[18]

AARP did not become a major power in Washington until the late 1970s or early 1980s, which leads to my second qualification. AARP is decidedly weaker when it says "yes, more" than when it says "no, not less." In other words, over the last quarter century, AARP has generally been less successful in winning new benefits from government than in defending existing benefits against cutbacks.*

Medicare offers good evidence for this pattern. Though modeled in several ways on Social Security, Medicare developed very differently. Medicare covered most of the elderly from the start, so legislators had fewer opportunities to expand eligibility than they had with Social Security in the 1940s and 1950s. The main change came in 1972, when eligibility for Medicare was extended to the disabled and to individuals with end-stage renal disease, regardless of age. These changes were due largely to the efforts of specific members of Congress and to organized groups connected to kidney disease and research, not to AARP. Where elected officials did have room to improve Medicare was on the benefits side, and for the most part they declined to do so. "The two decades following Medicare's enactment witnessed few significant changes in program benefits," according to the best history of the program.[19] Consequently, there just isn't much of a record of success that we can credit to anyone, including AARP. The failure to expand benefits is surprising, considering that large majorities of Americans have repeatedly said that they want to spend more on Medicare and on long-term care for the elderly.

AARP appeared to score a major victory in 1988 when Congress passed and President Reagan signed the Medicare Catastrophic Coverage Act (MCCA). Major changes included longer coverage of hospital and nursing-home stays, a new prescription drug benefit, and various limitations on deductibles, co-payments, and out-of-pocket expenses paid by the el-

* Although the recent addition of prescription drug benefits to Medicare may seem like an exception to this pattern, I will show later in the chapter that it is not.

derly. "AARP's crucial role as the preeminent group backing the legislation is indisputable."[20] The MCCA passed by huge margins in both the House and the Senate. This was the first time in its history that AARP had worked hard to bring about a significant expansion of the American welfare state and succeeded. Nevertheless, barely six months later, legislators were besieged with demands to repeal the MCCA—most of them from senior citizens—and in 1989 Congress did just that.

What happened? The short answer is that AARP's leaders misread their members. Instead of financing the MCCA like a traditional social insurance program, with a flat tax rate applied to all workers, the architects of the bill relied more on a progressive rate structure applied solely to retirees. The poorest of senior citizens might pay only an additional $50 a year for the new benefit; the richest could pay up to $1,600. Leaders of AARP had assured members of Congress that this financing mechanism would generate little opposition among the elderly. They were very wrong. Thousands of angry seniors wrote letters to their representatives and made special trips to express their displeasure in person. In perhaps the most famous episode, several dozen people pounded on the car of Rep. Dan Rostenkowski (D-IL), chairman of the House Ways and Means Committee, calling him a coward and demanding repeal of the MCCA.[21] What looked like a historic victory quickly became a stunning defeat. From that point on, AARP started to hear questions about its ability to represent the elderly.

AARP's leaders acted more cautiously the next time a major expansion of government's role in health care was on the agenda. During debates over the Clinton health plan in 1993 and 1994, AARP laid out general principles that it felt should guide health reform. In particular, it supported the goal of universal health insurance, the addition of prescription drug coverage for the elderly, and greater spending on long-term care. These were all features of the Clinton plan and yet AARP's leaders refused to endorse it, even after a specific request by the president in February 1994. They worried that paying for universal coverage would require substantial cuts in future spending on Medicare, which in turn could generate animosity among retirees and a nasty replay of the MCCA debacle. AARP was one of several organizations that Clinton officials hoped would be strong allies and that instead offered little or qualified support for the health plan. In the meantime, opponents from the insurance industry, small business, Republican Party, and Christian Coalition mounted an impressive attack. By the summer of 1994, the Clinton plan was dead in Congress.[22]

The organization's failures have not been limited to health care. Each year, AARP endorses a broad set of domestic policies affecting major sections of the national budget, covering everything from tax policy to housing and transportation.[23] Conservatives like to use these recommendations to show AARP's strong left-wing leanings. The National Taxpayers Union calculated, for instance, that if Congress had enacted everything AARP wanted in 1998, each taxpayer would have owed an additional $7,800 per year.[24] But Congress did not come anywhere close to approving AARP's agenda. It did not cut the home mortgage interest deduction or increase estate taxes for the rich. It failed to boost spending for job training or low-income housing. It did not pass universal health insurance. The considerable gap between what policies AARP favored and what public officials actually did raises questions about the organization's political power.

In AARP's defense, any new spending initiative faced long odds during the 1980s and 1990s. At one point or another there were record budget deficits, tighter spending caps adopted by Congress, and Republican control of the White House, Senate, or House. Groups who wanted bigger government were bound to lose more often than they won. On the other hand, some additional social spending was approved during this period. National officials expanded the Earned Income Tax Credit three times, created the Child Tax Credit, and extended Medicaid coverage to several million more individuals, especially children (chapters 4 and 5). The last example is particularly telling, for it shows that policy makers were willing to expand government's role in health care. In none of these cases was AARP instrumental in producing victory. It may have endorsed these moves on paper, but AARP did little to rally its members, affect public opinion, or pressure elected officials.[25]

AARP has had more success in blocking policy changes that it opposes. During the 1990s, policy makers tried several times to curb the growth of Medicare. Doing so was politically difficult because large, organized groups were going to resist any cuts in spending, and elected officials were reluctant to increase taxes.[26] Although retirees bore some of the cost-cutting burden, most of the cuts were targeted at doctors and hospitals in the form of lower reimbursement from the national government. This is one reason Jonathan Oberlander, an expert on Medicare, says that "by 1990 the AARP had arguably replaced the AMA as the most prominent interest group engaged in Medicare politics."[27] In addition, there is evidence that AARP helped to defeat proposed cuts in Social Security benefits in the 1980s and 1990s, and to shield assorted smaller programs targeted at the elderly from budget cuts.[28]

That said, the veto power of AARP has its limits. For example, the organization opposed many changes to Social Security that eventually became law in 1983. This was the first time that policy makers agreed to retrench Social Security, a historic turning point. Among the changes approved were the first increases in the retirement age (from 65 to 67), partial income taxation of benefits, and a temporary freeze on cost of living adjustments to benefits. And yet, "AARP was simply brushed aside during the restructuring debate."[29]

Nor can we assume that AARP's opposition was always decisive. Shortly after taking control of Congress in the mid-1990s, GOP leaders announced plans to cut Medicare spending by $270 billion over seven years. If approved, these changes would have represented the single largest cuts in the program's history. Although AARP sharply criticized the GOP proposal, the organization was occupied for much of this debate with defending its tax-exempt status. The key opponents to Medicare cuts were President Clinton and congressional Democrats, and the proposal died. Much the same thing happened with the GOP's plan to transform Medicaid into a block grant, which also failed in 1995.[30] More recently, AARP has opposed proposals to carve out a portion of Social Security in order to create individual retirement accounts. Such proposals have not gained much political traction, despite being endorsed by President Bush and a number of prominent Republican leaders and policy analysts. The main barrier could be AARP. On the other hand, the waning appeal of privatization could be due to the substantial drop in the stock market, the growing budget deficit, or the shift in attention and dollars triggered by the war in Iraq and on terrorism in general.

AARP offers proof that being the biggest does not mean being invincible.[31] The organization has lost a number of policy battles over the last two decades, and it played almost no role in building the American welfare state prior to 1980. It makes more sense to say that the welfare state created AARP than vice versa. The organization did not become politically engaged until *after* Medicare and Medicaid had been created and *after* Social Security had been significantly expanded—in short, until after there were sizable government benefits worth defending.[32]

Why Isn't AARP Stronger?

There is a sizable gap between AARP's size and political clout, and one reason is the emergence of rival organizations. If AARP ever had a monopoly on speaking for the elderly, it certainly does not now and probably has not for many years. Many groups now claim to represent the interests of older Americans. Some of these groups take positions that are diametrically opposed to AARP's. The Seniors Coalition bills itself as "*the* responsible alternative to the AARP." It favors privatization of Social Security, curbs on domestic spending, and significant tax cuts. It is certainly not as large at AARP, but with 3 million members it is by no means a small organization.[33] The 60 Plus Association and United Seniors Association

BOX 7.1

Other Seniors' Groups

Historically, AARP has not been the only organization representing the elderly, and demonstrating its limited impact is not the same thing as showing that all "gray lobbies" lack influence. Prior to the New Deal, the main interest groups that were instrumental in creating or expanding benefits for the elderly were the Grand Army of the Republic, a veterans' organization that pushed for Civil War pensions in the late nineteenth century, and the Fraternal Order of Eagles, which helped pass state-level old age pensions in the 1920s. Probably the first organized group of older Americans of any size appeared during the 1930s when thousands of Townsend clubs popped up around the country, animated by a plan to give the elderly $200 a month as long as they retired from work and spent the entire amount within a month. In theory, this plan would have helped the elderly combat poverty and jump-started the economy at the same time. While the Townsend movement probably deserves some credit for making President Franklin Roosevelt focus on the problems of the elderly, nothing in the original Social Security Act looked anything like the Townsend plan. After the Act passed, the key actors were senior leaders within Congress and the Social Security bureaucracy. In general, "the two decades following the passage of Social Security . . . witnessed a marked decline in organized political activity by older people" (Day, p. 23). Before 1960, it is hard to find evidence that organized groups of senior citizens were integral to building the American welfare state.

The influence of senior groups was more evident in subsequent decades. The National Council of Senior Citizens (NCSC) formed in 1961 in large part to help enact Medicare. The group was an offshoot of the labor movement, and initially its members consisted primarily of retired union members, so it was not as "pure" an example of an elderly organization as AARP. Although some scholars credit the NCSC with a major role in enacting Medicare, the most comprehensive analyses of the program's origins (e.g., by Oberlander) say little about the group. There is very little evidence that the NCSC or other similar groups played even a minor role in enacting Medicaid, the Older Americans Act, or the major benefit increases to Social Security in the late 1960s and early 1970s.

These groups became more visible and more influential beginning in the 1980s. Although AARP opposed many of the Social Security reforms passed in 1983, the NCSC was one of the key interest groups involved in supporting the compromise forged by top officials in the Reagan White House and Congress. In fact, AARP was about the only group representing the elderly to strongly oppose the final package. Later in the decade, the National Committee to Preserve Social Security and Medicare and the National Association of

(boxed text continued on following page)

Retired Federal Employees led the drive to repeal the Medicare Catastrophic Coverage Act, which again put them squarely at odds with AARP. Without clear support from groups representing the elderly, it is hard to imagine elected officials voting to take back additional benefits to Medicare that they had authorized one year earlier. On the other hand, these groups were not strong enough to prevent the Act from passing in the first place—and they did try.

Sources: Christine L. Day, *What Older Americans Think: Interest Groups and Aging Policy* (Princeton, NJ: Princeton University Press, 1990); Martha Derthick, *Policymaking for Social Security* (Washington, DC: Brookings Institution, 1979); Richard Himelfarb, *Catastrophic Politics: The Rise and Fall of the Medicare Catastrophic Coverage Act of 1988* (University Park, PA: Pennsylvania State University Press, 1995); David M. Kennedy, *Freedom From Fear: The American People in Depression and War, 1929–1945* (New York, NY: Oxford University Press, 1999), ch. 9; Paul Light, *Artful Work: The Politics of Social Security Reform* (New York, NY: Random House, 1985); Theodore Marmor, *The Politics of Medicare* (Chicago, IL: Aldine, 1973); Jonathan Oberlander, *The Political Life of Medicare* (Chicago, IL: University of Chicago Press, 2003); Henry J. Pratt, *The Gray Lobby* (Chicago, IL: University of Chicago Press, 1976); Theda Skocpol, *Protecting Soldiers and Mothers: The Political Origins of Social Policy in the United States* (Cambridge, MA: The Belknap Press of Harvard University Press, 1992); Theda Skocpol, *Social Policy in the United States: Future Possibilities in Historical Perspective* (Princeton, NJ: Princeton University Press, 1995), ch. 4.

hold similar views and recently lobbied for repeal of the estate tax. The emergence of these groups is most welcome for elected officials, especially conservatives, who favor policy changes that AARP does not. These officials can now claim that their positions have the backing of seniors' groups. Even groups broadly sympathetic to AARP, such as the National Council for Senior Citizens (NCSC), sometimes take opposing stands on specific issues.

The smaller size of these rival groups can work to their advantage. They find it easier to speak with one voice. The Seniors Coalition, 60 Plus Association, and United Seniors Association deliberately target more conservative (and more affluent) retirees. Membership in the National Association of Retired Federal Employees is limited to certain occupations, and the organization is dedicated to preserving a special retirement pension. This is a second reason for AARP's underwhelming record: its huge size makes it quite likely that its members will be divided on most issues. If AARP leaders take a strong stand and play an active role, they risk alienating some sizable fraction of their members—witness the catastrophic coverage debacle of the late 1980s. A safer course is to espouse general principles that few can disagree with, as AARP did during debates over the Clinton health plan, and avoid making detailed recommendations. Another strategy is to go on record in favor of certain policies but do little to rally members to push for those policies. This seems to be the status of the annual policy book, which even AARP staffers describe more as a "wish list" than a blueprint for action.[34]

A corollary is that large size can hurt one's credibility during negotiations. Paul Light explicitly contrasted the large, lumbering AARP to the smaller and more focused National Council of Senior Citizens in his case study of the 1983 Social Security reforms. At one point he quotes a congressional committee aide saying, " 'There was never any doubt about whether you could trust the Council. . . . They would not break an agreement. We were not as sure about the American Association.' "[35] This difference is one reason the NCSC was much more influential than AARP in shaping reform. Whatever concerns policy makers had about AARP were amplified after the catastrophic coverage episode later in the decade. In the words of one legislative staffer, " 'while there once would have been a willingness to accept whatever AARP said about an issue, now everybody checks everything three times from Sunday.' "[36]

One more reason why AARP has trouble converting mass to muscle is that most of its members do not belong to it because of the organization's political activities. AARP is a classic source of what political scientists call selective material benefits. These include significant discounts on travel, entertainment, and prescription drugs; options to buy health, life, and home owners' insurance; and subscriptions to a monthly magazine and newsletter. All these benefits are available only to AARP members, and at $12.50 a year, membership is an incredible bargain. Senator Alan Simpson (R-WY), a frequent critic of the organization, once described it as "33-million people bound together by a common love of airline discounts, automobile discounts, [and] discounts on pharmacy."[37] Harsh, but not far from the truth. Almost 40 percent of AARP's revenue comes from what the organization refers to euphemistically as "royalties and service provider management fees." When AARP members buy these goods and services, either from an AARP subsidiary or a separate company, AARP gets paid. Annual dues, in contrast, represent a little over one-quarter of the organization's revenues.[38]

When AARP polled its own members, it found that only one in six joined because the organization worked to influence policy on behalf of seniors. The vast majority mentioned instead the discounts and subscriptions. Later polls have found that "no particular reason" is the leading explanation individuals give for renewing their AARP membership.[39] In this sense AARP is akin to the American Automobile Association (AAA), whose members join more for travel discounts and roadside assistance than for AAA's efforts to win federal money for highway repair and construction. Both organizations are multimillion-dollar businesses first and political actors second.

Take a look sometime at AARP's website. In August of 2003, the front page invited members to attend Life@50: A Celebration of You. This three-day event featured celebrities such as Dr. Phil and Ray Charles and more sessions about health and lifestyle than political advocacy. A few months later, the section of the website devoted to *AARP: The Magazine* gave the lead spot to an article called "Seeking Love," which declared that the "50-plus dating game has never been hotter." Other features included a list of the fifteen best cities in which to reinvent your life and a quiz about Harley-Davidson products and culture. About the closest thing to political advocacy was a profile of Nancy Reagan's efforts to promote stem cell research that might one day help victims of Alzheimer's disease. The March/April 2004 magazine cover included the provocative heading, "Help! My Husband Loves Porn."[40]

From the perspective of organizational maintenance, relying on selective benefits makes perfectly good sense, and lots of organizations besides AARP use the same strategy. The sheer size of the organization makes it doubtful that any ideology or cause will hold everyone together, so it must keep offering members a large basket of goodies. Nevertheless, the diversity of AARP's membership also means that most members may not respond to calls to political action. Granted, a small fraction of them could still represent a large number of people, but not necessarily larger than that mobilized by smaller, more homogeneous groups.

If AARP is not as strong as many people think, and we understand some of the reasons why, we still need to explain why AARP has had more success preventing cutbacks than winning expansions. Part of the answer is that the American political system is designed to preserve the status quo. The fragmentation of political authority, both across different levels of government and within each level, creates an intricate web of checks and balances. Any group that does not like a proposed change can find many possible veto points in the system. Losing in one house of Congress? Try the other. Losing in both houses of Congress? Try the courts. Losing in the states? Try Washington, D.C. Opposing change is easier than achieving it, for AARP or any other group.

The other part of the answer is based on how individuals typically perceive gains and losses. Interest groups generally find it easier to mobilize people against loss because "the goal is more clearly focused, the moral reaction to potential inequity is stronger, the perception of fairness outweighs that of selfishness, and losses are felt more acutely than gains of comparable magnitude."[41] In other words, people may or may not appreciate a little extra help from the government, but they get really agitated when they see government taking away something that they feel rightly belongs to them. (This behavior appears early in life: contrast the willingness of your average child to write a thank-you note for a gift with the child's sadness if that gift is later broken or taken away.) The opposition of small-business owners, who faced additional taxes and mandates from the Clinton health plan, was far more intense than the rather modest efforts of individuals who stood to gain health insurance coverage.[42] All else being equal, AARP members are more likely to become politically active when programs like Medicare are on the chopping block than when additional benefits are proposed.

Both of these factors help account for the "stickiness" of public programs, and in particular their ability to resist retrenchment. Once Social Security and Medicare were well established, it became very difficult to restrict eligibility or cut benefits.[43] The historical record suggests that AARP deserves little credit for creating or expanding Social Security, Medicare, Medicaid, or any other part of the American welfare state. But it does deserve some credit for defending major social programs from attack. To the extent that such attacks become more common in the future, as policy makers search for ways to rein in spending, AARP may exercise its power more often. The odds of winning are in its favor, just as they are for any large group trying to preserve an existing public program. Although vivid depictions of AARP as an eight hundred-pound gorilla may not be accurate now, the gap between its reputation and reality could diminish in the future. Looking back, one is led to conclude that AARP's power has been overrated. Looking ahead, however, is another matter.

Admittedly, my portrait of AARP's power is at odds with that of the journalists and Washington insiders mentioned at the start of this chapter. I am not entirely comfortable with that gap because I respect the political acumen of people who spend their working lives in the nation's capital. One way of reconciling these two images is to suggest that journalists and insiders use AARP as a ready symbol for the elderly. AARP is the tip of a giant iceberg, the most visible expression of a larger political phenomenon called, for lack of a better term, senior power. References to AARP give the story a certain familiarity, and concreteness, that references to "the elderly" would lack. If this is true, then a narrow focus on AARP's record of success and failure is not enough. Like the bulk of the iceberg, the political might of the elderly may be greater below the surface than above, where AARP resides. In that case, we should examine other ways in which seniors influence public policy.

Voting and Public Opinion

Old people vote, and in a democracy voters have power. Between 1980 and 2000, two-thirds of individuals age sixty-five and older reported voting in the most recent presidential election. About 60 percent reported voting in the most recent congressional off-year election. Turnout is lower among younger cohorts. By the time you get to adults age eighteen to twenty-four, only about one in three votes in presidential elections, and about one in five votes in off-year elections. The age gap in turnout is larger than that between whites and blacks or between the employed and the unemployed. It is roughly the same as the gap separating high school dropouts and college graduates. Moreover, the age gap is growing. While turnout among the elderly increased during the 1980s and 1990s, it decreased among younger adults.[44] Age is also positively correlated with campaign contributions, interest in public affairs, and interest in the current election campaign.[45]

We would expect senior citizens to vote for candidates who promise to defend their entitlements and perhaps even expand them. Younger adults might be more interested in education and child care policies, but because they do not vote, their voices will not be heard in Washington. Given that the elderly vote more often than other age groups, racial minorities, the unemployed, and the less educated, it is no wonder that Social Security and Medicare dominate the American welfare state.

Is this a good account of senior power? Again, a historical perspective helps to refine a piece of accepted wisdom. Looking back in time, we can see that the elderly were not always so active in electoral politics. During the 1950s, 1960s, and 1970s, when legislators enacted Medicare and repeatedly expanded Social Security, the elderly were no more likely to vote than the nonelderly. Nor were the elderly more likely to work in campaigns, give money to candidates or campaigns, be contacted by political parties, or write to their representatives in Washington. As Andrea Campbell carefully demonstrates, the growth of the American welfare state helped to mobilize seniors politically. Their heightened participation might help explain why Social Security and Medicare were able to resist cutbacks starting in the 1980s, but not how those programs grew so large in the first place.[46]

A second and related problem is that many of the elderly are not instinctively drawn to parties or candidates who push for a greater government role in social welfare. In the most recent National Election Studies (NES) polls, anywhere from 30 to 40 percent of older Americans called themselves conservatives, and a similar percent identified with the Republican Party. Exit polls conducted after the 2000 presidential election found that voters age sixty-five and older split pretty evenly between Democrat Al Gore (50%) and Republican George W. Bush (47%). Apart from 1964, Republican presidential candidates consistently won more of the senior vote in the 1950s, 1960s, and 1970s. The only recent election in which a Democrat won older voters by a large margin was Bill Clinton's victory in 1992.[47]

There is also an important difference between voter turnout and the turnout rate. When you start out as 16 percent of the voting-age population, which is what the elderly were in 2000, you need high turnout to have much of an impact. While the elderly are better at getting to the polls than any other age group, the number of elderly voters has been only 20–25 percent of total voters in recent national elections. A large majority of voters are not elderly. In the 2000 presidential election, there were more voters aged eighteen to thirty-four than over the age of sixty-five.[48] If senior citizens are going to influence national elections, they are going to need some help (and, as we shall see, they get it).

Most important, we need to know whether the elderly want government to do things that the rest of the nation does not. Just because the elderly have a loud voice does not mean that they have a distinctive voice. If the elderly work hard to make pecan pie the nation's official pie, then this middle-aged author will be delighted because we love the same pie. If the elderly have basically the same views toward social policy as the rest of the country, it does not matter if the only people who vote are over sixty-five. We need evidence of a generation gap in policy preferences before we become suspicious of how much is spent on programs such as Social Security and Medicare.

The General Social Survey (GSS) and the National Election Studies (NES) have been asking people for years what they think government's responsibilities should be, and how much should be spent on various policies. Figure 7.1 summarizes the results for several questions relevant to social policy, starting at the top with policies aimed at the elderly and ending with policies aimed at families with children. The respondents are grouped into three age categories (18–34, 35–64, and 65 and over). The numbers cited for each group are net support scores, like those used in the previous chapter. On the government responsibility questions, the scores refer to the difference between agreement and disagreement. On the spending questions, the scores refer either to "too little" minus "too much" or "spend more" minus "spend less," depending on the survey. Except for unemployment benefits, the figures come from 2002.

If senior citizens are somehow hijacking the nation's priorities, then they should show substantially more support than younger adults on questions related to retirement and Social Security. The numbers say otherwise. When asked if government has a responsibility to provide a decent

**Government Should Provide
Elderly with Decent Standard of Living**

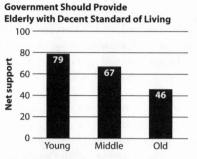

More Spending on Social Security

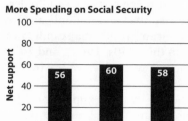

**Government Should
Help Pay Medical Bills**

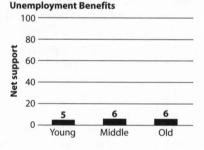

Too Little Spending on Health

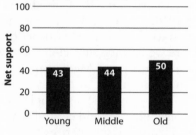

**More Spending on
Unemployment Benefits**

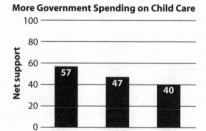

More Spending on Poor People

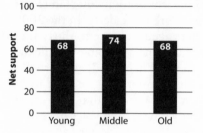

More Government Spending on Child Care

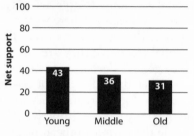

More Spending on Public Schools

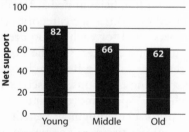

Figure 7.1 Support for Social Policy by Age (Generational Warfare?).
Sources: General Social Survey; National Election Studies.
Note: Young = 18–34; middle = 35–64; old = 65+. All figures are from 2002 except unemployment benefits, which are pooled from 1985–96.

standard of living for the old, a large majority of people over the age of sixty-five agreed in 2002 (net support of +46). While this figure may seem high, it is lower than comparable figures for middle-aged (+67) and younger adults (+79). That year was no fluke. After pooling answers from surveys conducted between 1980 and 2002, I discovered that younger adults have consistently expressed greater support. The generational gap has grown wider over the last two decades, which is almost entirely due to declining support among the elderly. If we shift from the question of government responsibility to spending, support for Social Security was quite strong and quite similar among the age groups in 2002. Over the last two decades, Americans under the age of sixty-five were a little more likely than Americans over the age of sixty-five to call for more spending on Social Security.

The story does not end there. When asked whether most of the projected budget surplus should be used to protect Social Security and Medicare, four out of five adults under the age of sixty-five agreed in 2000 (GSS) and 2002 (NES). In 2002 nonelderly adults were more likely than the elderly to say that government should do more to help the elderly with long-term care.[49] If politicians listened exclusively to senior citizens, they would hear no more demand for government action on behalf of retirees than if they listened to the entire country.[50]

Other surveys indicate little resentment toward the elderly. In 1999 the *Los Angeles Times* conducted a special nationwide poll specifically about aging. Asked if "the elderly in this country are generally ignored and not treated with respect," 73 percent of young adults (age 18–44) agreed, compared to 57 percent of those over the age of sixty-five. Asked if "older people should be encouraged to retire early to make room for younger, more energetic workers," only 13 percent of young adults agreed, compared to 15 percent of senior citizens.[51] Another survey conducted that year, this time targeted at adults under the age of thirty-five, found only 12 percent agreeing that "senior citizens generally get more than their fair share of benefits, and that is unfair to young people."[52] This hardly qualifies as generational combat.

Perhaps the battles are occurring elsewhere. Younger, middle-aged, and older Americans may agree that government should do a lot to help the elderly, yet disagree on how much help should be offered to younger adults and children. In particular, we might wonder if senior citizens do not show much enthusiasm for national health insurance, unemployment benefits, child care, education, and the like since they already have Medicare and Social Security and are no longer raising children. There is some evidence of generational gaps in these areas. The older you are, for example, the less you think government should reduce income differences between rich and poor. There was a 22-point gap in net support for this question in 2002, with younger adults in the lead.

The biggest disagreement is over child care. Senior citizens overwhelmingly oppose the idea that government should provide child care to everyone who wants it (−68), and they are generally opposed to extending child care benefits if both parents work (−11). The elderly feel more negatively toward government-provided child care than welfare, which is no mean feat. In contrast, younger adults are evenly divided on the question of public child care for all (+3) and strongly embrace benefits for two-earner families (+56). When asked whether government should spend more on child care, however, older Americans agree much more than they disagree (figure 7.1).

Before we think of our parents and grandparents as greedy or uncaring, consider attitudes toward education. By 2002 a larger number of senior citizens said they wanted more spending on education than said they wanted more spending on Social Security (figure 7.1). Between 1984 and 2002, the elderly's net support for spending on public schools (+47) was practically the same as for Social Security (+49). Moreover, middle-aged and older Americans are expressing more support for spending on education than they did ten or twenty years ago.[53] The gap between young and old on this issue (figure 7.1) should continue to narrow. Support for education is correlated with years of formal schooling, and a large number of the elderly today never graduated from high school.[54] As they die off and are replaced by people who have more schooling, seniors' support for education should go up.

Likewise, as more people who grew up with working mothers start to reach their sixties and seventies, senior citizens' support for child care should increase. It already has on the question of government spending for child care. The main reason to expect change has to do with views toward gender and family roles. At the end of the twentieth century, older Americans were two to three times more likely than younger adults to believe that women should take care of home and family while men work and run the country. By a similar margin, older Americans felt that preschool children were likely to suffer if their mothers worked outside the home.[55] These attitudes make sense for people who grew up in the 1930s, 1940s, and 1950s. Basic differences in life experiences, more than simple greed, may help explain some of the major generational gaps in attitudes toward social policies. Senior citizens show less support for what they have not gone through and thus do not understand or value.

We can also see from figure 7.1 that young, middle-aged, and old people agree on many issues. Clear majorities of each group believe that government should help people pay their medical bills, and those majorities have grown larger in recent years. Substantial majorities of all groups believe that the United States spends too little on health. When asked specifically about national health insurance, however, support drops off across the board. Regardless of age, Americans want government to do more for the poor but not spend more on welfare. Americans are fairly evenly divided when it comes to offering more help to the unemployed.

In addition to comparing across age groups for a given social policy, we can also compare across policies for a given age group. Younger adults are more likely to say that government should provide the elderly with a decent standard of living than should help pay medical bills, reduce income differences, or provide a decent living for the unemployed. Younger adults are more likely to say that government should spend more on Social Security than on poor people. The numbers of young adults who want more spending on Social Security are very close to those wanting more government spending on child care. Middle-aged adults, many of whom are still raising children, express similar views. By the end of the twentieth century, seniors were expressing more support for education than for Social Security. Overall, then, age does not have much impact on Americans' views toward policies that target the elderly or that cut across generational lines. Even on policies aimed at the nonelderly (education, unemployment, child care), there is as much agreement as disagreement, and what gaps do exist between young and old are narrowing.

Students of public opinion will remind us, however, that we need to consider more than policy preferences. We also need to account for the intensity of those preferences, and here we can see differences across the generations. Older Americans care more about Social Security and Medicare, and younger Americans care more about education, the economy, and jobs. In the 2000 NES, pollsters asked individuals to name the single most important problem facing the country. Because this question was open-ended, respondents gave many answers and no one answer topped 20 percent. Older Americans mentioned Social Security or Medicare twice as often as middle-aged Americans and three times more often than young Americans. Older Americans mentioned education about half as often as Americans under the age of sixty-five. Younger adults were more likely to be worried about poverty, and practically no one mentioned day care or child care as the most important problem.

Exit polls conducted by the Voter News Service after the 2000 elections asked a similar question, but this time forced people to choose from a short list of problems. Excluded from this list were child care and poverty, in part because they had failed to generate much support in open-ended surveys. Almost a quarter of senior voters listed Social Security as the most important issue in the election, and another 17 percent said Medicare or prescription drugs. Only about 11 percent of younger voters (ages 18–29) mentioned Social Security, Medicare, or prescription drugs. Results for education and the economy were virtually the mirror image. Almost a quarter of younger voters listed education as their most important issue and a fifth opted for the economy/jobs, while only 12 percent of older voters ranked these issues at the top of their list. Only 7 to 8 percent of each age group listed health care as the most important problem. Andrea Campbell examined polls from the 1980s and 1990s and found similar results.[56]

Results from the massive Citizen Participation Study show how different social programs affect political activity. Fully one-quarter of Social Security and Medicare recipients said they based their voting decisions on these programs. Only about 10 percent of welfare, Food Stamps, or Medicaid recipients factored their programs into their decisions. Social Security and Medicare recipients were also more likely to donate money, contact a public official, or belong to an organization that worked on behalf of their programs.[57]

The combination of policy preferences and intensity helps us make sense of recent patterns in policy making. Older Americans vote more often than any other group, and they send a clear message to policy makers in Washington—pay attention to Social Security and Medicare. When policy makers think about making cuts to these programs, the whole nation, and not just the elderly, says no. When policy makers think about spending more, the whole nation, and not just the elderly, says yes. All the monies we spend on Social Security and Medicare are very important to the elderly and quite acceptable to everyone else.

Adults in their working years do not worry as much about direct support from the government. They want public officials to keep the economy growing and spend more on education. They are not pressing the government to do more for the poor or the unemployed. In short, younger and middle-aged adults want government to create favorable conditions for self-sufficiency. Policy makers can do much of this through monetary policy, tax policy, and regulations; they do not have to boost social spending. The national government has never been a major source of K–12 educational funding (7–8%). It might issue regulations, such as the recent No Child Left Behind Act, but it will not spend much money relative to state and local governments. Thus, the age bias in social spending reflects the contours of public opinion.

THE NEW MEDICARE DRUG BENEFIT

Earlier in the book, I maintained that any useful generalization about the American welfare state ought to cover the largest individual programs. I should therefore explain how the recent Medicare prescription drug benefit came to pass if the elderly are less powerful than most people think. The Bush administration initially estimated that the Medicare Prescription Drug, Improvement, and Modernization Act of 2003, as it is officially known, would cost $400 billion over ten years.* Almost all of that money is to pay for a new drug benefit for seniors, formally known as Medicare part D. This program is financed through a mixture of monthly premiums and general revenues (not payroll taxes). Starting in 2006, the government pays for 75 percent of the first $2,250 a year in prescription drug costs, 95 percent of any drug costs over $5,100, but nothing for drug costs between $2,250 and $5,100 (the so-called doughnut hole in coverage). The new benefit also includes subsidies for low-income recipients who may not be able to afford the monthly premium. This was the only significant social spending initiative of the Bush administration. By way of comparison, the State Children's Health Insurance Program that passed during the Clinton administration (1997) had a ten-year price tag of "just" $40 billion.

It is hard to imagine better proof that seniors rule. But take a look at what Americans wanted. In a survey conducted right before the 2000 elections, 79 percent of senior citizens said they favored a general proposal to guarantee prescription drug coverage to everyone on Medicare. That figure looks pretty remarkable until we realize that 87 percent of adults under the age of sixty-five also expressed support for this proposal.[58] Like Social Security, Medicare drug benefits generate broad support among people who will not receive them for many years. In the summer of 2003, pollsters asked Americans whether Congress should approve the prescription drug bill, or whether the bill had so many problems that it should not be enacted. Thirty-three percent of the elderly and 24 percent of the nonelderly said it should not be enacted.[59] Three months after the law was enacted, a CNN/USA Today/Gallup poll found that only 36 percent of the elderly favored it, compared to 42 percent of the nonelderly. Another survey taken at about the same time found that the elderly were more likely to worry that the new benefit would cost government too much in the long run, give seniors too little help, be too complicated to understand, force Medicare beneficiaries into HMOs, and benefit drug companies too much.[60] Evidently, seniors did not lead the charge for these new drug benefits.

AARP was involved, though not wholly on behalf of senior citizens. Important changes have taken place in recent years that have redefined

---

* It was later revealed that administration officials had good reason to believe that the total cost of drug benefits would be closer to $500–600 billion and chose not to disclose these estimates to Congress or the general public. Robert Pear, "Inquiry Confirms Top Medicare Official Threatened Actuary over Cost of Drug Benefits," New York Times (July 7, 2004), p. 12.

AARP's identity and political behavior. The name change, mentioned previously, was one signal that the organization would no longer be tied so closely to retirees. Having lowered its membership age to fifty, AARP opened its doors to millions of younger members. In the general population, individuals between the ages of fifty and sixty-four started to outnumber individuals age sixty-five and over in the mid-1990s. By 2003 a majority of AARP members were working and not retired. "Boomers are the future of AARP," according to AARP's chief executive officer, William Novelli. The organization introduced a new magazine in 2001, *My Generation*, to appeal to members in their early fifties. When that failed, AARP developed three different editions of *AARP: The Magazine*, one each for members in their fifties and sixties and one for those seventy and older. The celebrities on the cover are getting younger; in 2004, they included Billy Crystal (57), Cybill Shepherd (54), and Kevin Spacey (44). The term "senior citizen" has reportedly been banned from the magazine.[61]

Shortly after Novelli took over in 2001, AARP centralized control. No longer do local chapters elect the board of directors. State AARP officials who disagree with headquarters have been asked to resign. Historically, AARP has polled its members before taking a stand on a major piece of legislation. Not this time. When attention turned to Medicare drug benefits, AARP conducted polls and focus groups of people over the age of forty-five, regardless of whether they belonged to the organization. AARP's leaders were interested in the views of prospective members and current workers at least as much as the opinions of retirees. The polls cited above show that support for the prescription drug plan was greater among the nonelderly, and AARP officials decided to weather any criticism from its older members in order to appeal to the next generation.[62]

The backlash was swift. By July 2004, less than eight months after the bill became law, some eighty thousand members left AARP to protest its support for the drug bill. One of the main criticisms was that AARP had traded its endorsement for financial gain. Medicare's greater coverage of drug costs may bring hundreds of millions of dollars of additional revenues to AARP's insurance ventures. "AARP's big money comes from insurance kickbacks—cancel ALL your AARP insurance policies," wrote one frustrated member on a message board connected to the AARP website. Many Democrats in Congress were dismayed over AARP's actions and started using language similar to that employed by Republicans just a few years earlier. Rep. Pete Stark (D-CA) decried the "huge conflict of interest" between AARP's political activities and commercial ties. Senator Jay Rockefeller (D-WV) declared that "the AARP is a business, first and foremost. They have a product to sell." AARP officials strongly deny the charge. They also realize that many members are angry and have taken steps to win them back, such as endorsing Democrats' plans to ease restrictions on importing prescription drugs from Canada.[63]

Some observers believe that the Medicare drug episode was just the most visible sign of a historic shift in AARP's partisan leanings. Beginning in the mid-1990s, congressional Republicans led by House Speaker Newt Gingrich started to court AARP while other Republicans, notably Senator Alan Simpson, held high-profile hearings challenging the group's tax-exempt status. The combination is supposed to have muted AARP's opposition to GOP plans for cutting Medicare and adding more forms of managed care to the program. The selection of Novelli—who once worked in the Nixon administration and recently wrote a foreword to Gingrich's book on health reform—as CEO is seen as proof that the organization is losing its pro-Democrat, pro-government identity.[64]

My reading of events is a little different. I believe AARP president James Parkel, who was interviewed shortly after Congress passed the Medicare drug bill: "We had to change. We had the boomers coming and you didn't want to be perceived by the boomers as just being for old people."[65] The demographic winds are blowing against the generation raised under FDR and Truman and blowing with the generation raised under Eisenhower, Nixon, Ford, and Reagan. When AARP endorsed the GOP's Medicare drug bill, it was thinking about the tens of millions of middle-aged Americans who are now or will soon be the organization's core market. This group is less likely than the New Deal generation to be Democratic and less likely to be strongly attached to either major party. That is one reason why AARP can endorse the GOP's Medicare drug plan one year and the Democrats' drug import plan the next. What it also means, however, is that AARP aims to represent people in the second half of life, not the fourth quarter. As a result, AARP should no longer be viewed as an instrument of gray power, or its victories as proof that senior citizens run the country.

CONCLUSION

This chapter has offered evidence that AARP's power is historically fairly recent and more apparent when it plays defense than offense. Policy makers did not expand Social Security or create and expand Medicare because of pressure applied by organized groups of senior citizens. At key moments in the development of these programs, AARP did not exist, was not involved, or acted on behalf of middle-aged citizens. Social Security and Medicare originated and grew because of a relatively small number of political elites located in the White House, key congressional committees, and the Social Security Administration.[66] AARP does deserve credit for helping to protect those programs against cutbacks after they had become so important to senior citizens.

Likewise, the recent creation of Medicare part D reinforces the point that the elderly are not alone is asking for the government's help. Americans under the age of sixty-five want government to take care of Americans over the age of sixty-five. While citizens may not have liked what was in the final Medicare bill, young and old agreed that government ought to help the elderly pay for prescription drugs—just as they have long agreed that government ought to provide a decent standard of living for the elderly and ought to spend more on Social Security. When the elderly push for government help, the rest of the nation pushes right along with them. One classic definition of power is the ability of A to make B do something that B does not want to do. By that standard, the elderly are not that powerful because they have not been forcing the rest of us spend lots of money on Social Security and Medicare.

The main findings of this chapter pose a real challenge to those who have been trying to highlight generational conflict. Efforts to generate resentment or even concern about the amount of money spent on senior citizens will probably fail with the general public. Calls to cut Social Security and Medicare in any significant way are unlikely to find a receptive audience when most people, including most young people, want government to spend more. Critics such as Kotlikoff and Peterson and organizations such as the Concord Coalition and Third Millennium are literally spitting into the wind of public opinion. President Bush learned just how strongly Americans feel about protecting the elderly when he tried to sell the idea of Social Security privatization in the first half of 2005. Despite dozens of well-orchestrated appearances around the country, the number of people who distrusted the president's handling of Social Security increased. By the time he was through, only about one-third of the nation approved of what he was trying to do to Social Security.[67] In the future, it may make more sense for advocates of privatization or retrenchment to try persuading other political and economic elites rather than the general public. Or they might try to bury privatization so deep in a budget bill that few will notice.

By the same token, this chapter shows some of the difficulties facing those hoping to build support for social policies aimed at workers and families with children. Some observers look at the mix of social spending and argue that the country does not need less spending on the elderly but more spending on the rest of us.[68] And yet, Americans do not want government to do more for the unemployed, and they are generally skeptical of national health insurance. Although most Americans want government to spend more on the poor and on child care, it is not clear how deeply they feel about these issues. Instead, any such change may have to be driven largely by political elites, as was the case with the Child Tax Credit (chapter 4) and with recent expansions in Medicaid and the Earned Income Tax Credit (chapter 5). Another possibility, more distant in time, is that today's baby boomers will remember what it was like to worry about health insurance and to pay for child care when they start receiving Social Security and Medicare. Organizations like AARP might take a serious interest in the 8 million Americans between the ages of forty-five and sixty-five who lack health insurance, and might throw their weight behind efforts to expand coverage. Older Americans in the future may ease up on defending their own benefits, or go more on offense to win support for working families. Such a future would require a healthy dose of empathy and altruism, and I am not about to predict that it will happen.

PART III

Checkpoints and Roadblocks

CHAPTER 8

The American States

LABORATORIES OF DEMOCRACY
OR CRYOGENIC CHAMBERS?

ALMOST ALL THE ACTION IN the book thus far has occurred at the national level. The main officials responsible for building the American welfare state were presidents, especially Franklin Roosevelt and Lyndon Johnson, senators such as Jacob Javits, and representatives such as Henry Waxman. The main agents of retrenchment were President Ronald Reagan and congressional Republicans. Key interest groups such as AARP mattered to the extent they tried to influence policy debates in the nation's capitol. The same goes for public opinion. So much emphasis on national developments could easily leave readers with a distorted picture of the American welfare state. After all, the states are heavily involved in financing and administering many social programs, from unemployment insurance and workers' compensation to Medicaid and welfare. This chapter and the next will partly redress this imbalance by analyzing developments at the state level more fully.

Many analysts view the American states as a liability. State officials are supposed to have little incentive to help the poor because doing so requires higher taxes that might chase affluent individuals and businesses away. When state officials are white and many of the poor are black, some states (e.g., in the South) may have even less incentive to act. The phrase "race to the bottom" captures the worst-case scenario in which states compete to have the smallest safety net. Even if inclined to help those in need, state governments have limited capacity because they cannot run deficits in times of recession, which the national government can. And running fifty separate programs requires more bureaucracy and more administrative costs than running a single national program. From this perspective, relying on the states to make social policy leads predictably to the kinds of inequities and inadequacies discussed in chapter 2.[1]

A somewhat different version of this chapter appeared as "Workers' Compensation, Federalism, and the Heavy Hand of History," *Studies in American Political Development* 16, 1 (Spring 2002): 28–47.

Other observers believe that the American states are a real asset. Rather than implement some unwieldy "one-size-fits-all" solution crafted in Washington, states can tailor social policies to the particular needs of their residents. The kind of job training someone needs in Wyoming, for example, is probably different from the training someone needs in Massachusetts. Wide variations in social policy should therefore be expected in a large, heterogeneous nation. Alternatively, no one may know how to remedy certain social problems, and allowing fifty states to experiment may be the most efficient way to find the best approach. Law professor John Yoo of the University of California, Berkeley, has stated the argument succinctly: "expand federal power and you retard the innovation that can answer difficult national problems."[2] The American states, to paraphrase Justice Louis Brandeis, help the country by serving as "laboratories of democracy."[3]

In practice, giving responsibility to the states is quite common. Many of the social programs established during the New Deal and the Great Society rely on partnerships between national and state governments. Since the Reagan administration, the national government has given states waivers to experiment more with their welfare and Medicaid programs. Officials in the 1980s spoke glowingly about "new ideas," "fresh strategies," and "state and local energy." Although devolution might seem like a Republican stratagem to reduce the size of the national government, its appeal crosses party lines. After floundering a bit under the first President Bush, waivers gained momentum under President Clinton. States were trying a variety of approaches to reduce welfare dependency and out-of-wedlock births by the mid-1990s. The 1996 welfare reform law gave states added flexibility in determining eligibility and spending monies (the law also took some flexibility away). The following year, officials tried to expand health insurance coverage among children by creating the State Children's Health Insurance Program (SCHIP). States could use federal monies to expand their existing Medicaid programs, establish a separate SCHIP program, or do both. The George W. Bush administration has been quite willing to continue granting welfare and Medicaid waivers.[4]

In many cases these experiments are so new or the data so incomplete that it is hard to evaluate how well the states have performed. Instead, this chapter analyzes one of the longest-running experiments in social policy at the state level. Workers' compensation was the first social insurance program to gain widespread acceptance in the United States, years before Social Security. Most states passed compensation laws between 1911 and 1920, and all but two states did so by 1935. Some authors argue that in the early twentieth century, workmen's compensation* and mothers' pensions (the forerunner of welfare) established the foundation of the two-tiered welfare state.[5] In contrast to welfare and virtually every other social program, workers' compensation remained almost exclusively the responsibility of state governments. Workers' compensation laws "are unlike other social insurance programs in the United States— such as Social Security, Medicare, and unemployment insurance—in that they have no federal involvement in financing, administration, or mandatory minimum coverage standards."[6] This feature makes workers' compensation a terrific case to study, for we can attribute whatever strengths and weaknesses we observe to the states. With programs like welfare and Medicaid, it can be difficult to figure out which problems are the states' fault and which are due to national officials and agencies.

Although it may not get much attention from the media or scholars, workers' compensation is an important program. Total spending on income support and medical care was close to $50 billion in 2001, making workers' compensation larger than unemployment insurance and larger than every single means-tested social program except Medicaid. Compensation laws covered 127 million workers that year, or about 93 percent of the employed labor force. Such laws are crucial when 5,000 Americans die on the job and another 3 to 4 million workers suffer disabling injuries each year.[7]

Evidence cited earlier in the book indicates that our prolonged experiment with workers' compensation has turned out badly. We would expect similar states to adopt similar practices, especially given decades to learn from each other's successes and failures. And yet, comparisons of Alabama to Mississippi and Indiana to Illinois showed huge variations in benefits (chapter 2). Other weird discrepancies are easy to find. Death benefits in Virginia are three times those in North Carolina. Employers with fewer than five employees are exempt from workers' compensation laws in Kansas City, Missouri, but not in Kansas City, Kansas. While injured workers get to choose their own doctor in Ohio, those in New York have to pick a doctor approved by a state agency, and those in Pennsylvania must pick one approved by their employer. A couple of states compel employers to pay into a single public compensation fund. A few states give employers the choice between the state fund and self-insurance. About half the states have no public fund and compel employers to buy insurance from private carriers or self-insure, making workers' compensation closer to social regulation than social insurance. The rest of the states allow employers to choose between public and private insurance.[8] Work-

---

* The more gender-neutral term "workers' compensation" did not become common until the 1970s. I will use both names in this chapter, depending on the context.

ers' compensation differs on so many dimensions that learning from other states is all but impossible. "Even practitioners, who may be familiar with the application of the law within their own states, often have little knowledge about the workings of the laws in other jurisdictions."[9] Probably the most uniform feature of the program is the sizable amount of money that never reaches injured workers and goes instead to administration, litigation, and insurers' profits. Employers paid $65 billion for workers' compensation in 2001, but workers received only $50 billion in benefits.[10]

Some variation might be acceptable if most states provide adequate benefits, but they do not. By the late 1990s, the average worker who was temporarily but totally disabled received benefits that were just barely enough to keep a family of four out of poverty. Because benefits are tied to wages, this means that many families of injured workers with below-average wages fall into poverty. If we measure adequacy against the Model Act adopted by the Council of State Governments, then workers' comp benefits are less than half of what they should be. The nonpartisan National Academy of Social Insurance examined benefits in several states and found that while injured workers could in theory have received two-thirds of their previous income, in practice benefits replaced only one-third to one-half of their income.[11]

From an international perspective, leaving workers' compensation to the states is highly unusual. Virtually every nation in the world with workers' comp, including some with federal systems (e.g., Germany and India), has a single program operating within its borders. In most countries, workers' compensation is integrated into a larger social insurance system administered by the national government.[12] If the United States has found a particularly clever solution to the problem of injured workers, the rest of the world has not noticed.

It is hard to imagine a good justification for allowing injured workers to be treated so poorly and so differently from one state to another. The only plausible explanation is historical and political. As we shall see, the flaws of workers' compensation have been evident for a long time, and critics have suggested increasing the role of the national government to help remedy these flaws. By the time they tried to do something, however, compensation laws were so firmly entrenched in the states that major change was politically costly.

For a multitiered system, the enactment of policies at a decentralized level may constrain the options available to authorities in the central tier. Once adopted, policies go through a gradual process of institutionalization. Established programs generate sunk costs and networks of political interests that diminish the prospects for radical reform. The possibility of policy preemption suggests that an important source of variation among multitiered systems arises from the timing of interventions by constituent members and central authorities.[13]

Though written with European integration in mind, these words apply equally to federal systems like the United States. In the case of workers' compensation, the relevant "networks of political interests" consisted primarily of private corporations and public, state-level bureaucracies. Respecting their power was more important than fixing the program.

Other parts of this book identify patterns across thousands of individuals, fifty states, many nations, or a handful of programs. This chapter analyzes a series of decisive moments in the history of a single program. One key question in the 1910s was how best to implement workmen's compensation—by creating new public bureaucracies or by building on existing institutions in the private sector. Once that question was answered in favor of the private sector, policy makers from the 1930s on faced a new dilemma, how to deal with the program's shortcomings. National officials repeatedly recognized that state-level control of workmen's compensation was deeply flawed but chose not to deal with those failings directly. Instead, they advocated creation of disability insurance and national standards for workplace safety, new programs that might indirectly remedy some of the flaws in workmen's compensation. Expecting a bitter fight from stakeholders in both the private and the public sectors, national officials chose not to take over workers' compensation or even to set minimum standards for state programs. The cumulative effect of these decisions has been to embed workers' compensation at the state level and perpetuate its problems.[14]

Origins of Workmen's Compensation

Before workmen's compensation, the courts handled disputes over industrial accidents, and prevailing legal doctrine was heavily biased in favor of employers.[15] If the injured worker or fellow workers were even slightly to blame, or if the injury could have been expected given the nature of the job, the employer was not liable for damages. The system created a perverse kind of uniformity. Rarely could workers in any state overcome these defenses and win in court. The costs of industrial accidents were thus borne primarily by injured workers and their families, and also by the local community if and when these individuals had to rely on poor relief.

Starting with railroads and mining, two of the most hazardous industries, state legislatures began to restrict employers' defenses in the middle of the nineteenth century. By 1910 most states had abolished or substantially modified at least one of the major legal defenses favoring employers. The result, from the perspective of injured workers, was a small improvement. For the majority of injured workers and their families, compensation still varied between too little and nothing at all. Two workers injured in similar circumstances might be treated very differently depending on the quality of their legal representation and the specific judge or jury they drew. In Minnesota, court awards for loss of an eye ranged from $290 to $2,700 in the early twentieth century; for loss of a foot, the range was $50 to $3,000.[16] Those who managed to win in court often had to wait years from the time of injury to the time of payment.[17]

Employers objected to the unpredictability of the new laws, which occasionally produced a large judgment against them. Companies started to buy private accident insurance for the first time. Employers did not, however, do much to enhance workplace safety. "Industrial accident rates reached their all-time peak in the first decade of this [the twentieth] century. For example, in 1907 over 7,000 workers were killed in just two industries—railroading and bituminous coal mining."[18] Employers worried, too, about the potential for fostering labor unrest at a time when unions were growing in influence.

Elected officials were troubled by all these flaws as well as the strain that the growing number of lawsuits placed on their court systems. Workers, employers, and public officials all viewed the legal system as wasteful. Attorney fees and insurance company profits and overhead consumed a large fraction—often more than half—of the monies spent. Soon after the turn of the century, many state legislatures created special industrial accident commissions to analyze the situation and recommend changes.

In most instances, these commissions suggested an entirely different approach—industrial accident insurance, modeled after laws in Europe. The new system was based on the principle of liability without fault. Employers would pay, not because they were negligent, but because accidents were inherent in an industrial society and therefore a cost of doing business. Injured workers and their families would now be guaranteed compensation. Although the benefits would be lower than the largest court awards, they would also be more predictable, more widespread, and paid more rapidly.

State courts overturned the first pieces of compensation legislation. One problem was that many laws compelled employers to participate, which was termed a violation of the due process clause in the Fourteenth Amendment.[19] To mollify the courts, states started to make participation in workmen's compensation elective while at the same time keeping benefits low and restricting employers' legal defenses so much that most employers would "freely" elect to join the new system. This approach withstood judicial scrutiny and diffused rapidly across the nation. Ten states passed compensation laws in 1911 and four more followed suit in 1912.[20] Some of the early adopters were important industrial states (Massachusetts, New Jersey), and some were not (Arizona, Kansas). Forty-two states had passed workmen's compensation laws by 1920, and by 1935 only Arkansas and Mississippi had failed to adopt.[21]

While many of the affected parties wanted workmen's compensation laws, they clashed over how big a role government should play in running the new program. Organized labor and left-wing politicians pushed for monopolistic state funds, arguing that the reduction in operating expenses and lack of profit would free up monies to enhance coverage and benefits. They were strongly opposed by the insurance industry, which raised the twin specters of patronage politics and creeping socialism.[22] Insurers claimed that the private sector would be better at ferreting out the "fraud, malingering, and simulation characteristic of [workmen's compensation] claimants."[23] This was not exactly an impartial judgment. For insurers, compensation laws were a source of new business.

Private insurers prevailed, giving most employers the choice of buying insurance from a private carrier or self-insuring. If employers chose the latter route, they had to demonstrate that they possessed the financial resources to compensate accident victims, and in some states the standard of proof was fairly low. Private insurers did not win in every state. By the mid-1930s, a handful of states operated monopolistic public funds, and eleven states had public funds competing with private insurers.[24]

Even so, private insurance companies and self-insured employers dominated the market for workmen's compensation from the beginning. Insurance companies enjoyed advantages because they could deny coverage to the worst risks, which by law the state-operated funds had to cover; they could better serve companies operating in more than one state; and they could offer employers discounts on other types of insurance if purchased in combination with a workmen's compensation policy. Private insurers paid about 50 percent of workmen's compensation benefits in the late 1930s, and self-insured companies accounted for another 20 percent. The rest were paid by public funds, financed by payroll taxes.[25] No other social program from this era incorporated the private sector so closely.

The decision to rely heavily on corporations to implement workmen's compensation proved to be critical. This new social program gained a powerful set of stakeholders in addition to whatever state agencies were involved. Private insurers remained important for the rest of the century. By 2001 private carriers were paying out 55 percent of all workers' compensation benefits, self-insured companies 23 percent, and public funds the remaining 22 percent. The public-private mix at the start of the 21st century was virtually identical to that of the 1930s.[26]

State-level control led to substantial differences in coverage and benefits.[27] As a general rule, the more industrialized states covered a larger fraction of their workforce. By 1930 eleven states and the District of Columbia had extended coverage to at least some occupational diseases; the rest had not. Then, as now, states valued the loss of various body parts quite differently. Overall, compensation benefits were two to three times higher in the more generous states (e.g., New York and North Dakota) than in the less generous (e.g., South Dakota or Virginia). Although Progressive Era reformers were critical of these variations and pushed for uniform state laws, they failed. William Graebner argues that some states, notably in the South, resisted uniformity because they wanted to compete for business investment based on the relatively low cost of their workmen's compensation programs.[28] Thus, while it is true that workmen's compensation was the first social insurance program to gain widespread acceptance in the United States, it is also true that the program assumed a different form in every single state.

Workmen's Compensation and the Social Security Act

President Roosevelt's first response to the Great Depression was to extend immediate cash relief to millions of needy families and create public works programs for the unemployed. The Federal Emergency Relief Administration, Civilian Conservation Corps, and Public Works Administration were three of the many agencies created in 1933 to help citizens cope with hardship. The second wave of initiatives began in 1934 when Roosevelt created the Committee on Economic Security (CES). The committee's report, issued in January 1935, offered a blueprint for expanding significantly the national government's role in social welfare. After modifications by the president and Congress, many of these recommendations were incorporated in the Social Security Act that became law in August 1935. Widely viewed as the birth of the American welfare state, the Act committed the national government to old age insurance, unemployment insurance, and cash assistance to several categories of poor citizens (elderly, blind, and children of single mothers).

Why, then, was workmen's compensation excluded from the Social Security Act? Policy makers had their chances. FDR's original executive order (no. 6757), issued in June 1934, instructed the Committee on Economic Security to "study problems relating to the economic security of individuals." The CES narrowed the focus in August 1934, arguing that other parts of the administration were already developing proposals to promote economic recovery and prevent a repeat of the Depression. Still, the committee's scope included workmen's compensation, also known as accident insurance: "The field of study to which the committee should devote its major attention is that of the protection of the individual against dependency and distress. This includes *all* forms of social insurance (*accident insurance*, health insurance, invalidity insurance, unemployment insurance, retirement annuities, survivors' insurance, family endowment, and maternity benefits) and also problems of providing work (or opportunities for self employment) for the unemployed, and training them for jobs that are likely to become available."[29]

A study commissioned and circulated within the CES, but never made public, recommended major changes to existing compensation laws. The overriding emphasis was on the need for national standards. In almost every case, these standards would force states to make their programs more comprehensive and more generous. The study called for all state laws to be compulsory rather than elective; an end to exemptions for small employers and nonhazardous occupations; blanket coverage of occupational diseases; shorter waiting periods for compensation; higher minimum and maximum weekly benefits; longer duration of benefits; and unlimited expenses for medical care.[30] The American Association of Labor Legislation, a leading progressive reform group, had made of these same recommendations years earlier, without success.[31]

Important policy makers were well aware of workmen's compensation and its problems. On the very first page of its final report to the president, the CES noted that 14,500 workers had been killed and another 55,000 had been permanently injured on the job in 1933 alone.[32] Secretary of Labor Frances Perkins, who chaired the CES, had previously helped administer workmen's compensation in New York. Edwin Witte, executive director of the CES, and Arthur Altmeyer, head of the CES technical board, had similar experience in Wisconsin. Among Witte's papers at the State Historical Society of Wisconsin is an article describing problems in New York. A committee created by then governor Franklin Roosevelt found that over half of all injured workers were being denied adequate medical care in order to keep costs down. Before coming to Washington, Altmeyer had found that in any given year, 40 percent of all new cases reported in Wisconsin in the 1920s were still pending by the end of that year. That did not exactly constitute a swift response to the problem of industrial accidents.[33]

Altmeyer was also disturbed by the "random quality" of workmen's compensation in Wisconsin. Workers with minor injuries received too much, workers with major injuries received too little, and workers with identical injuries received different amounts of compensation.[34] As the final CES report noted, workmen's compensation laws across the nation "were sadly lacking in uniformity." This was not just the view from Washington. Speaking before a meeting of the International Association of Industrial Accident Boards and Commissions, the chairman of Maine's Industrial Accident Commission offered a scathing indictment: "the amounts paid for the losses of certain members in each State often bear no consistent relationship at all to the amounts paid for the losses of other members, nor are they in proportion to the value of the body as a whole. The various systems of such compensation in the United States, or lack of system, have been characterized as a veritable crazy quilt. The schedules themselves have been declared over and over again, by commissioners and other competent authorities, as haphazard, unscientific— even as absurdities."[35]

Officials did not believe, however, that the national government was well equipped to remedy these problems. Altmeyer found that as workmen's compensation spread in Wisconsin, administrative costs per case failed to drop significantly, an indication that economies of scale were not materializing. Perhaps most tellingly, Altmeyer discovered that private insurers consistently lost money on workmen's compensation during the 1920s.[36] The only reason insurers stayed in business was because they offset these losses with profits from other lines of insurance that they sold to employers as part of a package deal. Such a strategy would be unavailable to the national government.

As a matter of principle, "Wisconsin school" reformers like Altmeyer and Witte often resisted national uniformity. They designed unemployment insurance, for example, to vary from state to state. They were also willing to accommodate powerful interests in order to pass legislation. They believed that, in politics, half a loaf was better than none.[37] Despite its reputation as a pioneer in social policy, Wisconsin relied solely on private insurers for its workmen's compensation policies. Officials there deliberately resisted pressures from the state federation of labor to establish a state fund.[38]

As if these reasons were not enough, the involvement of doctors proved troublesome. Unlike old age or unemployment insurance, workmen's compensation provided both income support and medical benefits. In the majority of cases involving serious injury, workers had to be examined by doctors approved by their employer or the insurance company, leading to complaints that the extent of disability was often understated. The reverse was also possible. A committee investigating workmen's compensation in New York in the early 1930s discovered that doctors chosen by workers usually found major injuries and recommended the maximum benefits under law, while doctors chosen by employers or insurers often found no reason for an award. Because disability is often subjective, doctors could legitimately disagree on its severity even when a conflict of interest was absent. At a 1935 conference, medical experts from several states analyzed evidence from actual cases of permanent partial disability and determined the severity. "Estimates on one case ranged from nothing (hysteria) to 80%, while another case saw estimates from 25 to 90%."[39]

These difficulties reinforced policy makers' general unwillingness to tackle issues of medical care. Greater national involvement was likely to generate opposition from powerful groups of medical providers such as the American Medical Association. It could also lead the government into the thicket of identifying and quantifying medical disability. With important new forays into unemployment and old age insurance on the agenda, as well as greater support for several existing means-tested programs, the national government's capacity to provide social welfare could be stretched to the breaking point if it took on workmen's compensation as well.

Given less than six months to survey, repair, and redesign the entire social safety net, and a relatively modest budget, CES officials had to make priorities. Even a ragged patchwork collection of state compensation laws was better than what existed for the elderly and the unemployed. Existing work relief programs were of minimal help to the elderly; unemployment remained at record high levels from 1933 to 1934. No state had old age insurance, and only Wisconsin had adopted unemployment insurance prior to 1935. One-quarter of the states lacked any special program for the poor elderly, and some states with such programs made them county optional.[40] Workmen's compensation laws, in contrast, had spread to almost every state by the early 1930s and were never county optional, always statewide. Though coverage varied by state, roughly 50 percent of all employees were subject to workmen's compensation laws in 1930.[41] Ironically, the early introduction and rapid spread of workmen's compensation may have contributed to its neglect during the formative stages of the Social Security Act.[42]

Conceivably, national officials might still have elected to tackle workmen's compensation if pressured to do so by organized groups. No such pressure materialized. Although business and labor groups were not necessarily happy with existing compensation laws, they were accustomed to working through state legislatures to make any changes. Business and labor directed their attention toward the old age and especially the unemployment insurance titles in the Social Security Act. For their part, private insurers wanted states to authorize higher rates, not national involvement.[43] No one came forward during legislative debates to elevate the problems of injured workers and their families after the CES issued its final report and the Roosevelt administration developed its proposed bill.

In light of other commitments and two decades of experience with workmen's compensation, the architects of the Social Security Act decided to leave well enough alone. National involvement might have helped, for existing state laws were not working well. But it would have been administratively complex and politically risky. The final CES report to the president mentioned workmen's compensation only briefly and toward the very end. Its two main recommendations were to encourage the few states without compensation laws to adopt them, and to have the Labor Department do whatever it could to make state laws more uniform and adequate. The government would offer states neither carrot nor stick; its main tools would be persuasion and exhortation. Though minor, these recommendations were later dropped from the final bill.

Omitting workmen's compensation from the original Social Security Act was a pivotal moment in the history of the program. The framework established by the Act proved remarkably durable. Social Security started as a purely national program and has remained so ever since. Unemployment insurance and Aid to Dependent Children (later AFDC) started as federal programs and still require the national and state governments to administer and finance them. Even when officials replaced AFDC with Temporary Assistance for Needy Families (TANF) in 1996, they continued the national government's role in helping to finance the program and set eligibility rules. Workmen's compensation was left to the states in 1935 and has remained there ever since.

Nonetheless, change was possible. When officials created SSI (Supplemental Security Income) in 1972, they effectively nationalized aid to the blind and old age assistance. At a few junctures after 1935, policy makers also considered greater national involvement in workmen's compensation. With only minor exceptions, they declined to modify the previous decision to leave workmen's compensation to the states. The rest of this chapter analyzes the most important of these episodes.

WORKMEN'S COMPENSATION AND DISABILITY INSURANCE

The growth and development of Social Security were in many ways more important than its enactment. Social Security initially covered a little over half of the workforce and paid no benefits. Beginning in the late 1930s, policy makers started to use Old Age Insurance as a platform, adding survivors insurance (1939), disability insurance (1956), and medical insurance for the elderly (Medicare, 1965). They also started to expand the range of occupations covered by Old Age Insurance, with the most notable successes coming in 1950. That same year marked the first of many benefit increases, the largest of which occurred in the late 1960s and early 1970s. The overall pattern of expansion was driven not by interest groups of the elderly but by a dedicated and capable cadre of bureaucrats who developed alliances with powerful members of Congress.[44]

Edward and Monroe Berkowitz argue that this history of expansion can be understood partly as an effort to compensate for the deficiencies of workmen's compensation laws.[45] With job-related fatalities so common and death benefits so meager in the 1930s, policy makers pushed hard for survivors insurance. They designed survivors insurance so that benefits would be paid even if workers were killed on the job. The inadequacy of workmen's compensation benefits was one reason that bureaucrats and legislators felt a continuing need to make old age and survivors insurance benefits more generous.

The most direct link was to disability insurance, the design of which began shortly after the Social Security Act became law. A number of policy makers in Washington saw no good reason why identically disabled workers in Georgia and California, or any other state, should be treated differently. They saw no good reason why the government should limit coverage to disabilities "arising out of and in the course of" employment, as stipulated by states' compensation laws. Someone who accidentally fell at home while repairing a roof was as much in need of help as someone who fell while building a roof at a construction site. Indeed, one of the fundamental sources of friction in workmen's compensation had been the need to prove that a given injury was work related. Employers and insurers regularly denied claims because they felt the injuries had occurred away from the job. Workers regularly accused them of violating the law, and the disputes ended up before a state commission or court.

The logical thing to do was to create a single national disability program with uniform benefits and no distinction between occupational and nonoccupational injuries. There was some initial support for this approach. In 1938 and 1939, President Roosevelt's Interdepartmental Committee to Coordinate Health and Welfare Activities surveyed the nation's health needs and issued five major policy recommendations. One of these was for "Federal action to develop a program of compensation for wage loss due to temporary and permanent disability," regardless of the source of disability.[46]

Key policy makers ignored these proposals and decided instead to design a more limited disability program that would operate alongside workmen's compensation. To understand why, we start with the Social Security Board, which became the main engine for expanding social insurance programs within the administration.[47] Social Security officials preferred a more incremental approach to reform, one designed to dampen opposition from conservative politicians, special interests, and a public still suspicious of big government.[48] In the process of designing disability insurance, they picked their battles carefully.

One can observe policy makers' sense of the possible as early as 1936. That year I. S. Falk, a well-respected expert on health policy whose research later influenced the design of disability insurance and Medicare, published a book titled *Security against Sickness*. Though quite critical of workmen's compensation and in favor of a single disability program, Falk recognized the difficulties of modifying the existing network of state programs and recommended instead that new programs for nonoccupational disability and health insurance be created. Researchers working directly for the Social Security Board in the late 1930s expressed similar views. Their hope was that a new, more generous, and more uniform program covering nonoccupational disabilities would prompt states to improve their workmen's compensation laws.[49]

Even after limiting their objectives to nonoccupational disabilities, policy makers faced considerable resistance. In its 1938 report to the Senate Finance Committee, the Advisory Council on Social Security was divided over the desirability of national action. Some council members worried that disability insurance would depart from old age insurance in several respects: its costs would be less predictable; disability determination would require more subjective judgments than verification of age and work history; and medical expertise would be required to determine eligibility. To address these concerns, Social Security officials restricted their proposals in the 1940s to the permanently and totally disabled. In 1948 the Advisory Council further stipulated that eligibility for the disability program would depend on "recent and substantive attachment to the labor market," and that benefits would be paid only after a six-month waiting period.[50] Both provisions were by design more restrictive than those found in states' compensation laws.

These changes were enough for the House, which approved a single, national disability insurance program in 1950 as part of a series of amendments to the Social Security Act. They were not enough for the Senate, which approved instead a means-tested grant program for the permanently and totally disabled, administered jointly with the states. The Senate wanted more public assistance, not more social insurance. Senators were responding in large part to pressures from the American Medical Association (AMA), which portrayed disability insurance as the first step toward the complete socialization of American medical care. Joining the AMA in opposition were the U.S. Chamber of Commerce and various insurance companies. This pattern repeated in 1952.[51]

In such a hostile political environment, it was hard to imagine tackling workmen's compensation at the same time. Doing so might have been good policy, but it would have heightened the resistance of some powerful groups and generated additional enemies. "Despite social security planners' disapproval of workers' compensation inequities and complexities and their desire to eliminate them under their new laws, they were not free of the older program. Workers' compensation had one big advantage over the new program [disability insurance]: it already existed. Both labor and management had invested a lot of political energy into shaping it to their ends. As a result, the program had well-defined interest groups."[52] Labor and management were not the only interested parties. Insurance companies made millions of dollars from selling products that included compensation policies, and several states had established their own monopolistic or competitive funds. National involvement posed a direct threat to their existence. A number of doctors and trial attorneys in every state also counted on business from injured workers. State accident boards and industrial commissions had existed since the 1910s, long enough to form their own professional associations and professional identities. Located in every district of every state, opponents to national involvement were in an ideal position to pressure Congress. Insurance for nonoccupational disabilities, by contrast, had no established network of interests. Such insurance was virtually nonexistent in the private sector.

If anyone doubted the power of established interests, further proof came just as officials were finalizing disability insurance. Arthur Larson, Eisenhower's undersecretary of labor, was leading an effort in 1954 to develop a standard for states' compensation programs. Intended to motivate improvements in coverage and benefits, the plan triggered fears of a national takeover. "By 1956, Larson's model compensation act . . . lay totally discredited, the victim of political sniping by state officials, businessmen, and their allies in the administration."[53]

To advocates of disability insurance, the political legacy of workmen's compensation was clear—stay away. Advocates viewed these concessions as the price they had to pay to gain acceptance for the basic principle of disability insurance. As with old age insurance, officials planned on starting with a fairly limited program and later making disability benefits more generous and more widely available. After 1956, they worked hard to make incremental improvements and cope with the complicated administrative challenges inherent in a disability program.[54] In retrospect, the decision to create a separate disability program was another milestone in the development of workmen's compensation. Since the 1950s, any move toward greater national involvement has been linked not to social insurance but to regulation involving occupational safety and health.

THE BLACK LUNG PROGRAM

In December 1969, Congress approved and President Nixon reluctantly signed a bill to extend benefits to victims of black lung (pneumoconiosis), a common and often fatal occupational disease of coal miners.[55] This program was the national government's only formal intrusion into the realm of workers' compensation since the 1920s. The question is why national officials made an exception in this case, and how they were able to triumph over stakeholders at the state level.

By way of background, it is important to remember that the national government already operated two workmen's compensation programs.[56] The first, passed in 1908 and expanded in 1916, provided coverage to employees of the national government. It was administered initially by the Department of Commerce and Labor, then by an independent commission. Since 1950, responsibility has been housed in the Labor Department—perhaps reinforcing the image of workmen's compensation as an occupational program rather than social insurance. The second program, created in 1927, covered workers engaged in interstate commerce who were excluded from state compensation programs (originally, longshoremen and harbor workers). In neither case did the U.S. government intrude on existing state-level programs.

The most visible trigger for the national Black Lung program was a disastrous explosion in a Farmington, West Virginia, coal mine. For ten days in November 1968, the nation watched and waited as rescue crews tried to free 99 miners trapped underground. Seventy-eight of those miners eventually died. This was not an isolated tragedy. A total of 150 West Virginia coal miners died on the job that year, and another 159 coal miners died in twelve other states. The rate of on-the-job fatalities in the late 1960s was approximately eight times higher for coal miners than for other workers.[57]

In September of 1968, President Johnson proposed new health and safety regulations for coal mines. Members of Congress initially did nothing, but in the wake of the Farmington disaster they quickly made the topic a priority for their next session.[58] In a special message to Congress in March 1969, newly elected President Nixon endorsed new health and safety measures for coal mines. The result was the Coal Mine Safety Act of 1969. The Act required the Department of the Interior to set safety standards and the Department of Health, Education, and Welfare to set health standards for coal mines. It authorized funds for health and safety research. It required each mine to be inspected at least four times a year, and established civil and criminal penalties for those who violated the Act. These provisions of the Act were relatively uncontroversial given the recent spate of mining disasters and the national government's prior involvement in mine safety. What was novel, and more controversial, was the inclusion of compensation benefits for the victims of black lung disease and their families. Legislators devoted an inordinate amount of time debating this section of the bill. Nixon at one point considered vetoing the entire package because of the Black Lung program.

It is important to understand why officials considered involvement by the national government to be acceptable. One reason was that organized labor backed the new program. For a number of years, unions such as the United Mine Workers (UMW) had overlooked occupational health and focused instead on wages and benefits. In the wake of the Farmington disaster, the head of the UMW publicly "absolved Consolidation Coal of responsibility, explaining that 'as long as we mine coal, there is always this inherent danger. . . . This happens to be one of the better companies.' "[59] The leadership's response angered many rank-and-file members, who succeeded in passing a series of resolutions at the 1968 UMW convention directing union leaders to push employers for better compensation for various dust diseases. Nevertheless, when the union finalized a new contract with mine operators in October 1968, there was no mention of workplace safety or occupational disease.

Union leaders' intransigence prompted some miners to create local Black Lung Associations. By the end of 1968, a handful of doctors, consumer advocate Ralph Nader, and a variety of activists linked to VISTA and other Great Society programs had joined them. By early 1969, legislation had been introduced but not approved in the West Virginia state legislature. Miners staged a wildcat strike in February, prompting legislators to pass and the governor to sign a bill adding coverage for coal dust diseases to that state's compensation program. Only then did the mines reopen.

UMW leaders realized that in order to maintain the support of their members, they had to produce a major victory concerning occupational health, and black lung in particular. UMW officials looked to Washington, where coal mine safety legislation was already working its way through Congress. The bill that reached the Senate floor in September 1969 made no mention of compensation for black lung. With the help of West Virginia's two senators (Byrd and Randolph, both Democrats), the UMW managed to attach language creating a national Black Lung program to the bill. It received bipartisan support, particularly from legislators in key coal-producing states such as Alabama, Kentucky, Ohio, and Pennsylvania, several of whom occupied important leadership positions in Congress.

Support from labor was not enough. Advocates of a new Black Lung program also had to win support from other powerful interests, or at least neutralize them. The medical community by and large stayed on the sidelines. The government was not proposing to usurp doctors' role in diagnosing or treating black lung disease; it was proposing to help infected miners, who in turn might be better able to pay for medical care. Private insurers did not feel threatened, for occupational diseases were one of the more troublesome parts of their business. The costs were hard to predict because the state of scientific knowledge linking specific job hazards to specific diseases kept changing. And the costs were potentially large if afflicted workers lived for many years with the disease.

Legislators found a way to minimize the fiscal impact on employers. Part B of the Black Lung program extended benefits to miners who filed claims before the end of 1972, and was financed entirely out of general revenues. Officials expected it to account for most of the spending. Legislators never seriously considered a payroll tax, the traditional means of financing a social insurance program, because they worried that the regulatory measures contained elsewhere in the Act would already impose a significant burden on an industry that had struggled in recent years. Part C of the program extended benefits to affected miners and their dependents who qualified starting in 1973. It was financed by coal companies or by employers more generally if states expanded their workers' compensation programs to include black lung disease. Coal companies were not obligated to pay for Part C, however, after 1976. Policy makers expected state compensation laws to change by then, and all subsequent cases to be handled at the state level. Given the adoption of stronger health and safety regulations, many people expected that the number of future cases of black lung would be relatively small, so Part C would not entail much change to states' programs or employers' costs over the long run.

Administrators of state programs were the main stakeholder to testify in Congress against the measure. They made dire predictions about "the abandonment of our 55-year-old workmen's compensation system." They implied that the national government was ill equipped for the task because "workmen's compensation administration is a professional specialty demanding experience and dedication and an intimate knowledge of local problems. This proposed legislation would replace local control with a centralized administration impairing development in the various regions of the country."[60] To counter these attacks, supporters included language that made parts of the program temporary.[61] They made a number of statements indicating that Black Lung would not set a precedent, that it was emergency aid to a tiny but deserving segment of the population. Although these tactics did not prompt state bureaucrats to change their position, they did make opposition to Black Lung benefits less potent in Congress.

In retrospect, it is hard to see just how the Black Lung program threatened the status quo. For one thing, the national government was stepping in to cover a disease that states had historically excluded. Neither doctors nor private insurers felt threatened. For another, the program hardly qualified as social insurance. The Black Lung program was not only financed differently than disability insurance or Social Security. As a practical matter, benefits were available only to coal miners, which excluded much of the country. The Black Lung program was, in effect, regional aid for Appalachia. Its unique design, and the UMW's strong but historically specific need for a legislative victory, paved the way for the national government to become involved, ever so modestly, in compensating civilians for work-related disabilities.

WORKERS' COMPENSATION AND OSHA

The struggle over Black Lung benefits was part of a larger movement to improve working conditions. Shortly after passing the Coal Mine Safety Act, Congress approved and President Nixon signed the sweeping Occupational Safety and Health Act (OSHA) of 1970. The Act applied to every nongovernmental employer in the country and created strict standards, new enforcement mechanisms, and new rights for workers. One section of this Act created a commission to study problems with workers' compensation and recommend changes. In this section, I explain why substantive changes to workers' compensation were not part of the original OSHA, and why the commission's work later failed to produce any change in state-level control of workers' compensation.[62]

The general issue of workplace safety gained greater visibility in the mid-1960s. Organized labor provided one impetus. At the very top, union leaders were generally uninterested in better working conditions. They believed that workers in risky occupations should be paid more, rather than have a safer workplace. Several staff members at AFL-CIO headquarters were more interested in working conditions and fought hard to make the issue a priority among union leaders. The staff had little trouble winning support from the rank and file, who were increasingly motivated to strike over working conditions. These union activists forged alliances with public health specialists within the national bureaucracy to make the case for greater government involvement.

Labor's interest in workplace safety coincided with the Democratic Party's search for new issues that would enhance its electoral prospects. In the wake of increased spending for social programs and the war in Vietnam, social regulation appeared to be a relatively cheap tool of reform at a time when Congress was becoming more cost conscious. Moreover, OSHA strengthened Democrats' ties to organized labor, which increasingly felt that the party was devoting too much attention to racial minorities. President Johnson's involvement was decisive. It was Johnson who lobbied union leaders to make workplace safety a priority, not labor who lobbied Johnson. And it was Johnson's Bureau of the Budget (BOB) that led the way in drafting a bill in 1966 and 1967.[63]

One justification for any new legislation was that existing compensation programs and workplace regulations had done too little to prevent accident rates from rising. As with disability insurance, national officials had two primary options: try to reform existing state laws or design a new program. They considered reforming states' compensation laws early in the process of crafting OSHA, then dismissed the idea for political reasons.

> The administration . . . decided against reforming the workers' compensation system, although that program's manifest failures made reform logical. Organized labor considered this as important, if not more important, than a federal regulatory program, and Johnson's own advisers were attracted to the idea of rehabilitating the system to provide economic incentives to employers to improve working conditions. But [Labor Secretary] Wirtz met with insurance industry representatives to test the waters and returned to recommend two very limited reforms: a grants-in-aid program to improve state research and administration, and a congressionally appointed National Commission on Workmen's Compensation.
>
> Johnson's advisers clearly understood the economic and political interests at stake and the problems they faced if they chose to tackle workers' compensation directly. After reviewing the history of the program, both the Council of Economic Advisers (CEA) and BOB concluded that comprehensive changes were unlikely to succeed in Congress. Gardner Ackley, chair of the CEA, wrote [Joseph] Califano [Johnson's top domestic policy adviser] that "even innocuous government efforts to improve the system have been vigorously assailed and strongly resisted as precursors to a Federal 'take-over' of the system. . . . Given the entrenched power of the defenders of the status quo," he concluded, minor gains were all that could be expected.[64]

The outcome was virtually identical to that for disability insurance. Although there was a constituency for reform and evidence of poor performance, existing stakeholders were too strong. If policy makers wanted to pass a meaningful bill, they had to shorten the list of enemies and accept workmen's compensation, warts and all.

Creation of a National Commission on State Workmen's Compensation Laws was one of those "minor gains" in the Act. Admittedly, such commissions are frequently symbolic gestures, creating the appearance of official activity but ultimately changing nothing. Every once in a while, such commissions give elected officials the ideas and political cover needed to address difficult issues; the recent military-base-closing commissions are a good case in point. At a minimum, commissions need to have a clearly defined topic, adequate technical support, and a range of views represented among their members if they are to have any tangible impact on policy.[65] The National Commission on State Workmen's Compensation Laws seemed to qualify on all counts, and was later credited with a number of improvements in states' compensation programs during the 1970s. Nevertheless, none of these improvements fundamentally challenged state-level control.

The commission's final report (1972) and three volumes of supplemental studies were the most thorough indictment of workers' compensation in the twentieth century.[66] They faulted state laws for failing to cover the entire workforce, provide adequate cash benefits, provide adequate and timely medical benefits, help rehabilitate injured workers, promote safety on the job, and keep administrative and legal costs in line. The final report identified nineteen "essential elements" of a good workmen's compensation program. On average, state programs possessed only seven of the nineteen elements, and many states had fewer than five. The report estimated that the cost to comply with these elements would be minimal in a few states and substantial in many others. In fourteen states, largely but not exclusively in the South, total compliance would entail a 40 to 60 percent increase in current spending for workers' compensation.

Given the commission's detailed catalog of deficiencies in states' programs and its willingness to promote sweeping change, why was state-level control deliberately retained? The commission did discuss a greater role for the national government. One option was to disassemble workers' compensation and combine several of the parts with existing national programs. Total, permanent disability claims could be handled by disability insurance, medical care by Medicare or a future national health insurance plan, and safety objectives by OSHA. The commission found several problems with this option, such as the lack of coverage for permanent partial disabilities, the time delay in receiving disability benefits, and the prospect of injured workers shuttling among multiple agencies for help.

The commission openly rejected a national takeover of the program, though the reasons cited were rather curious. The commission noted that "a Federal takeover would substantially disrupt established administrative arrangements" without ever saying whether it was injured workers or state-level bureaucrats and private insurers who would suffer.[67] And it declared that the national government had shown no special skill in administering workers' compensation for its own employees, but offered little supporting evidence.

Instead, the commission recommended that states be given three years to comply with the nineteen essential elements "and, if necessary, Congress with no further delay . . . should guarantee compliance."[68] All commission members agreed that states had the technical and economic capacity to comply quickly. The main impediment was political will. If states failed to comply, a minority of the commission advocated a complete national takeover of workers' compensation. The majority felt that national standards would be more appropriate. But they left it up to Congress to decide if such standards were necessary.

The combination of detailed criticism yet unwillingness to depart from state-level control was understandable given the background of commission members. Of the eighteen members, four (including the vice-chairman) had direct connections to state agencies responsible for workmen's compensation, two were from the insurance industry, one administered workmen's compensation for the Ford Motor Company, and one represented the American Medical Association. A few others were academics who had never challenged the basic structure of workmen's compensation in their writings. They had heard criticism before and wanted another chance to make things right. Though diverse in occupational background, the majority of commission members shared a strong preference for state-level control. The only members who went on record with serious reservations about the ability of states to administer workmen's compensation were the two representing organized labor.

It is tempting to view the commission's composition as evidence that national policy makers were not serious about comprehensive reform. Why else would they ask the foxes to inspect the henhouse? Nevertheless, an equally plausible explanation is that, by 1970, workmen's compensation had developed into such a specialized field of knowledge, and state laws varied on so many dimensions, that well-established experts in the field were about the only ones capable of conducting a systematic analysis. National officials who were well versed in compensation laws may have been prominent in Roosevelt's Committee on Economic Security and even in the Social Security Board of the late 1930s and the 1940s, but their numbers dwindled over time. This less conspiratorial view highlights the importance of information and learning effects in reinforcing the path taken by a given program or policy.[69]

Three years after the commission's report, states were nowhere near complying with all nineteen essential elements. Congress did nothing. Six years after the report, same story. Ten years after, no change. Democrats and Republicans introduced bills, in the House and Senate, calling for national standards in the late 1970s. Each time, opponents successfully pointed to recent progress in the states and asked for more time. States did, in fact, make significant improvements to their programs in the wake of the commission's report. Starting with compliance on an average of 6.9 out of 19 elements in 1972, states improved to 9.4 elements by 1975 and 12.1 by 1980. State laws covered more workers. Benefits were higher and in many cases were indexed to inflation for the first time. The glass may be half full, supporters of state control argued, but it was filling up.

The threat of national action was real but limited in duration. As stakeholders in workers' compensation looked around in the early 1970s, they saw a new Black Lung program, serious discussion of national health insurance and welfare reform, and the nationalization of means-tested programs (e.g., SSI). They saw how a sympathetic audience of commission members could produce an unflattering portrait of workers' compensation. They moved quickly to demonstrate some progress. Once the threat had passed, the rate of improvement abruptly stopped: the compliance score was 12.1 in 1980 and 12.2 in 1988. By then, most policy makers in Washington had already reverted to their old patterns of working around the edges of state compensation laws. The main issue during the 1980s was whether the national government should do more to help victims of occupational diseases, especially those related to asbestos. The window for substantial national involvement in workers' compensation, never large to begin with, had closed.

Little has changed since that time. The national government created two small programs for illnesses and injuries related to nuclear weapons. The Radiation Exposure Compensation Act of 1990 covers civilians who may have contracted cancer from the development and testing of nuclear weapons in the western states during the 1940s, 1950s, and 1960s. Individuals who qualify receive a lump sum cash benefit and in some cases medical treatment. The Energy Employees Occupational Illness Compensation Program, dating from 2001, covers only those people who worked directly or indirectly for the government but applies nationwide. Both programs are essentially extensions of the Black Lung model and pose no threat to states' compensation laws. Between the late 1980s and late 1990s, states' average compliance score rose from 12.2 to 12.8 out of 19 elements, a very modest improvement compared to the near doubling of the 1970s.[70]

CONCLUSION

The history of workers' compensation offers us at least two lessons. The first and more practical lesson is this: the next time someone says how adept states are at tackling social problems, ask that person about workers' compensation. States have had decades and decades to address the problems of injured workers, and their answers are about as wide-ranging and irrational now as they were seventy-five years ago.[71] The only time that states made meaningful improvements to their workers' compensation programs was when they felt pressured by the national government in the 1970s. The flaws of workers' compensation persisted in part because so many companies and insurers had a stake in preserving the status quo, a fact that anyone interested in contracting out social services to the private and nonprofit sectors might want to consider. The phrase "laboratories of democracy" is supposed to evoke undertakings like the Human Genome Project in which talented scientists at different institutions work to solve a complex puzzle and add to our collective understanding. With workers' compensation, the more appropriate image is baseball legend Ted Williams, who was decapitated and frozen in liquid nitrogen after his death in the hope that he might someday be revived—an act that provoked acrimony and lawsuits among his surviving relatives, tasteless jokes in the media, and disbelief in the general public.

If state-level experiments with welfare turned out as badly as workers' comp, we would be tempted to ascribe failure to the vulnerability of beneficiaries. Welfare recipients are uniformly poor, most of them are in single-mother families, many of them are black or Hispanic, and some of the adults do not work for wages. These individuals do not have much political power, and the rest of the nation is not always sympathetic to their plight. Failing to help the poor is, sadly, not a big surprise. Workers' compensation is completely different. This program originated in the early twentieth century to aid white male industrial workers. While eligibility has expanded and the labor force has changed, many of the beneficiaries are still white, male, and not poor. They are all wage earners, and many of them are hurt doing dangerous jobs. It is difficult to stereotype workers' compensation as a poverty program, and yet it has many of the drawbacks associated with welfare. If states cannot do the right thing for injured workers, why should we trust them to take care of poor single-mother families?[72] Giving states more responsibility over social programs makes sense if the main objective is keeping benefits low, but not if we want to promote adequacy, equity, efficiency, or effectiveness.

The second lesson concerns the policy-making process. Most journalistic and academic treatments of the process focus on the stage when authoritative decisions are made, such as congressional votes or court rulings. These are important and highly visible moments. Some scholars have tried to show that earlier stages in the process, when issues move onto the public agenda and the range of policy alternatives is defined, can be just as significant.[73] These scholars stress asymmetries of power that enable particular individuals and groups to influence what problems are taken up and what remedies are considered legitimate.

Empirically, it can be difficult to show what happened at these earlier stages, and whether those events were decisive. With workers' compensation, the evidence ranges from strongly circumstantial to clear and compelling. Comprehensive reform of workers' compensation never came to a vote in Congress during the twentieth century, so our focus must be on these earlier stages. Clearly, such reform was considered more than once. Each time, key individuals within the executive branch—Franklin Roosevelt's Committee on Economic Security, Social Security officials in the late

1930s and the 1940s, and White House staff under Lyndon Johnson—decided that a fundamental challenge to states' programs was politically unwise. They repeatedly noted how poor a job states were doing with workers' compensation, and how formidable the stakeholders were. It is striking that policy makers deemed a major expansion of the national government's role in regulating workplace safety (OSHA) more likely than a national takeover of workers' compensation, or even than legislating uniform standards for state laws. The only times that national officials created compensation programs were when they were sure they would not upset the basic framework of state-level control (e.g., Black Lung). The appropriate metaphor here is not the dog that did not bark. Workers' compensation is the mean-tempered dog that everyone learned to walk around. It is hard to imagine a better example of the "second face of power," in which fundamental challenges to the status quo are never attempted, because the chances of success seem so low.[74]

Policy makers' sense of the possible was in turn shaped by decisions made much earlier, which is one of the main insights from scholars who stress path dependence in policy making.[75] At the time, these decisions may not even have seemed that consequential. In the 1910s and 1920s, most states did not create public compensation funds. They relied instead on private insurers and self-insurance. Although a number of scholars have focused on the initial adoption of workers' compensation laws, the less-studied debates over public versus private insurance proved to be highly consequential. In the 1930s, policy makers agreed to increase the national government's responsibility for several groups—the elderly, the unemployed, the blind, poor mothers and children—but not injured workers. Once the program had been excluded from the Social Security Act, it became so entrenched politically and institutionally at the state level that future reformers found it almost impossible to imagine a successful campaign to nationalize or even federalize the program. Workers' compensation has not evolved over the years to a technically efficient or effective form. The program has been and remains deeply flawed because vested interests have discouraged fundamental reform.

CHAPTER 9

Race Still Matters

IN 1903 W.E.B. DUBOIS DECLARED that race would be the fundamental problem of the twentieth century, and many journalists, novelists, and social scientists writing after DuBois agreed. By the end of the century, however, a number of voices were suggesting that race had lost much of its significance in the United States. The real optimists in this group see signs of progress everywhere. The Supreme Court's *Brown* decisions (1954–55) outlawed segregated schools. Passage of the Civil Rights Act (1964) and Voting Rights Act (1965) signaled the end of legal discrimination. Blacks and then Hispanics started winning elections to local, state, and national office. Presidents appointed racial minorities to lead important government agencies. A new black middle class emerged, firmly rooted in professional employment. Racial intermarriage became more common. Racial animosity diminished.[1] Recently, Harvard sociologist Orlando Patterson, an authority on slavery and race relations, wrote that "the racial divide that has plagued America since its founding is fading fast—made obsolete by migratory, sociological, and biotechnological developments that are already under way. By the middle of the twenty-first century, America will have problems aplenty. But no racial problem whatsoever."[2]

Although few scholars are this bold, a fair amount of evidence indicates that the impact of race on social policy has diminished. Robert Lieberman argues that racial considerations influenced many parts of the Social Security Act (1935), leaving African-Americans excluded or poorly served by new social programs. Over time, particularly as domestic and agricultural workers became eligible, blacks were gradually incorporated into Social Security.[3] We saw in chapter 2 how survivors insurance (enacted in 1939) helps compensate for blacks' shorter life expectancy. Disability insurance (1956) likewise serves a disproportionate number of African-Americans. The addition of these programs, combined with the progressive benefit formula in Social Security, means that blacks and Hispanics have been treated about the same as whites in the major social insurance programs. Medicaid (1965), the largest of the means-tested programs, helps to narrow the racial gap in health insurance because blacks and Hispanics are less likely than whites to have coverage through their employers.

The big exception is welfare. Numerous studies have documented how badly welfare policies have treated blacks throughout the twentieth century. Southern states were among the last to adopt mothers' pension laws in the 1910s and 1920s, and when they did they offered some of the lowest benefits in the nation. Because the vast majority of blacks lived in the South at the time, poor black families were much less likely to receive help than poor white families. After the Social Security Act created Aid to Dependent Children, southern states continued to discriminate against black applicants, declaring them to be unfit mothers and thus ineligible for aid. More recent work by Martin Gilens shows how racial attitudes affect support for welfare. Because many whites believe that welfare recipients are usually black, and blacks are usually lazy, whites believe that welfare spending should be cut. Racial attitudes are more important than education, income, partisanship, or general political ideology in shaping public opinion toward welfare. In contrast, whites are willing to support more spending on virtually every other social program. Other scholars have found that welfare benefits are lower and eligibility requirements are tougher in states with large numbers of racial minorities.[4] Apart from welfare, few contemporary social programs are supposed to be influenced by racial considerations.

This chapter demonstrates that the influence of race on U.S. social policy has not disappeared, nor is it limited to welfare. Like the previous discussion of workers' compensation, this chapter draws evidence from policy making at the state level, with emphasis on the benefits that people receive from social programs. Unlike the last chapter, the approach here is more quantitative than qualitative, more in keeping with the behavioral tradition than the historical. Using simple statistical techniques, I will assess the influence of race on benefit levels for a number of social programs financed and administered by the American states. We will see that benefits for welfare, Medicaid, and unemployment insurance are lower in states with large minority populations, even controlling for other economic and political variables. Race also affects the overall adequacy of a state's workers' compensation program. Much has changed in state politics over the last few decades: state legislatures have professionalized; interest groups have proliferated; campaign finance laws have toughened.[5] Nevertheless, race remains an important influence on social policies in the American states.

The usual approach to this kind of analysis is to present the hypotheses, the data, and the results that emerged at the very end of the research process. Everything seems so logical and inevitable. What is missing is some sense of how the author tried to think through the problem. Much of the frustration, and creativity, of quantitative analysis gets lost. Moreover, in my experience, some of these studies drain the life out of political analysis by overwhelming readers with numbers and technical jargon. This chapter tries to address those problems through an unconventional format. The following dialogue about race and social policy takes place between a Student and a Teacher, starting in the Teacher's office.

• • •

Student (knocking on door): Professor?

Teacher: Come in, come in. What can I do for you, my friend?

Student: Well, like I said in my e-mail, I wanted to talk with you about some ideas for my research paper.

Teacher: OK. Uh, remind me again which class you're in.

Student: Your seminar on the American welfare state.

Teacher: Right.

Student: I don't have a definite idea yet for my topic, but basically I want to show that the modern American welfare state is racist.

Teacher: Racist? What do you mean, racist? Do you think that social policies today are based on innate genetic differences between whites and blacks?

Student: Um . . . no.

Teacher: Do you think that the officials making these policies believe in the biological superiority of one race over another?

Student: Probably not.

Teacher: So what are you talking about?

Student: Well, I remember taking a sociology class where the teacher talked a lot about how U.S. social programs treat whites a lot better than blacks, and I thought I'd do a little more research on that. Did you know that the poverty rate for African-Americans and Hispanics is almost three times that for whites, and has been for decades?

Teacher: Actually, I do know that. Listen, I see two problems here already. First, let's start by dropping "racist" from your project. Scholars who think like you do might talk about "racial hierarchies" or "racialized policies," but they usually save "racist" and "racism" to describe a time before even I was born. Second, there's a difference between what social programs give people and what they accomplish. Benefit checks are outputs that government can more or less control, whereas poverty is an outcome that is much harder to control. Did your sociology professor happen to mention how many blacks and Hispanics drop out of high school or have illegitimate children? Those things can have a pretty big impact on poverty, too, and separating out the effects of these different factors can get pretty complicated.

Student: So what should I do?

Teacher: I think you should stay aware from comparing outcomes like poverty and stick to benefits. Do you know much statistics?

Student: I took a stats class last year.

Teacher: Well, why don't you use some statistics to see if race helps explain the variations in benefits from state to state?

Student: Hmmm, maybe I'll do that. Any other suggestions?

Teacher: I'm supposed to teach you, not tell you. You go off and do some research and come back when you've got something. I'll give you one hint: look ahead in the syllabus for our course and see if anything I've assigned looks useful.

• • •

A Few Weeks Later

Student: OK, I went ahead and read all the stuff on race and social policy for our class. I looked at the footnotes, found a couple of recent journal articles that compared welfare programs in the states, and read those. A couple of authors mentioned *Statehouse Democracy* and *Faces of Inequality*, so I read/skimmed through those.[6] I really liked those books, so what I want to do is somehow combine them and use more recent data. A lot of what I read was about race and the old AFDC program, and I want to figure out if race is still important for TANF.

Teacher: Sounds good so far. Have you started looking at the numbers?

Student: Yes. First, I correlated states' African-American population and the average monthly TANF benefit. I took data from as close to 2000 as possible so no one could complain that I was digging up old history. Based on past studies, my hypothesis is that there ought to be an inverse relationship—the higher the percentage of blacks in the state, the smaller the benefits. And that's what happens. I brought some numbers to show you. See, the relationship between race and welfare benefits is negative, quite strong ($r = -.57$), and statistically significant ($p < .01$).* To give you an example, Alabama is about one-quarter African-American, and the average welfare benefit for a family of three was \$164 a month in 2000. In New Hampshire, which is less than 1 percent black, benefits were \$575 a month.

But some authors don't think that the average welfare benefit is a good measure. It can be affected by things that state governments can't really control, like family size and applicants' incomes. So I correlated race to the maximum possible TANF benefit allowed by the state and found that the relationship was basically unchanged ($r = -.54$, $p < .01$). Conceivably, states might use federal Food Stamps benefits to compensate for their low TANF benefits, so I also correlated race with the maximum combined value of the

---

* The r refers to the Pearson correlation coefficient, whose values can range from -1 to $+1$, with 0 indicating no relationship. The p refers to the probability that we mistakenly detect a relationship when in fact none exists; in this case, there is less than a 1 in 100 chance of error, so we can be very confident of the results.

two benefits. Again, not much change ($r = -.52$, $p < .01$). The bottom line is that race still matters for welfare.[7]

Teacher: Is that it? I hate to be harsh, but this isn't exactly headline news.

Student: I know; that's why I did more. Next stop is Medicaid, which (as you know) is the biggest means-tested program in the American welfare state. Medicaid basically serves three groups of poor people—the elderly, the disabled, and families with kids. Because the cost of caring for each group is much different, it makes sense to analyze each separately.[8] First I looked at Medicaid spending per person for each of these groups. There's a lot of variation in Medicaid spending across the states, and a lot of variation in the percent of residents who are African-American. And guess what I found.

Teacher: Oh, surprise me.

Student: The relationship is negative in all three instances. More blacks in the state mean lower Medicaid spending. The relationships between race and spending on Medicaid children ($r = -.32$) and on Medicaid disabled ($r = -.31$) aren't quite as strong as between race and welfare, but they do meet the usual test of statistical significance. The relationship between race and Medicaid benefits for the elderly barely misses ($r = -.27$, $p < .06$). It's not as strong as welfare, but still pretty strong. Compared to Alabama, New Hampshire spent an average of three times more money on every one of its Medicaid children.[9]

Teacher: It looks like you analyzed SCHIP, too.

Student: That's right. The State Children's Health Insurance Program was created in 1997, which is why it didn't show up in any of the past studies I read. SCHIP is supposed to reach children who do not qualify for Medicaid but whose parents do not have health insurance through their job. Because SCHIP is targeted at the poor and near poor, I thought that it might look like welfare or Medicaid. It doesn't. The coefficients are positive, meaning more blacks in the state are associated with higher, not lower, SCHIP spending per child ($r = .24$, $p < .10$). It's also positively associated with the scope of the program, which is the ratio of enrolled SCHIP children to total poor children in each state. Neither coefficient is statistically significant, but they're close. These results mean that I can't say that race has a major influence on every program for the poor. But it does mean that creating SCHIP might have been a smart way of compensating for the racial inequalities in Medicaid.[10]

Teacher: Interesting.

Student: It gets better. I also found evidence that race matters in places that scholars rarely examine—the upper tier of social insurance programs. Most people think of social insurance as Social Security and Medicare, and they're both national programs. But the states do have a lot of control over unemployment insurance and workers' comp, so I correlated some features of those programs with race. Turns out that race is negatively related to average unemployment benefits per week ($r = -.23$, $p < .11$). While I can't be 95 percent sure that a relationship exists, I'm almost 90 percent sure, which is good enough for most people. The biggest surprise was workers' comp. States with a large percentage of African-Americans consistently have fewer of the nineteen essential features of a good workers' compensation program, as stipulated by the U.S. Department of Labor (see chapter 8). The relationship is stronger than any I found in Medicaid, and highly significant ($r = -.43$, $p < .01$). Race matters, even in programs that are not targeted at the poor.[11] To my knowledge, no one has ever really looked at the relationship between race and these two programs, at least not using state-level data. Have you seen anything?

Teacher: Hmmm, nothing comes to mind right away. Lieberman's work on race and unemployment insurance is more historical, and I think he stops in the 1960s.[12] Listen, if you read Hero's book and the Soss chapter, you must have seen that "race" doesn't mean "black" anymore.[13] There are as many Hispanics as blacks in this country now. Did you see if there is any relationship between a state's Hispanic population and your social programs?

Student: I did, but didn't find much. Most of the relationships are statistically insignificant, with coefficients close to zero. I do think it's interesting that SCHIP spending per child appears to be inversely related to the state's Hispanic population ($r = -.23$, $p < .11$), yet positively related to the state's black population.[14] I'm not sure what's going on there. I guess the main message is that when we talk about race and social policy in the American states, we really mean African-Americans and not Hispanics. That's an important point.

Teacher: If you had a halfway decent stats class, you know what I'm going to ask next. Lots of things in this world are correlated, but the relationship turns out to be spurious. Alabama is not exactly the wealthiest state in the nation. Maybe all you're seeing is the difference between rich and poor states. Does race still matter when you control for affluence?

Student (pulling out a second sheet of numbers): OK, just like Hero, and like Erikson, Wright, and McIver, I did control for the effects of per capita income, as well as education levels and urbanization using multiple regression.[15] After I did that, race remained a strong influence on welfare, regardless of whether you look at average benefits, maximum benefits, or maximum combined TANF/Food Stamps benefits. In every case the unstandardized regression coefficient for percent black was negative and statistically significant. More blacks in the state mean lower welfare benefits, even when you take these other factors into account. Georgia is a little more affluent than North Dakota, but its welfare benefits are a lot lower. Guess which state has more black people? Put another way, every 1 percent increase in the black population is associated with a five to six dollar decrease in monthly benefits. Moving from a racially homogeneous state to a more diverse state would mean losing a hundred dollars a month in welfare benefits. That's a big effect.

If you compare the standardized coefficients, which give you some sense of the relative importance of each variable, then race has a stronger impact than any other variable. Together, these four factors explain 50 to 60 percent of the variation in welfare benefits from state to state, which is a pretty powerful model. In addition, race remains a significant influence on the workers' comp "nineteen essentials" variable after controlling for income, education, and urbanization.

All those results support my case. Then there's Medicaid. The significance of race disappears for spending per child and spending per disabled once I control for the other factors. Income and urbanization are both statistically significant, but not percent black. Income has a very strong effect on Medicaid spending on the elderly, and race does not. In general, it looks like Medicaid spending is driven more by affluence and welfare spending more by race.

Teacher: Sounds to me like you're back to square one. There is no relationship between race and SCHIP, and the apparent relationship with Medicaid is basically masking a wealth effect. You didn't find any clear relationship between race and unemployment insurance. So what you're left with is welfare, which is old news, and one aspect of workers' comp, a program that most people don't know or care much about.

Student: Isn't this good enough?

Teacher: You could write up what you've done so far and have a perfectly respectable paper for class. From what you've shown me in class, though, I bet you could create something special. It looks like you've spent the last month thinking a lot about dependent variables. You've been pretty thorough, even creative, in finding different measures for your dependent variables. But I don't think you've spent nearly enough time thinking about your independent variable, race. If I understand you correctly, race is measured by some fraction of the population that belongs to a minority group. Just how, exactly, do more black or brown bodies affect policy making? What's your theory? I can easily imagine that having more blacks in a state might lead to their having more political power, and in turn more generous social benefits. You seem to think that more blacks leads to less power—why? If I were you, I wouldn't spend more time looking for new social policy variables to test; I'd think more about how race matters.

Student: I know that population is kind of a crude measure. I'd love to know the racial composition for each social program. The government keeps those numbers for welfare, but not for unemployment insurance or workers' comp, and I'm not sure they exist for Medicaid. I looked around and couldn't find them. So I went with the best numbers around, which are population figures.

Teacher: You still need some theory to make sense of whatever numbers you use.

• • •

One Month Later, in the Teacher's Office

Student: Hey, I think I've made some real progress since we last talked about my research paper. Do you have a few minutes?

Teacher: Uh, just a second. Let me finish this e-mail. OK, what have you got for me?

Student: I've done a couple of things differently. First, I've added a couple more control variables to my regression equations. I got to thinking that social policies might legitimately differ if some states faced worse social problems than others, so I added measures of objective need. When looking at welfare and Medicaid, I controlled for the state's poverty rate. For unemployment benefits and workers' comp, I controlled for the state's unemployment rate.[16] The other new variable is an index I created for party control of state government. Basically, I looked at which parties controlled the legislature and the governor's office during the period from 1994 to 2000. The values range from 1, pure Republican control, to 5, pure Democratic control. A state that consistently experienced divided government earned a score of 3, and if it was mostly Republican or mostly Democratic it earned a 2 or a 4. My working hypothesis is that greater Democratic control should be associated with more generous social programs.[17]

Teacher: Well, there are lots of different ways to measure party control, but yours sounds reasonable. I thought we talked last time about thinking through the relationship between race and social spending.

Student: I did that, too. First, I created a new measure by adding the percent black and the percent Hispanic. Before, I just tested each separately and found that black mattered a lot more than Hispanic. While I assumed that combining them would simply average their effects, I realized that the combination could matter more than black alone. So I tried out both population measures.

I also thought more about how race matters and decided to explore two different mechanisms. Many studies show that public opinion affects public policies, so I decided to try that route.[18] Maybe states with the largest minority populations have less tolerance for blacks, which leads to lower social spending. Erikson, Wright, and McIver developed a general measure of policy liberalism for the states, but that can conceal lots of policy-specific variations in attitudes. I found a more precise measure of racial attitudes based on a pooled set of responses from the General Social Survey, taken between 1972 and 1998. Paul Brace and his coauthors created an index based on answers to questions about racial integration in the schools, racial intermarriage, and a few other things. The index goes from 0 to 1, from less to more tolerant. The most tolerant state turns out to be Rhode Island (0.88). Several of the other top scorers come from the Northeast or West. The three least tolerant states are Kentucky, West Virginia, and Alabama (0.50).[19] My old population measure and this new measure of racial attitudes are related, but not perfectly ($r = -.30$). In general, states with larger black populations do have more negative racial attitudes. The basic theory is that having more minorities in a state might translate into more racial animosity, in which case benefits could be lower. The attitude measure isn't perfect for my purposes, because it focuses on blacks and not Hispanics. But it's better than nothing.

The other mechanism is through elective office. We know from past studies at the local, state, and national levels that having more blacks and Hispanics in office can make governments more responsive to the needs of racial minorities.[20] I found the number of black and Hispanic elected officials in each state, and divided that by the total number of elected officials to create a measure of minorities' political power in each state. This number includes people elected to Congress, the state legislature, and local offices. I tried to get voter turnout numbers, too, but data were missing for so many states, and so many of the same kind of states, that I decided to drop this measure. Basically, we don't get reliable turnout numbers for states like Maine and North Dakota, because if one black guy doesn't vote, black turnout in the state drops 10 percent. I'm exaggerating, but you get the idea. We have complete data for black elected officials, less so for Hispanics.[21] These two new measures of race—attitudes and elected officials—ought to satisfy you more than the old population measures because they pinpoint specific processes.

Teacher: This is sounding good. What did you find?

Student (pulling out some papers): What I found is that race matters in a variety of U.S. social programs, though not always in the same way. I'll show you a few examples. The first table here (table 9.1) summarizes a series of regression models where the dependent variable is the maximum TANF benefit in each state for the year 2000. Earlier, when I regressed maximum benefits against only the population measure, I found that every 1 percent increase in the state's black population was associated with a drop of $8.77 in monthly benefits. The relationship was statistically significant, and the black population alone accounted for over 25 percent of the variation in benefits among the states.

To make sure that race really matters, I need to control for the effect of other variables, which in my case means per capita income, education, urbanization, poverty, and party control of state government. In the first two equations (Models 1 and 2), I tested two different measures of population,

TABLE 9.1
Race and Welfare Policy in the American States

Independent variables	Maximum Monthly TANF Benefits (2000)				
	Model 1	Model 2	Model 3	Model 4	Model 5
Income	0.013	0.014	0.016*	0.010	0.012
Education	11.050*	14.189*	5.401	13.714*	6.136
Urban	−1.764	−1.355	−3.454**	−2.369*	−2.978**
Poverty rate	−1.930	4.100	−4.914	−2.489	−0.952
Party control	18.193	3.577	0.982	13.558	15.839
Black population	−7.458**	—	—	—	—
Black + Hispanic population	—	−4.568*	—	—	—
Racial attitudes	—	—	6.474**	—	6.195**
Black elected officials	—	—	—	−12.835**	−10.760*
Adjusted R²	.552	.448	.524	.509	.590
N	49	49	44	49	44

Note: Figures for each variable represent unstandardized regression coefficients. The number of cases (N) in each model is less than 50 because Nebraska has a nonpartisan state legislature and is thus omitted from the party control variable, and because we do not have measures of racial attitudes for Hawaii, Idaho, Maine, Nebraska, Nevada, and New Mexico.
* $p < .05$; ** $p < .01$

one just black and the other black and Hispanic combined. As you can see, each measure was statistically significant, even after controlling for these other variables. Of the two, percent black had the bigger impact. Every 1 percent increase in the black population was associated with a drop in monthly benefits of $7.46, holding the other factors constant. That's not much of a drop in impact versus the earlier model where race was the only independent variable. In contrast, a 1 percent increase in blacks and Hispanics lowered benefits by $4.57. The explanatory power of Model 1 was also greater than Model 2. As a result, I restricted the race variables in the subsequent models to African-Americans.

Models 3 and 4 test different ways that race might matter, through attitudes or through elected officials. Each of these race variables is statistically significant. More tolerant attitudes do mean higher welfare benefits, and the effect is pretty large: moving from the least tolerant to the most tolerant state is worth about an extra $250 a month in benefits. Even though Model 3 explains less of the variance in benefits than Model 1, I suspect you'd still find Model 3 more satisfying theoretically.

These results are very consistent with Gilens's research. He found that racial attitudes affect welfare attitudes nationally, even after controlling for a variety of other influences. I've found that racial attitudes affect welfare policies at the state level, controlling for economic development and objective need. He found that negative racial attitudes were aimed more at blacks than Hispanics. I've found that welfare benefits vary more based on the black population than on the combined black and Hispanic populations.[22]

The coefficient sign for my black elected officials variable, however, is negative, which means that having more officials is associated with lower welfare benefits (Model 4). That's not what we would usually expect. It turns out that the percent of officials who are black is very highly correlated with the percent of the population that is black ($r = .90$). My best guess is that states with lots of black officials, often from the South, are also states where conservative Democrats or Republicans control government. As a result, black officials are in the minority and have less power than their numbers might indicate.

The final step was determining which of the two new race variables is more important (Model 5). It turns out that racial attitudes and the percent of black elected officials have independent and statistically significant effects on TANF benefits. The only other variable that appears to have a clear effect is urbanization (the more urban the state, the lower the benefits). Based on a comparison of the standardized coefficients, racial attitudes, black elected officials, and urbanization all have roughly the same impact.

Teacher: So you're more sure than ever that the conventional wisdom about race and welfare is right. Did you find any other programs where race matters besides welfare? That's the $64,000 question.

Student: I sure did. The next table shows the same kind of numbers for Medicaid spending per elderly patient (table 9.2). I thought this would be a better test than spending on Medicaid kids, many of whom also receive welfare, where any race effect wouldn't be too surprising. But grandmas in nursing homes? That would be news. This part of Medicaid has less racial content than welfare.

If you remember, I didn't find any correlation between Medicaid spending on the elderly and the size of minority populations (percent black or percent Hispanic). Add in the control variables, and percent black still isn't significant (Model 1). But, if you substitute percent black plus Hispanic, then race is significant. Every 1 percent increase in the minority population is associated with a decrease of $126 in annual spending per elderly patient. The only other variable to consistently achieve statistical significance was per capita income. Therefore, the impact of race does go beyond welfare.[23]

TABLE 9.2
Race and Medicaid Policy in the American States

Independent variables	Annual Medicaid spending per elderly (1999)			
	Model 1	Model 2	Model 3	Model 4
Income	0.692**	0.707**	0.744**	0.680**
Education	−179.833	−165.205	−322.497	−118.379
Urban	−36.174	2.274	−29.815	−50.623
Poverty rate	40.834	307.230	−94.555	71.260
Party control	−943.237*	−884.181*	−1014.878*	−865.562
Black population	−36.166	—	—	—
Black + Hispanic population	—	−126.430*	—	—
Racial attitudes	—	—	13.241	—
Black + Hispanic elected officials	—	—	—	−233.981
Adjusted R^2	.352	.420	.374	.315
N	49	49	44	34

Note: Figures represent unstandardized regression coefficients. The number of cases (N) is less than 50 for reasons cited in table 9.1 and because we do not have accurate numbers for Hispanic elected officials in many states.
* $p < .05$; ** $p < .01$

Exactly how race matters in Medicaid, I'm not sure. Neither the attitude measure nor the percent of minority elected officials proved significant (Models 3 and 4). I can rule these two out, which is useful, but I'm not yet sure how race matters. What I can say is that race matters in different ways for Medicaid than it does for TANF.

Teacher: That's a more sophisticated and convincing argument than you had before.

Student: This last table shows the same kind of analysis for weekly unemployment benefits in 2001 (table 9.3). Again, there's no obvious racial content to this policy. This time, instead of the poverty rate, I use the unemployment rate to measure objective need. Otherwise, the rest of the independent variables are just what you've seen before. The first two equations (Models 1 and 2) are quite similar to the first two for Medicaid in that both measures of race in the population have a negative sign. So again, a larger minority population means less spending on benefits. The combined percent of black and Hispanic has a bigger impact than percent black alone. Again, I'm not sure what the precise mechanism is. Neither the attitude nor the elected offi-

TABLE 9.3

Race and Unemployment Insurance in the American States

Independent variables	Average weekly unemployment benefits (2001)			
	Model 1	Model 2	Model 3	Model 4
Income	0.003	0.002	0.004	0.002
Education	0.712	1.176	0.898	2.541
Urban	0.479	0.991**	0.311	0.491
Unemployment rate	−4.720	−1.068	−5.889	−3.629
Party control	2.028	2.305	−3.761	−1.864
Black population	−1.179*	—	—	—
Black + Hispanic population	—	−1.716**	—	—
Racial attitudes	—	—	−.133	—
Black + Hispanic elected officials	—	—	—	−2.733
Adjusted R^2	.432	.529	.384	.332
N	49	49	44	34

Note: Figures represent unstandardized regression coefficients. The number of cases (N) is less than 50 for reasons cited in tables 9.1 and 9.2.

* $p < .05$; ** $p < .01$

cial variables performed well, much like Medicaid (Models 3 and 4). None of the other variables works particularly well, and I'm really not sure what influences unemployment benefits beyond the state's racial population.

I also tested the effects of race on the percent of unemployed workers in each state who received unemployment benefits in 2000. This is a coverage measure rather than a spending measure, like I did a while back for SCHIP. Perhaps states with more minorities make it harder to qualify for benefits. That does seem to be the case. Controlling for the same variables as before, I found that the percent of blacks plus Hispanics in the states was inversely related to the scope of unemployment benefits ($p < .01$). Again, neither the racial attitude nor the elected officials variables worked that well when substituted for my population variable.

More important, I have evidence that the impact of race extends to the upper tier of social insurance programs. It isn't limited to your classic anti-poverty programs. And it's not just unemployment insurance, either. I don't have the numbers with me right now, but I did test for the effects of race on the overall adequacy of states' workers' comp programs, defined as how many of the "nineteen essentials" each program had. Controlling for income, education, percent urban, party control, and the unemployment rate, I found that both of my racial population measures were significant, and the sign of both was negative—more minorities, fewer essentials. The impact of blacks plus Hispanics was slightly larger than blacks alone. In this case, racial attitudes were not significant, but the percent of minority elected officials was. The sign was negative, which again might reflect holding office but not power. Nevertheless, I don't think I have to nail down every loose corner to make a convincing case that race matters in many parts of the American welfare state.[24]

Teacher: No, you don't. It sounds like you can write a great paper now. You know, at the end of a paper like this one, I want students to suggest avenues for future research. Have you given some thought about what you might do with this project if you had more time?

Student: Well, one refinement might be to develop a better measure of minority political power. Instead of just counting how many minority officials there are in each state, I might be able to determine how many were mayors of major cites or chairmen of important legislative committees.[25] If I had even more time, I might collect similar data from other decades. What I'm saying here is that race isn't just a 1950s thing; it's still important to social policy at the beginning of the twenty-first century. But I don't really know whether the significance of race is declining, or how fast. I'd need to run similar models for earlier years and compare the results. The other thing I could do is conduct a careful case study or two to figure out better how race matters in social policy making. The statistics help me identify which variables are related to each other; now I could shift to a more qualitative approach to figure out the process that links race to various social policies. For instance, California has fewer blacks than the national average and more generous welfare benefits, but a very high percentage of blacks plus Hispanics and some of the lowest unemployment benefits in the country. How come?

Teacher: Well, I'm not sure that's the best example since California is unusual is many ways, including its racial composition. But I definitely like the way you're thinking. One last thing: I never said this explicitly in class, but when you're writing up your results, use one of the journal articles assigned in class as a model. The basic formula is Intro, Lit Review/Theory, Data/Variables, Results, Conclusions. Don't try to be too creative. You have plenty of substance here, and you don't need to compensate with some off-the-wall presentation.

Student: Will do. Thanks.

CHAPTER 10

Change versus Progress

> Change is one thing, progress is another. "Change"
> is scientific, "progress" is ethical; change is indubitable,
> whereas progress is a matter of controversy.
>
> —*Bertrand Russell*

> Progress is not an illusion, it happens, but it is slow and
> invariably disappointing.
>
> —*George Orwell*

YOU CAN MAKE A GOOD CASE that the ultimate test of a welfare state is not how many social programs are created, or how much money government spends on those programs. It is not whether most people support the welfare state and want government to do more. The real test is whether a welfare state does a good job of helping needy individuals and families. Earlier we heard from critics who fault the American welfare state for doing too much to help the elderly at the expense of everyone else (chapter 7). In their more passionate moments, these individuals rail against greedy geezers and raise the specter of generational warfare. We also encountered a fair amount of evidence that most people, young and old, want government to do a lot to help senior citizens. And the billions of dollars spent on Social Security and Medicare have kept millions of older Americans out of poverty. The final chapter of this book takes a closer look at poverty and inequality, the most widely used indicators of how well a welfare state is working. In the process, this chapter pulls together some of the main findings and themes of the book.

If moderate and conservative elites worry about generational equity, prominent liberals are troubled by poverty and inequality. According to economist and *New York Times* columnist Paul Krugman, the growing gap between haves and have-nots is part of the "great unraveling" of American society. Other scholars contend that the U.S. economy operates on winner-take-all principles that exacerbate poverty and inequality. Recent waves of economic growth have been "lifting the yachts [and] swamping the rowboats," or at least causing the rowboats to run aground.[1] Liberal politicians and commentators do not hesitate to use phrases like "class warfare" when discussing recent trends.[2] They draw unflattering comparisons to the Roaring Twenties and the Gilded Age.

Somewhat more temperate voices refer to the United States as a two-tiered society with well-paid, well-educated professionals on top and poorly paid, less-educated service workers below.[3] The Carnegie Corporation, the Economic Policy Institute, the Russell Sage Foundation, and similar organizations have been sponsoring ambitious research programs designed to uncover the full scope and many causes of inequality.[4]

Any way you look at it, economic inequality in the United States is substantial. The most recent figures from the U.S. Census Bureau show that median household income was $44,389 in 2004. Many people, however, lived well above or well below the median. The poorest 10 percent of households had less than $11,000 in income. The richest 10 percent had more than $120,000. Collectively, the poorest quintile had only 3.4 percent of total income, while the richest quintile had 50.1 percent. Thus, one-fifth of the nation controlled one-half of the income. If we consider not just income but overall wealth, the disparities are much greater. According to economist Edward Wolff, the richest 5 percent of Americans controlled over half of the nation's wealth in 2001, while the richest 20 percent controlled over 80 percent of the wealth. The bottom 40 percent of Americans had essentially no net worth.[5]

To put these numbers in perspective, we can compare inequality over time and among countries. Although inequality diminished somewhat in the United States in the decades after World War II, it began to increase in the early 1970s. Between 1974 and 2004, the share of aggregate income held by the upper quintile increased from 43.5 to just over 50 percent. Every other quintile saw its share diminish. These shifts in income caused the Gini index* to rise from .395 to .466.[6] The Luxembourg Income Study (LIS) is probably the best source of cross-national data on inequality. In 2000, the most recent year available, the Gini index was higher in the United States than in Austria, Belgium, Canada, Germany, Ireland, Italy, Norway, Spain, Switzerland, Sweden, Taiwan, or the United Kingdom. One would have to visit Mexico or Russia to find more inequality than in the United States.[7]

Similar patterns hold true for poverty. After declining substantially in the 1960s and early 1970s, the U.S. poverty rate has fluctuated between 11 and 15 percent. In 1974, when the U.S. economy was officially in a recession, the poverty rate was 11.2 percent. In 2004, when the economy was not in a recession, the poverty rate was 12.7 percent (i.e., 37 million poor people). Making cross-national comparisons is a little complicated because the U.S. government defines poverty differently. Whereas the pov-

---

* The Gini index is a common way of measuring income inequality. The number ranges from 0 (everyone has the same income) to 1 (one person has all the income); the higher the number, the greater the inequality.

erty line in the United States is a fixed dollar amount, the poverty line in Europe and Canada is typically one-half of median income. To Europeans, poverty entails both material deprivation and social exclusion; anyone with less than half the income of the average person is something less than a full member of society. Scholars have recalculated the U.S. poverty line using a relative measure and discovered that poverty at the end of the twentieth century was twice as high in the United States as in Germany, and almost three times the rate in Scandinavia. Poverty was more prevalent in the United States than in Hungary, Ireland, Poland, Slovenia, or Taiwan. Canada and the United Kingdom, the countries most similar to the United States in culture and history, had considerably less poverty. The United States was also a leader in poverty among children and the elderly. Factor in differences in standards of living, and poverty was still higher in the United States than in most affluent democracies.[8]

There is no shortage of explanations for the high levels of poverty and inequality in the United States. Some analysts highlight the shift from a manufacturing economy to a service-based economy, the pressures of increased global competition, or the weakness of labor unions. Others point to growing gaps in skills and education, immigration, or the rise of single-parent families.[9] I lack the time, space, and frankly the mental equipment needed to figure out which of these explanations is most important. But I do know that the causes are not solely economic and demographic. What we might call "market inequality," meaning the distribution of income before government taxes and transfers, is actually *lower* in the United States than in Belgium, France, the Netherlands, or the United Kingdom. Market inequality is only slightly higher in the United States than in Sweden, of all places. The U.S. economy is by no means the only one capable of generating significant inequality. But once governments finish redistributing income through taxes, social insurance, and other transfer programs, inequality is a good bit higher in the United States than these other countries. Similarly, the United States does less to reduce "market poverty" than many other countries. Inequality and poverty are, to some degree, the result of political decisions. U.S. officials choose to do less about poverty and inequality than their counterparts in Europe and Canada.[10]

This seems like a strange, perhaps even contradictory way to end the book. Am I saying that even though the American welfare state is in many ways less exceptional than it was a few decades ago (box 10.1), it is still less effective at reducing poverty and inequality than European welfare states? Am I really saying that despite the wide range of tools used to make U.S. social policy; despite how often social programs have been created and expanded; despite significant growth in means-tested programs such as Medicaid and the Earned Income Tax Credit; despite strong

BOX 10.1

American Exceptionalism in Decline

The American welfare state is less exceptional than it used to be. In some respects the American welfare state has become more like its European counterparts, and in some ways European welfare states have come to resemble the American model. Although a complete analysis of these developments could take another book, consider the following changes in public opinion and public policy.

Public Opinion

Many scholars believe that the American welfare state is relatively small because public support is relatively low (chapter 6). Ladd, Lipset, and other analysts of public opinion based their conclusions in part on the first ISSP Role of Government survey, conducted in 1985. By comparing the answers given in the 1985 and 1996 surveys, we can see evidence of convergence. While support for government jobs for all declined by 2 percentage points in the United Kingdom, 7 points in West Germany, and 12 points in Italy, it increased by almost 5 points in the United States. Support for reducing the income gap between rich and poor dropped by 5 points in West Germany, 7 points in the United Kingdom, and 9 points in Italy, while increasing by almost 10 points in the United States. The percent of people wanting to spend more on unemployment benefits increased slightly in the United States while dropping by 5 to 7 percentage points in the other three countries. Support for spending more on health jumped by over 9 points in the United States, and on Social Security by 7 points. The trend in other countries was a mix of small increases and decreases in support. In short, American attitudes toward the welfare state were less distinctive in the 1990s than the 1980s (see also table 10.2).

Public Policy

For a long time, observers have contrasted the universalism of European welfare states with the heavy reliance on means-tested programs in the United States (chapter 2). Confronted with a growing number of elderly individuals and single-parent families, more expensive medical care, high unemployment, and a host of other pressures, officials in Europe have been devising ways to target scarce resources at their neediest populations. Robert Cox describes how Denmark and the Netherlands have been "moving away from universalism, either by placing more responsibility on individuals to secure their own welfare or by targeting only the truly needy for support." He points to important policy changes in the 1990s involving unemployment benefits and retirement pensions. Summarizing developments in a number of countries (including Great

(boxed text continued on following page)

Britain, Italy, and Sweden), Neil Gilbert concludes that "over the last decade many social welfare policies have been redesigned to narrow the scope of recipients by targeting benefits through means tests, income tests, claw-back taxes, diagnostic criteria, behavioral requirements, and status characteristics." Another study, using data from the mid-1990s, calculated the share of total social spending devoted to means-tested programs. The United States was quite similar to Denmark, Canada, and the Netherlands, and less reliant on means-testing than Great Britain. However big the gap between the United States and other nations might have been with respect to means-testing, it appears to be getting smaller.

In the early twentieth century, new ideas about social policy flowed from Europe to the United States. Now we are seeing some countries adopt American innovations. Australia (1992) and Great Britain (1995) modeled their disability laws explicitly after the U.S. Americans with Disabilities Act (1990). Germany passed a constitutional amendment in 1994 that extended antidiscrimination protection to the disabled. In all three nations, advocates adopted the language of equal opportunity and self-sufficiency that had been used in the United States (chapter 4). Similarly, the British modeled their Working Families Tax Credit explicitly after the U.S. Earned Income Tax Credit. Perhaps social regulation and tax expenditures will become more traditional tools of social policy in the future, not just in the United States but in other nations as well.

Sources: International Social Survey Program (ISSP), *Role of Government I, 1985* computer file and codebook (Cologne, Germany: Zentralarchiv für Empirische Sozialforschung, 1993); ISSP, *Role of Government III, 1996* computer file and codebook (Cologne, Germany: Zentralarchiv für Empirische Sozialforschung, 1999); Robert Henry Cox, "The Social Construction of an Imperative: Why Welfare Reform Happened in Denmark and the Netherlands but Not in Germany," *World Politics* 53 (April 2001): 466; Neil Gilbert, introduction to Gilbert (ed.), *Targeting Social Benefits: International Perspectives & Trends* (New Brunswick, NJ: Transaction, 2001), xviii (other chapters in this volume have country-specific evidence of targeting); Aya K. Abe, *Universalism and Targeting: An International Comparison Using the LIS Database*, Luxembourg Income Study Working Paper no. 288 (December 2001), available at http://www.lisproject.org/publications/wpapersf.htm; Katharina C. Heyer, "The ADA on the Road: Disability Rights in Germany," *Law & Social Inquiry* 27, 4 (Fall 2002): 723–62; Elizabeth Lightfoot, "A Comparative Study of Social Policy Transfer: The Adoption of Anti-discrimination Policy in the United Kingdom and Australia," *Social Policy Journal* 1, 4 (2002): 5–22; Pat Strickland, "Working Families Tax Credit and Family Credit," Research Paper 98/46 (London, U.K.: House of Commons Library, 1998), available at http://www.parliament.uk/commons/lib/research/rp98/rp98–046.pdf.

public support for many parts of the American welfare state; despite the willingness of Democratic and Republican officials to champion new and existing programs; in short, despite all the signs of vitality described in parts 1 and 2 of this book, the United States has made little headway in reducing poverty and actually lost ground in the fight against inequality?

That is exactly what I am saying. There has been change, yes, but not much progress. One is tempted to think of the American welfare state as a treadmill or a stationary bike where you work hard but don't get anywhere. That's not quite right. If you spend enough time on this equipment, you might not physically move forward, but your body will get into better shape. For all its huffing and puffing, the American welfare state does not seem to be in any better shape now than it was thirty years ago. This, in my view, is the most important puzzle of contemporary social policy.

Some analysts would point to the two-tiered shape of the American welfare state and maintain that the problem is too little social insurance and too much public assistance. This argument is counterintuitive considering that public assistance programs are aimed squarely at the poor. Spending a lot of money on public assistance should be the most efficient way to reduce poverty and inequality. The problem is that such programs are politically vulnerable, so they never end up spending enough money on the poor. Welfare is the classic example. The right way to fight poverty and inequality is by creating broad-based social insurance programs like Social Security. This argument is not entirely convincing. The rather sorry state of unemployment insurance and workers' compensation indicates that whether a program is designed according to social insurance principles matters less than how much authority is wielded by the states (chapters 2, 8). Some means-tested programs, namely Medicaid and the Earned Income Tax Credit, did develop bipartisan support and expand in recent decades, and they are much larger and arguably more important than welfare (chapter 5).

The federal structure of the American welfare state is a more likely suspect. When officials let state governments play a major role in financing and administering social programs, a number of bad things can happen. The people in charge might be unwilling or unable to remedy the flaws in these programs, as happened in workers' compensation. Social programs might differ so much from state to state that learning is quite difficult. Business interests, like insurance companies and firms that self-insure, might be quite powerful at the state level (chapter 8). In addition, we have seen that benefits might vary from state to state more because of race than objective differences in poverty or unemployment (chapter 9). In contrast, the national government appears to have created social programs that do not systematically disadvantage African-Americans (chapter 2). The historical development of Medicaid (chapter 5) and workers' compensation (chapter 8) demonstrates that major improvements to social programs happen when the national government gets involved. I am not suggesting that the national government should have sole responsibility for all social programs. Social conditions do differ across the country, and there are times when intelligent experimentation is needed. But the national government could certainly do more to ensure that those experiments go well, such as creating decent minimum standards for eligibility and benefits. Such a change would improve the adequacy and equity of welfare, unemployment insurance, and workers' compensation.

Nevertheless, federalism cannot be the only barrier to progress. Canada and Germany manage to reduce poverty and inequality more than the United States, and they too are federal. One of the largest barriers, in the opinion of most political scientists, is political inequality. If the poor and the near poor had more political power, the U.S. government would do more to help them. A recent report by the Task Force on Inequality and American Democracy, sponsored by the American Political Science Association, drew clear connections between political participation and public policy. The authors did not think it mere coincidence that the elderly are politically active and the government spends so much on Social Security and Medicare, or that the affluent participate more than average and often reap the benefits of tax cuts. After reviewing a number of national and cross-national studies, Sidney Verba, Kay Lehman Schlozman, and Henry Brady conclude that "one factor in explaining the weakness of redistributive policy is the absence of political clout of those lower on the socioeconomic scale" in the United States. Lawrence Jacobs, writing about health care, notes that "Americans with lower income and blue-collar occupations are most in need of government assistance and most supportive of government activism. The hitch is that . . . [they] are also the least likely to vote, attend political meetings, join political organizations, write to their elected officials, contribute to candidates, and influence policy makers."[11]

Political participation is strongly related to income in the United States. The less affluent are less likely to engage in virtually every kind of political activity, and they are less active than their counterparts in other nations. But, if the have-nots in the United States somehow gained a greater political voice, would they really tell officials anything new? Recall from chapter 6 that fewer than half of all Americans said that government should be responsible for closing the gap between rich and poor. In contrast, two-thirds to three-quarters of Britons, Germans, Italians, Norwegians, and Swedes said that government has that responsibility. Thus, while the average American might be like the average European in wanting government to care for the old and the sick, the average American does not necessarily want government to redistribute income. That might help explain why

Table 10.1
Support for Redistribution in the United States

	Support (1–2)		Support (1–3)	
	1980	2000	1980	2000
Income group				
Lower	39%	38%	59%	53%
Lower middle	29	31	45	50
Middle	23	24	40	41
Upper middle	19	19	34	36
Upper	10	18	20	30
Total	27	28	43	44
Class group				
Lower	41	50	62	58
Working	31	30	48	47
Middle	22	25	38	41
Upper	21	19	36	27
Total	27	28	44	44

Question wording: "Some people think that the government in Washington ought to re-duce the income differences between the rich and the poor, perhaps by raising the taxes of wealthy families or by giving income assistance to the poor. Others think that the govern-ment should not concern itself with reducing this income difference between the rich and the poor. Here is a card with a scale from 1 to 7. Think of a score of 1 as meaning that the government ought to reduce the income differences between rich and poor, and a score of 7 meaning that the government should not concern itself with reducing income differences. What score between 1 and 7 comes closest to the way you feel?"

Source: General Social Survey 1972–2002 cumulative data file, accessed via http://sda.berkeley.edu:7502/archive.htm.

Note: Support (1–2) means those individuals who answered "1" or "2" to this question. Support (1–3) means those who answered "1," "2," or "3." The total figures for income and class are not identical, because of rounding or because of people who refused to answer one question versus the other.

the Gini index of inequality is higher in the United States. Differences in the performance of welfare states might reflect differences in public atti-tudes toward inequality and redistribution.

Of course, it is quite possible that the average American is a statistical fiction, a mixture of people who embrace redistribution and others who reject it. We would expect lower-income Americans to voice the most support for redistribution and upper-income Americans the least. And we would be right—to a point. Once again we return to the General Social Survey (GSS), which for years has asked Americans to rate their support for income redistribution on a scale of 1 to 7, with 1 representing the most support and 7 the least. Table 10.1 displays their answers at two points in time, 1980 and 2000. The top half of the table groups Americans into five income categories: lower, lower middle, middle, upper middle, and upper.[12] The bottom half of the table divides respondents based on their self-reported class position. The vast majority of Americans call themselves working class or middle class.

Determining how many Americans favor redistribution from rich to poor is not straightforward. Counting just those individuals who replied "1" or "2" on the 7-point scale, we find that fewer than 30 percent of Americans want government to redistribute income. Counting those who answered "1," "2," or "3," support is over 40 percent. But, of that group, a large number expresses rather modest support, meaning that they answered "3."[13] Which numbers are more valid? I am not sure; that's why I report both sets of figures in table 10.1. I have seen other versions of this question in which individuals had their choice of five possible answers, and about one-third supported redistribution, which is right in between the numbers cited here. As a ballpark estimate, one-third seems pretty reasonable.

No matter how you calculate support for redistribution, it clearly goes down as income goes up.[14] The differences among the income categories are large enough to be statistically significant. This makes intuitive sense and fits with what Verba, Jacobs, and others have argued. The crucial question, though, is whether the differences are politically significant. Under the broader definition of support, over half of the lower-income group now supports redistribution, but that includes a sizable number (20%) whose support is weak. Support among the lower-middle-income group barely reaches 50 percent. Under the stricter definition of support, fewer than 40 percent of lower-income Americans favor government redistribution. Fewer than a third of lower-middle-income Americans share this opinion. Dividing Americans according to their self-perceived class position produces much the same result. Given that very few people call themselves lower class, the more telling figures in the bottom half of table 10.1 are for the working class. Whether the definition of support is strict or broad, most members of the working class say they do not support redistribution. In short, the people who have the most to gain from redistribution are not exactly clamoring for government to do something.[15]

Note, too, how stable these numbers are. As inequality has worsened in recent decades, the public's views toward redistribution have not changed. In 1980, 39 percent of the lower-income group and 27 percent of the total population were clearly in favor of redistribution. By 2000, 38 percent of the lower-income group and 28 percent of the total felt this way.[16] The low levels of support for redistribution and the failure of support to increase over time do not fit the conventional wisdom. If the have-nots gained a greater voice in U.S. politics, it is not obvious that they would push government to close the gap between rich and poor.

On the other hand, maybe we need to consider inequality and redistribution from a different angle. Social scientists and polling organizations almost always frame the issue in terms of rich and poor. Some research suggests that it might be more useful to think in terms of rich, middle class, and poor. For example, Lars Osberg and Timothy Smeeding have reexamined surveys about equality that the International Social Survey Program (ISSP) conducted in the 1980s and 1990s. Several questions asked what people in several different occupations (e.g., doctor, skilled factory worker, secretary) do earn and should earn. Osberg and Smeeding used the answers to estimate the acceptable gaps between high and low earners, high and average earners, and average and low earners in various countries. Table 10.2 captures some of their key findings.[17]

For my purposes, the most important results involve changing attitudes toward inequality in the United States. Between 1987 and 1999, the earliest and latest surveys, Americans' views about acceptable gaps between high and low earners did not change. Americans thought that high earners should make 6.7 times as much as low earners (i.e., the max-min ratio). The apparent stability of opinion concealed two opposing trends. During that same period, the acceptable gap between high and average earners (the max-mean ratio) dropped from 2.7 to 2.0, and the acceptable gap between average and low earners (the mean-min ratio) rose from 2.4 to 3.3. Americans are apparently becoming less tolerant of inequalities at the upper end of the income distribution and more tolerant of inequalities at the lower end. Whereas Americans used to think that the distance between the best-paid and average workers should be larger than the distance between the average and least paid, now the reverse is true. Attitudes in Great Britain, Germany, and Australia exhibit the same patterns (table 10.2).[18] Greater sensitivity to the distance between the rich and the middle class is a general trend. Moreover, the max-min ratios in these other countries and the United States were more alike in 1999 than they were in 1987. This is further evidence that American exceptionalism is on the decline (box 10.1).[19]

If we look more closely at U.S. census data, we see that all the increase in inequality in recent decades has occurred in the upper half of the income distribution. Between 1974 and 2004, the ratio of household income between the 80th and 50th percentiles grew from 1.74 to 2.00. In other words, to qualify for the top quintile, you now need at least twice as much income as the median. The ratio of household income between the 95th and 50th percentiles grew even faster, from 2.76 to 3.56, as the very rich distanced themselves from the middle class. In the lower half of the income distribution, the ratio between the 20th and 50th percentiles

TABLE 10.2
Acceptable Income Inequality in Four Nations

	1987	1999
United States		
Max-min ratio	6.7	6.7
Max-mean ratio	2.7	2.0
Mean-min ratio	2.4	3.3
United Kingdom		
Max-min ratio	5.6	6.7
Max-mean ratio	2.7	2.1
Mean-min ratio	2.0	3.3
Germany (West)		
Max-min ratio	4.8	6.0
Max-mean ratio	2.4	2.0
Mean-min ratio	1.9	2.9
Australia		
Max-min ratio	3.8	5.0
Max-mean ratio	2.1	1.8
Mean-min ratio	1.7	2.7

Source: Lars Osberg and Timothy Smeeding, " 'Fair' Inequality? An International Comparison of Attitudes to Pay Differentials" (June 2005), manuscript accessed via http://www-cpr.maxwell.syr.edu/faculty/smeeding/, tables 3 and 5.

Note: In common parlance, the max-min ratio measures the acceptable gap in income between rich and poor; the max-mean ratio measures the acceptable gap between the rich and the middle class; and the mean-min ratio measures the acceptable gap between the middle class and the poor.

has not changed during the last three decades. The income gap between the poor and the middle class has stayed the same.[20]

Now we can start piecing together the puzzle of how U.S. social policy can do so much and accomplish so little. Americans seem increasingly attuned to inequalities between the rich and the middle class—between the have-lots and the haves—and understandably so. That is where inequality has been worsening. As for the have-nots, well, they have been losing ground to the rich but not to the middle class, and the latter might be the more salient inequality in the minds of ordinary citizens. Major cuts to means-tested social programs, like those enacted in 1996, might not provoke much opposition from a public that believes the acceptable gaps between the middle class and the poor could be larger. Expansions to programs such as Medicaid and the EITC might be tolerated as long as they were not big enough to make a real dent in inequality.

In fact, many of the legislative milestones in recent decades do relatively little for the have-nots and, in that sense, might reflect the public's concerns. Consider several of the social programs discussed in chapters 3 and 4. The main objective of ERISA is to shore up retirement pensions offered by employers, through a combination of regulations, insurance, and tax expenditures. According to the U.S. Census Bureau, employers' pension plans covered 43 percent of all workers in 2001. Managerial and professional workers were almost twice as likely to have pensions as sales workers, and almost five times more likely than agricultural workers. Pension coverage was much higher among full-time than part-time workers, and much higher among large employers than small businesses. Pensions are more common among unionized and public-sector employees. A lawyer will probably have a pension, but not the man he hires to care for his lawn. A college professor will probably have a pension, but not the woman who dry-cleans his shirts.[21]

A recent study by the Congressional Budget Office (CBO) provides more evidence of this upward skew. The CBO found that only 20 percent of all workers earning under $20,000 participated in an employment-based retirement plan, compared to 72 percent of workers earning between $80,000 and $120,000. The recent growth of Individual Retirement Accounts and Keogh plans has done nothing to alter this pattern. Two percent of workers earning under $20,000 and 7 percent of workers earning $20,000 to 40,000 participated in one of these alternative retirement plans. Among the most affluent workers, the participation rate was over 20 percent.[22] Thus, when the U.S. government offers tax breaks for private pensions—to the tune of $120 billion in 2005—it is largely subsidizing the haves and the have-lots.[23] When the Pension Benefit Guaranty Corporation bails out pension plans, it is helping airline pilots and steelworkers more than child care providers and cabdrivers.

Congress approved COBRA regulations in 1985 in order to make private health insurance more affordable and available. Those regulations allow individuals to keep their health insurance after they leave their job. That, of course, assumes that individuals have coverage in the first place, and many low-income workers do not. The effect of COBRA is further limited by the requirement that employees pay the full insurance premium, including whatever their employer formerly paid. Even at the lower group rates, many employees cannot afford to continue their health insurance.

Likewise, the Americans with Disabilities Act may be "most likely to improve work opportunities . . . for people who are employed and have good job skills."[24] Studies have found that few people who qualify for disability insurance or SSI ever return to work. The main effect of the ADA may be to help the disabled who are already employed to stay employed. Who are these people? Prior to the ADA, disabled black men were much less likely to be employed than disabled white men. Similar but smaller gaps separated black and white women. Disabled men and women without a high school education were much less likely to be employed than those with a high school education. Thus, whites and the better educated may reap more tangible benefits from the ADA.

Many observers welcomed the Family and Medical Leave Act (FMLA) when it became law in 1993. In some respects, the impact of the Act was impressive. Between 1993 and 1997, the percent of workers covered by parental leave policies increased substantially.[25] Nevertheless, the benefits of the FMLA have been distributed unevenly. Much of the problem is due to the program's original design. It mandated unpaid parental leave and limited that mandate to public entities and to private companies with fifty or more employees. It also limited coverage to individuals who had worked for their employer at least 1,250 hours in the previous year. Supporters felt that any measure requiring paid leave or extending coverage to small business would surely fail in Congress. The same reasoning applied to the Act's annual limit of twelve weeks of leave, which was shorter than in many other countries. Advocates hoped that if they got a foot in the door, they would be able to push later for expansion.

That has not happened, and no one in Washington is seriously discussing the possibility. Small businesses are still excluded, which meant that 42 percent of private-sector employees were not covered by FMLA in 2000. Another 11 percent of workers were in firms covered by the law, but they had not yet worked long enough to qualify. More than half of all workers in the private sector were therefore ineligible to take advantage of the FMLA. Compared to workers in large firms, those employed by small businesses are more likely to be high school dropouts and more likely to work in retail trade, construction, and agriculture.[26] Individuals who have these characteristics are not usually well-off financially, which gives us some reason to suspect that the FMLA is of less benefit to people with below-average incomes. The other reason that the FMLA benefits them less is simply that leave is unpaid. Low-income workers have a harder time living without a paycheck than do higher-income workers. Some people may be able to take twelve weeks off when a child is born, but others can afford only four weeks. When it comes to parental leave, the United States is still exceptional. In most affluent democracies, parental leave is universal and can last six months or longer, and workers are paid somewhere between 50 and 100 percent of their wages while on leave.[27]

The recently enacted Child Tax Credit (CTC) might not appear to have these problems. Eligibility is not tied to employment; you just need a child. Nevertheless, the CTC is very much a middle-class program. The total cost of the program was $47 billion in 2004, well above what the government spent on the child care block grant, TANF, or even the Earned Income Tax Credit. Of that amount, taxpayers with incomes below $20,000 claimed less than 5 percent. Taxpayers with incomes between $20,000 and $50,000 claimed a little over a third. Taxpayers with incomes between $50,000 and $100,000, who would be middle or upper-middle class almost anywhere in the country, took home not quite half of the tax credit. The rest went to people earning over $100,000. This last group benefited as much from the Child Tax Credit as those earning under $30,000. The CTC effectively negates much of the redistributive impact of the means-tested EITC.[28]

One can find older components of the American welfare state that are similarly biased in favor of the affluent. The tax expenditure for employer health insurance (estimated to cost over $75 billion in 2005) helps many of the same kinds of well-educated professionals as the tax break for employer retirement pensions. The most glaring example is U.S. housing policy. Tax expenditures for home owners cost the U.S. government an estimated $115 billion in 2005. The largest of these is the home mortgage interest deduction. It does less for poor and working-class Americans than any other major program in the American welfare state. Taxpayers earning less than $30,000 received a grand total of 2 percent of the benefits. Over half of the money went to those earning over $100,000. Taxpayers with incomes above $200,000 benefited more from this deduction than those with less than $50,000.[29] These are huge programs, surpassed only by the Big Three of Social Security, Medicare, and Medicaid. The combination of these programs and the newer ones discussed above means that a large and growing portion of the American welfare state does little to reduce poverty or narrow the gap between rich and poor.

Add together everything the United States spends on public assistance, from Medicaid and SSI to Food Stamps and welfare. Cast the net widely to include veterans' benefits and education. Make sure to count spending by national, state, and local governments. When you do all that, means-tested spending in the United States totaled about $525 billion in 2002. Now compare that figure to the cost of tax expenditures that went primarily to the middle and upper-middle classes in 2002: over $200 billion to subsidize fringe benefits such as health insurance and retirement pensions; about $100 billion for home owners; $35 billion for charitable deductions; and $27 billion for the Child Tax Credit. That sums to over $350 billion. If we include $100 billion in tax breaks for capital gains, which boost the incomes of the well-to-do, then the total is more than $450 billion. Tax expenditures thus negate a lot of the redistribution accomplished by traditional antipoverty programs.[30]

Earlier in the book, I noted that the American welfare state is more distinctive for its mix of policy tools than its overall size. That mix appears to have profound implications for the ability of welfare states to address poverty and inequality. Broadly speaking, the more that welfare states rely on social insurance and grants, the more successful they will be. Belgium, Denmark, Finland, and Sweden spend a lot of money on these traditional tools and very little on tax expenditures (tables 1.1, 1.2). The governments in these countries also do more than most affluent democracies to combat market inequality and market poverty.[31] The United States is the best example of a country that relies less on social insurance and grants and achieves smaller reductions in poverty and inequality. The largest social insurance program in the United States, Social Security, has had a large, positive effect on poverty among the elderly. The major grant programs (e.g., Medicaid, SSI, welfare) are targeted at the poor and by definition help close the gap between them and the rest of the nation. The positive impact of these tools is partly offset by the less traditional tools of social policy. Compared to other affluent democracies, the American welfare state relies unusually heavily on tax expenditures, social regulations, loan guarantees, and the like. While these programs are theoretically available to all, in practice they are tilted toward the middle and upper-middle classes. They are a thin but politically attractive version of universalism. Many of them are the mirror image of what we normally think of as means-tested programs. There are notable exceptions, but the general pattern is clear. By relying on these tools, the United States can still create and expand social programs when trust in government is low, control of government is divided, or deficits are high. But such flexibility, such adaptability, comes with a price. The American welfare state can do a lot, but not necessarily for the people who need help the most.

Before concluding, let me anticipate a few questions or reservations about my argument. Several scholars argue persuasively that social needs have changed in recent decades as employment and family patterns have changed. U.S. social programs might be doing a decent job of addressing needs that were important in the 1960s and 1970s, but policy makers may not have adapted those programs to the needs of single-parent families, two-earner families, part-time workers, frequent job-switchers, and other groups whose numbers have grown.[32] My argument, which I think complements theirs, is that policy makers have tried to help some of the people affected by these changes. Through the Family and Medical Leave Act and the Child Tax Credit, for example, officials have tried to help parents balance the demands of work and family—but mostly middle-class parents.

I am not saying that the less traditional tools of social policy are invariably biased in favor of the well-to-do. Because people with above-average incomes generate most of the income tax revenue in this country, tax expenditures are likely to benefit them the most. Policy makers who want to target benefits at those with below-average incomes need to use tax credits instead of tax deductions and need to make those credits refundable. Or, policy makers can phase out tax expenditures for higher incomes. The Earned Income Tax Credit is a shining example of how tax expenditures can be designed to help the poor and near poor. The United States uses tax expenditures to encourage employers to offer pensions and health insurance to their workers and then regulates the financing and administration of those benefits. But the government does not mandate pensions and health insurance, and in fact tries to ensure that the regulations are not so onerous that they discourage firms from providing these benefits. In contrast, the United States requires almost all employers to pay their workers a minimum wage. The government could use social regulation to mandate benefits as well.

Furthermore, I believe that understanding the impact of policy tools on the performance of welfare states is a starting point, not an end. Variations in the mix of policy tools across nations and over time might reflect the influence of business and labor, or institutional fragmentation. I have already suggested how political parties and public opinion might affect the choice of policy tools (chapters 3, 4, 6). That choice could be a crucial intervening variable between the kinds of influences that social scientists are accustomed to analyzing and outcomes like poverty and inequality. Not everything hinges on policy tools, however. Even if the American welfare state relied almost entirely on social insurance and means-tested grants, public opinion and federalism (and the interaction between federalism and race) would still limit our ability to reduce poverty and inequality.

Finally, some readers might wonder how one can discuss poverty, inequality, and redistribution without saying more about tax policy. One reason is that welfare states accomplish more redistribution through transfers than taxes. In the thirteen affluent democracies studied by Vincent Mahler and David Jesuit, government transfers accounted for three-quarters of government-sponsored income redistribution in the last decades of the twentieth century, and taxes the remaining one-quarter. The United States was an interesting outlier. Taxes were a more important source of redistribution in the United States than any other country, and the amount of redistribution via taxes was higher in the United States than the thirteen-nation average. The amount of redistribution via transfers in the United States was less than half the average. The data for this study ended in 2000, and the United States will probably look less unusual once the Bush tax cuts, which favor businesses and the rich, take full effect. For now, the United States' failure to make much of a dent in inequality is related more to transfer programs than taxation.[33]

FINAL THOUGHTS

I conclude with two observations, one historical and the other conceptual. The development of the American welfare state is often the story of proponents building up and critics tearing down. That is the story of Social Security: how public officials broadened eligibility in the 1950s and increased benefits in the 1960s and 1970s, and how they modeled disability insurance and Medicare after Social Security. That is the story of welfare: how state-level officials kept benefits low, and how national officials restricted eligibility in 1981 and 1996. This book offers a new twist to that history. Welfare is not the only part of the American welfare state to come under fire. It has been, however, the easiest to attack. In other cases, critics decided that direct confrontation was politically risky. They had to find another way.

Often the best these critics could do was build around or on top of programs that they did not like. At different points in the twentieth century, policy makers thought that workers' compensation was seriously flawed, believed that it could never be truly reformed, and decided to build anew. To varying degrees survivors' insurance, disability insurance, the Black Lung program, and even OSHA emerged from the shadow cast by workers' compensation (chapter 8). The recent enactment of the State Children's Health Insurance Program (1997) might fit this pattern as well. Despite expansion of Medicaid eligibility in the 1980s, millions of poor and near-poor children still lacked health insurance in the 1990s. There was no consensus as to why. Perhaps parents were unaware that their children were eligible for Medicaid; perhaps being on Medicaid carried a stigma; perhaps states could not afford to extend Medicaid to optional populations. Rather than trying to sort out and address various problems in Medicaid, elected officials created a new program, SCHIP. These critics believed that government should take the lead in promoting social welfare. In contrast, many of the key architects of ERISA, the Americans with Disabilities Act, and the Child Tax Credit wanted their new programs to curb the growth of existing social insurance and grant programs. To slow down Social Security, they tried to make retirement pensions in the private sector more widely available. To reduce the number of disabled people on public assistance, they tried to increase their odds of finding and keeping a job (chapter 4). Part of the history of the American welfare state, then, is critics being creative.[34]

Finally, I want to revisit the meaning of the welfare state. Starting with the first page of the first chapter, this book has tried to correct several misconceptions about where the United States stands in the family of welfare states. The United States is supposed to be a semi–welfare state, an incomplete welfare state, a welfare state laggard—in short, an underachiever. In many ways, this label is unfair. The American welfare state is larger and more popular than commonly believed. Although it lacks strong social insurance programs for people during their working years, it does subsidize their health insurance and home mortgages and it does regulate their wages and benefits. But, if the fundamental goals of a welfare state are security and equality, as many scholars contend, then the United States does indeed fall short.[35] Poverty and inequality are unusually high in the United States, and one of the main reasons why this is the case is that social policies do relatively little to mitigate the problems that market forces generate. While this book undermines a number of claims about American exceptionalism, it might reinforce the one claim that matters most. The American welfare state does not do much to lift people out of poverty or to close the gap between rich and poor. What redistribution there is occurs more across age lines than income lines.

This chapter opened with a quotation reminding us that the whole notion of progress is intrinsically controversial. Claims about progress require judgments about goals and how close you need to be to those goals in order to be successful. The main message of this chapter is how little progress the American welfare state has made in achieving key goals, and I realize that this judgment is problematic. The United States has done less to reduce poverty and inequality than other affluent nations; that is fact, not opinion. Whether the United States has made little progress in achieving these goals is a judgment call. There is no fixed or objective standard for how much poverty is too much, or how big the gap between rich and poor ought to be. The specific meanings of security and equality are political questions. Public policies in this country do reduce poverty and inequality, and whether that constitutes progress is something that must be decided collectively.

The increasingly middle-class character of the American welfare state is, in my view, a partial victory. I understand that middle-class families need help in paying for child care, affording health insurance, buying a home, and saving for retirement. I believe that parental leave for some is better than none at all. Nevertheless, millions more could use this same help, and the huge sums devoted to subsidizing the homes, pensions, and health insurance of the well-to-do are probably not money well spent. Going forward, the central question in my mind is whether major parts of the American welfare state can become truly inclusive, perhaps offering a little extra help to the less affluent (much like Social Security), or whether they will remain the province of more affluent Americans.

Notes

INTRODUCTION

1. For a more general introduction to these tools, see Lester M. Salamon (ed.), *The Tools of Government: A Guide to the New Governance* (New York, NY: Oxford University Press, 2002).

2. A partial list includes Edwin Amenta, *Bold Relief: Institutional Politics and the Origins of the American Welfare State* (Princeton, NJ: Princeton University Press, 1998); Martha Derthick, *Policymaking for Social Security* (Washington, DC: Brookings Institution, 1979); Linda Gordon, *Pitied but Not Entitled: Single Mothers and the History of Welfare* (Cambridge, MA: Harvard University Press, 1994); Michael B. Katz, *In the Shadow of the Poorhouse: A Social History of Welfare in America* (New York, NY: Basic Books, 1986); Robert C. Lieberman, *Shifting the Color Line: Race and the American Welfare State* (Cambridge, MA: Harvard University Press, 1998); Suzanne Mettler, *Dividing Citizens: Gender and Federalism in New Deal Social Policy* (Ithaca, NY: Cornell University Press, 1998); Gwendolyn Mink, *The Wages of Motherhood: Inequality in the Welfare State, 1917–1942* (Ithaca, NY: Cornell University Press, 1995); Frances Fox Piven and Richard A. Cloward, *Regulating the Poor: The Functions of Public Welfare*, updated ed. (New York, NY: Vintage, 1993 [1971]); Theda Skocpol, *Protecting Soldiers and Mothers: The Political Origins of Social Policy in the United States* (Cambridge, MA: The Belknap Press of Harvard University Press, 1992); Theda Skocpol, *Social Policy in the United States: Future Possibilities in Historical Perspective* (Princeton, NJ: Princeton University Press, 1995); Thomas J. Sugrue, *The Origins of the Urban Underclass: Race and Inequality in Postwar Detroit* (Princeton, NJ: Princeton University Press, 1996); Margaret Weir, *Politics and Jobs: The Boundaries of Employment Policy in the United States* (Princeton, NJ: Princeton University Press, 1992); Margaret Weir, Ann Shola Orloff, and Theda Skocpol (eds.), *The Politics of Social Policy in the United States* (Princeton, NJ: Princeton University Press, 1988); and Julian E. Zelizer, *Taxing America: Wilbur D. Mills, Congress, and the State, 1945–1975* (New York, NY: Cambridge University Press, 1998).

3. Andrea Louise Campbell, *How Policies Make Citizens: Senior Political Activism and the American Welfare State* (Princeton, NJ: Princeton University Press, 2003); Martin Gilens, *Why Americans Hate Welfare: Race, Media, and the Politics of Antipoverty Policy* (Chicago, IL: University of Chicago Press, 1999); Richard Himelfarb, *Catastrophic Politics: The Rise and Fall of the Medicare Catastrophic Coverage Act of 1988* (University Park, PA: Pennsylvania State University Press, 1995); Jonathan Oberlander, *The Political Life of Medicare* (Chicago, IL: University of Chicago Press, 2003); Theda Skocpol, *Boomerang: Health Care Reform and the Turn against Government* (New York, NY: W. W. Norton,

1996); R. Kent Weaver, *Ending Welfare as We Know It* (Washington, DC: Brookings Institution, 2000).

4. Important exceptions include Jacob S. Hacker, *The Divided Welfare State: The Battle over Public and Private Social Benefits in the United States* (New York, NY: Cambridge University Press, 2002); Paul Pierson, *Dismantling the Welfare State? Reagan, Thatcher, and the Politics of Retrenchment* (New York, NY: Cambridge University Press, 1994); and especially Michael B. Katz, *The Price of Citizenship: Redefining the American Welfare State* (New York, NY: Henry Holt, 2001).

5. To get a sense of these battles, see Jeffrey Friedman (ed.), *The Rational Choice Controversy* (New Haven, CT: Yale University Press, 1996); Donald P. Green and Ian Shapiro, *Pathologies of Rational Choice Theory: A Critique of Applications in Political Science* (New Haven, CT: Yale University Press, 1994); and Kristen Renwick Monroe (ed.), *Perestroika! The Raucous Rebellion in Political Science* (New Haven, CT: Yale University Press, 2005).

6. Notable books in this tradition include Sheldon H. Danziger and Robert H. Haveman (eds.), *Understanding Poverty* (New York, NY, and Cambridge, MA: Russell Sage Foundation and Harvard University Press, 2001); Sheldon H. Danziger, Gary D. Sandefur, and Daniel H. Weinberg (eds.), *Confronting Poverty: Prescriptions for Change* (New York, NY, and Cambridge, MA: Russell Sage Foundation and Harvard University Press, 1994); Sheldon H. Danziger and Daniel H. Weinberg (eds.), *Fighting Poverty: What Works and What Doesn't* (Cambridge, MA: Harvard University Press, 1986); David T. Ellwood, *Poor Support: Poverty in the American Family* (New York, NY: Basic Books, 1988); Michael J. Graetz and Jerry L. Mashaw, *True Security: Rethinking American Social Insurance* (New Haven, CT: Yale University Press, 1999); Christopher Jencks, *Rethinking Social Policy: Race, Poverty, and the Underclass* (Cambridge, MA: Harvard University Press, 1992); Theodore R. Marmor, Jerry L. Mashaw, and Philip L. Harvey, *America's Misunderstood Welfare State: Persistent Myths, Enduring Realities* (New York, NY: Basic Books, 1990); and William Julius Wilson, *The Truly Disadvantaged: The Inner City, the Underclass, and Public Policy* (Chicago, IL: University of Chicago Press, 1987).

7. Campbell, *How Policies Make Citizens*; Fay Lomax Cook and Edith J. Barrett, *Support for the American Welfare State: The Views of Congress and the Public* (New York, NY: Columbia University Press, 1992); Gilens, *Why Americans Hate Welfare*; Lawrence R. Jacobs, *The Health of Nations: Public Opinion and the Making of American and British Health Policy* (Ithaca, NY: Cornell University Press, 1993).

8. Good examples of this voluminous literature include Charles Barrileaux, Thomas Holbrook, and Laura Langer, "Electoral Competition, Legislative Balance, and American State Welfare Policy," *American Journal of Political Science* 46, 2 (April 2002): 415–27; Robert S. Erikson, Gerald C. Wright, and John P. McIver, *Statehouse Democracy: Public Opinion and Policy in the American States* (New York, NY: Cambridge University Press, 1993); Richard C. Fording, "The Political Response to Black Insurgency: A Critical Test of Competing Theories of the State," *American Political Science Review* 95, 1 (March 2001): 115–30; Rodney E. Hero, *Faces of Inequality: Social Diversity in American Politics* (New York,

NY: Oxford University Press, 1998); and Joe Soss, Sanford F. Schram, Thomas P. Vartanian, and Erin O'Brien, "Setting the Terms of Relief: Explaining State Policy Choices in the Devolution Revolution," *American Journal of Political Science* 45, 2 (April 2001): 378–95.

9. Some scholars known best for their qualitative historical work have used the behavioral approach to analyze social policies from the first half of the twentieth century. See, e.g., Edwin Amenta, Bruce G. Carruthers, and Yvonne Zylan, "A Hero for the Aged? The Townsend Movement, the Political Mediation Model, and U.S. Old-Age Policy, 1934–1950," *American Journal of Sociology* 98, 2 (September 1992): 308–39, and Theda Skocpol, Christopher Howard, Susan Goodrich Lehmann, and Marjorie Abend-Wein, "Women's Associations and the Enactment of Mothers' Pensions," *American Political Science Review* 87, 3 (September 1993): 686–701.

10. Amenta, *Bold Relief*; Edward D. Berkowitz, *America's Welfare State: From Roosevelt to Reagan* (Baltimore, MD: Johns Hopkins University Press, 1991); Edward D. Berkowitz and Kim McQuaid, *Creating the Welfare State: The Political Economy of 20th-Century Reform*, revised ed. (Lawrence, KS: University Press of Kansas, 1988); Derthick, *Policymaking for Social Security*; Marie Gottschalk, *The Shadow Welfare State: Labor, Business, and the Politics of Health Care in the United States* (Ithaca, NY: Cornell University Press, 2000); Hacker, *The Divided Welfare State*; Christopher Howard, *The Hidden Welfare State: Tax Expenditures and Social Policy in the United States* (Princeton, NJ: Princeton University Press, 1997); Katz, *In the Shadow of the Poorhouse*; Lieberman, *Shifting the Color Line*; Mettler, *Dividing Citizens*; Charles Noble, *Welfare as We Knew It: A Political History of the American Welfare State* (New York, NY: Oxford University Press, 1997); James T. Patterson, *America's Struggle Against Poverty in the Twentieth Century* (Cambridge, MA: Harvard University Press, 2000); Pierson, *Dismantling the Welfare State?* Jill Quadagno, *The Color of Welfare: How Racism Undermined the War on Poverty* (New York, NY: Oxford University Press, 1994); Skocpol, *Protecting Soldiers and Mothers*; Skocpol, *Social Policy in the United States*; Walter I. Trattner, *From Poor Law to Welfare State: A History of Social Welfare in America*, 6th ed. (New York, NY: Free Press, 1999); Weir, *Politics and Jobs*; Weir, Orloff, and Skocpol (eds.), *The Politics of Social Policy in the United States*.

11. Paul Pierson, "APD's Faustian Bargain," *Clio* 14, 1 (Fall/Winter 2003–4): 1+.

12. One side benefit of such eclecticism is that teachers can use this book in the classroom to introduce students to a wide variety of analytic debates and research strategies. This way, students have real choices when conducting their own research.

CHAPTER 1
SHE'S SO UNUSUAL

1. Harold L. Wilensky, "The Problems and Prospects of the Welfare State," introduction to the paperback edition of *Industrial Society and Social Welfare*, by

Harold L. Wilensky and Charles N. Lebeaux (New York, NY: Free Press, 1965), p. xii.

2. Edward S. Greenberg and Benjamin I. Page, *The Struggle for Democracy*, 4th ed. (New York, NY: Longman, 1999); Bruce S. Jansson, *The Reluctant Welfare State*, 4th ed. (Belmont, CA: Wadsworth/Brooks Cole, 2001); Michael B. Katz, *In the Shadow of the Poorhouse: A Social History of Welfare in America* (New York, NY: Basic Books, 1986); John W. Kingdon, *America the Unusual* (New York, NY: St. Martin's/Worth, 1999); Robert T. Kudrle and Theodore R. Marmor," "The Development of Welfare States in North America," in Peter Flora and Arnold J. Heidenheimer (eds.), *The Development of Welfare States in Europe and America* (New Brunswick, NJ: Transaction, 1981), pp. 81–121; Seymour Martin Lipset, *American Exceptionalism* (New York, NY: W. W. Norton, 1996); Diane Sainsbury, *Gender, Equality and Welfare States* (New York, NY: Cambridge University Press, 1996); Theda Skocpol, *Social Policy in the United States: Future Possibilities in Historical Perspective* (Princeton, NJ: Princeton University Press, 1995); Graham K. Wilson, *Only in America?* (Chatham, NJ: Chatham House, 1998); James Q. Wilson and John J. DiIulio, Jr., *American Government: Institutions and Policies*, 8th ed. (Boston, MA: Houghton Mifflin, 2001).

3. Martin Gilens, *Why Americans Hate Welfare: Race, Media, and the Politics of Antipoverty Policy* (Chicago, IL: University of Chicago Press, 1999); Jansson, *The Reluctant Welfare State*; Kudrle and Marmor, "The Development of Welfare States in North America"; Seymour Martin Lipset and Gary Marks, *It Didn't Happen Here: Why Socialism Failed in the United States* (New York, NY: W. W. Norton, 2000); Wilson, *Only in America?*

4. "Family allowances" are cash payments from a government to parents, usually monthly. Depending on the country, the exact amount can vary by the child's age, the family's income, or the parents' employment status.

5. The spending figures are taken from Willem Adema, *Net Social Expenditure*, 2nd ed. (Paris: OECD, 2001), and 1997 is the most recent year for which these data are available.

6. For exceptions, see Jacob S. Hacker, *The Divided Welfare State: The Battle over Public and Private Social Benefits in the United States* (New York, NY: Cambridge University Press, 2002), and Irwin Garfinkel, Lee Rainwater, and Timothy M. Smeeding, "Equal Opportunities for Children: Social Welfare Expenditures in the English-Speaking Countries and Western Europe," *Focus* 23, 3 (Spring 2005): 16–23.

7. One quick way to measure the extent of clustering or spread in the data is to calculate the coefficient of variation (CV), which is the standard deviation divided by the average. The smaller the CV, the more tightly bunched are the data. The CV for column A is 0.26 and for column B is 0.21.

8. The main policy tools used in public assistance programs are grants (e.g., Medicaid, TANF) and vouchers (e.g., Food Stamps, Section 8 rental assistance).

9. As a general rule, those who like tax expenditures refer to them as tax incentives, and those who dislike them speak of tax loopholes.

10. Christopher Howard, *The Hidden Welfare State: Tax Expenditures and Social Policy in the United States* (Princeton, NJ: Princeton University Press, 1997). Whether ordinary citizens think of tax subsidies and direct subsidies as

equivalent tools of social policy is an important but separate point. My argument relates to the definitions adopted by governments and professional analysts.

11. Adema, *Net Social Expenditure*. These figures reflect tax expenditures at the national level. Comparable data from the subnational level, such as the American states or Canadian provinces (which do offer their own tax expenditures), are not yet available.

12. For more in-depth analysis of national tax policies, see Sven Steinmo, *Taxation and Democracy: Swedish, British, and American Approaches to Financing the Modern State* (New Haven, CT: Yale University Press, 1993).

13. Similar arrangements exist in Australia, Austria, Belgium, Denmark, Germany, the Netherlands, Norway, Sweden, and the United Kingdom. Adema, *Net Social Expenditure*.

14. Ibid.

15. Anne Paternoster, "Minimum Wages: EU Member States, Candidate Countries, and the US, 2004," *Statistics in Focus* (October 2004), accessed via http://epp.eurostat.cec.eu.int/cache/ITY_OFFPUB/KS-NK-04-010/EN/KS-NK-04-010-EN.PDF.

16. I say "potentially" because key terms like "reasonable accommodation" and "otherwise qualified" workers are subject to interpretation, and the actual impact of the ADA depends considerably on court decisions.

17. U.S. Office of Management and Budget (OMB), *Analytical Perspectives, Budget of the United States Government, Fiscal Year 2006*, table 7–1, accessed via http://www.whitehouse.gov/omb/budget/fy2006/pdf/spec.pdf; Office of Policy Development and Research, "FHA's Impact on Increasing Homeownership Opportunities for Low-Income and Minority Families During the 1990s," *Issue Brief No. IV* (Washington, DC: U.S. Department of Housing and Urban Development, 2000); U.S. Census Bureau, *Statistical Abstract of the United States, 2004–2005* (Washington, DC: Government Printing Office, 2004), tables 524 and 961, accessed via http://www.census.gov/prod/www/statistical-abstract-04.html; Center on Budget and Policy Priorities, "Introduction to the Housing Voucher Program," available at http://www.cbpp.org/5-15-03hous.pdf (May 14, 2003). The Section 8 voucher program is probably the best-known of the housing choice vouchers administered by the U.S. Department of Housing and Urban Development.

18. David Fairlamb, "It's Sink or Swim for Germany's State Banks," *Business Week Online*, accessed via http://www.businessweek.com/magazine/content/01_12/b3724160.htm (March 19, 2002); Karl Soukup and Stefan Moser, "Further Developments on State Guarantees for German Public Banks," *EC Competition Policy Newsletter* 3 (October 2001): 75–76.

19. Robert A. Kagan and Lee Axelrad, "Adversarial Legalism: An International Perspective," in Pietro S. Nivola (ed.), *Comparative Disadvantages? Social Regulations and the New Economy* (Washington, DC: Brookings Institution, 1997), p. 171.

20. See, e.g., Theodore R. Marmor, Jerry L. Mashaw, and Philip L. Harvey, *America's Misunderstood Welfare State: Persistent Myths, Enduring Realities* (New York, NY: Basic Books, 1990), pp. 31–46. By my definition, social policies existed for centuries before welfare states emerged.

21. Cited in Michael B. Katz, *The Price of Citizenship: Redefining the American Welfare State* (New York, NY: Henry Holt and Company, 2001), p. 3.

22. Howard, *The Hidden Welfare State*, pp. 5–9.

23. Charles Noble, *Welfare as We Knew It: A Political History of the American Welfare State* (New York, NY: Oxford University Press, 1997), p. 7; Katz, *The Price of Citizenship*, ch. 1; Theda Skocpol, *The Missing Middle: Working Families and the Future of American Social Policy* (New York, NY: W. W. Norton, 2000), ch. 2. Another strategy has been to shift the conceptual focus from "welfare state" to some larger concept such as "welfare regime," "social citizenship," or "economic citizenship." Most of these scholars are inspired by the work of the British social scientist T. H. Marshall. Examples include Gosta Esping-Andersen, *The Three Worlds of Welfare Capitalism* (Princeton, NJ: Princeton University Press, 1990); Hacker, *The Divided Welfare State*; and Alice Kessler-Harris, *In Pursuit of Equity* (New York, NY: Oxford University Press, 2001). Hacker, for example, identifies three central elements of the American welfare regime: direct spending programs, typically social insurance and grants; indirect forms of government support such as tax expenditures, regulations, and loan guarantees; and the fringe benefits offered by employers and aid to the needy offered by charities. My notion of the American welfare state extends only to the first two of these elements.

24. For a similar approach to the overall size of government, see Richard Rose, "How Exceptional Is the American Political Economy?" *Political Science Quarterly* 104, 1 (1989): 91–115.

25. There is good evidence that in the late nineteenth and early twentieth centuries, and again in the late 1930s, social spending in the United States was comparatively generous. Thus, the status of the United States as laggard or leader may have fluctuated over time in ways that are not well understood. See Theda Skocpol, *Protecting Soldiers and Mothers: The Political Origins of Social Policy in the United States* (Cambridge, MA: The Belknap Press of Harvard University Press, 1992), and Edwin Amenta, *Bold Relief: Institutional Politics and the Origins of Modern American Social Policy* (Princeton, NJ: Princeton University Press, 2000).

26. Stanley Feldman and John Zaller, "The Political Culture of Ambivalence: Ideological Responses to the Welfare State," *American Journal of Political Science* 36, 1 (February 1992): 268–307.

CHAPTER 2
TRACKS OF MY TIERS

1. Bruce Miroff, Raymond Seidelman, and Todd Swanstrom, *The Democratic Debate*, 2nd ed. (New York, NY: Houghton Mifflin, 1998), accessed via http://college.hmco.com/polisci/miroff/chapters/chap17/overview.html.

2. Linda Gordon, *Pitied but Not Entitled: Single Mothers and the History of Welfare* (Cambridge, MA: Harvard University Press, 1994), pp. 4–5.

3. Michael K. Brown, *Race, Money, and the American Welfare State* (Ithaca, NY: Cornell University Press, 1999), pp. 4–5.

4. Ann Orloff, "Gender in the Welfare State," *Annual Review of Sociology* 22 (1996): 54.

5. Theda Skocpol, "The Limits of the New Deal System and the Roots of Contemporary Welfare Dilemmas," in Margaret Weir, Ann Shola Orloff, and Theda Skocpol (eds.), *The Politics of Social Policy in the United States* (Princeton, NJ: Princeton University Press, 1988), p. 296.

6. Robert L. Borosage and Roger Hickey (eds.), *The Next Agenda: Blueprint for a New Progressive Movement* (Boulder, CO: Westview, 2001); Stanley B. Greenberg and Theda Skocpol (eds.), *The New Majority: Toward a Popular Progressive Politics* (New Haven, CT: Yale University Press, 1997); Theda Skocpol, *The Missing Middle: Working Families and the Future of American Social Policy* (New York, NY: W. W. Norton, 2000).

7. See, e.g, the February 2005 issue of *The American Prospect*, which includes several critiques of privatization by well-known liberals.

8. Most states with mothers' pensions and old-age pensions simply allowed localities to offer such pensions, which meant variation in coverage within states as well. Christopher Howard, "Sowing the Seeds of 'Welfare': The Transformation of Mothers' Pensions, 1900–1940," *Journal of Policy History* 4, 2 (1992): 188–226.

9. U.S. Congress, Committee on Ways and Means, *2004 Green Book: Background Material and Data on the Programs within the Jurisdiction of the Committee on Ways and Means* (Washington, DC: Government Printing Office, 2004), table 7–10, accessed via http://www.gpoaccess.gov/wmprints/index.html.

10. Like Social Security spending, Medicare spending is not identical in every state, varying with the health status of the elderly, the price of medical care, and doctors' practice patterns. Nevertheless, two people in different states with identical medical conditions would be entitled to the same care. Bruce Vladek, "The Political Economy of Medicare," *Health Affairs* 18, 1 (January/February 1999): 22–36.

11. In the early 1990s, over 65 percent of initial disability applications were rejected in New Mexico and West Virginia, and over 60 percent were rejected in Michigan, Oklahoma, and several southern states. Less than 45 percent of DI applications were initially rejected in Massachusetts, Utah, and Vermont. I thank Andrew Houtenville of Cornell University's School of Industrial and Labor Relations for sharing these data with me. They originally appeared in The Lewin Group, *Labor Economic Conditions, Socio-economic Factors, and the Growth of Applicants and Awards for SSDI and SSI Disability Benefits* (Fairfax, VA: Lewin Group, 1995). For similar evidence of statewide variation in the percentage of DI applications denied and denials appealed, see Joe Soss and Lael R. Keiser, "The Political Roots of Disability Claims: How State Environments and Policies Shape Citizen Demands," Institute for Research on Poverty Discussion Paper 1292–05 (January 2005), available at http://www.irp.wisc.edu/publications/dps/dplist2005.htm.

12. U.S. Census Bureau, *Statistical Abstract of the United States, 2002* (Washington, DC: Government Printing Office, 2002), table 528; U.S. Census Bureau, *Statistical Abstract of the United States, 2003* (Washington, DC: Government Printing Office, 2003), table 639.

13. U.S. Congress, Committee on Ways and Means, *2000 Green Book: Background Material and Data on Programs within the Jurisdiction of the Committee*

on Ways and Means (Washington, DC: Government Printing Office, 2000), pp. 298–99.

14. AFL-CIO, "Workers' Compensation Comparisons, 2001" and "Workers' Compensation and Unemployment Insurance under State Laws, January 1, 2001," both accessed via http://www.afl-cio.org/.

15. U.S. Congress, Committee on Ways and Means, *2004 Green Book*, section 15, p. 31.

16. *Medicaid: A Primer* (Washington, DC: Kaiser Commission on Medicaid and the Uninsured, 2005).

17. Russell L. Hanson, "Medicaid and the Politics of Redistribution," *American Journal of Political Science* 28, 2 (May 1984): 313–39.

18. *Medicaid: A Primer*, p. 3.

19. Anna Sommers, Arunabh Ghosh, and David Rousseau, *Medicaid Enrollment and Spending by "Mandatory" and "Optional" Eligibility and Benefit Categories* (Washington, DC: Kaiser Commission on Medicaid and the Uninsured, 2005); Kaiser Family Foundation Medicaid Benefits database, accessed via http://www.kff.org/medicaidbenefits/index.cfm.

20. Teresa A. Coughlin, Leighton Ku, and John Holahan, *Medicaid since 1980: Costs, Coverage, and the Shifting Alliance between the Federal Government and the States* (Washington, DC: Urban Institute Press, 1994), ch. 4; Michael S. Sparer, *Medicaid and the Limits of State Health Reform* (Philadelphia, PA: Temple University Press, 1996).

21. Paul Pierson, "The Creeping Nationalization of Income Transfers in the United States, 1935–94," in Stephan Leibfried and Paul Pierson (eds.), *European Social Policy: Between Fragmentation and Integration* (Washington, DC: Brookings Institution, 1995), p. 302.

22. The SSI program went into effect in 1974.

23. Actual benefits may vary, depending on whether states opt to supplement the national benefit, and by how much. About one-half the states supplement the standard SSI benefit, and most of them by no more than 10 percent. U.S. Congress, Committee on Ways and Means, *2000 Green Book,* section 3.

24. Lewin Group, *Labor Economic Conditions.* Determination of disability in SSI is left to the states, with about as much variation in rejected applications as in disability insurance.

25. U.S. Congress, Committee on Ways and Means, *2000 Green Book,* pp. 865–89.

26. Some states do operate their own earned income credit, modeled after the national EITC.

27. Social Security and Medicare (A) benefits are not exactly alike. Whereas benefits are tied to past earnings in Social Security, they are not in Medicare. Workers with a history of higher earnings receive a larger pension but not more medical benefits.

28. This is more difficult than it looks. For instance, it does not make sense to arrange programs in each tier from largest to smallest and then compare those of similar rank. Social Security and Medicaid, the biggest programs in their respective tiers, are designed to address very different kinds of needs. So, too, are the smaller unemployment insurance and school lunch programs. While the more ap-

propriate comparison would involve social programs designed to serve similar needs, some programs have no equivalent in the other tier. All food and nutrition programs, for instance, are located in the lower tier. Another complication is that some needs are designed to be served by more than one social program. We may have to compare packages of assistance and not just individual programs. Families who qualify for TANF automatically qualify for Food Stamps and Medicaid. Some of them may also receive housing assistance. Disabled individuals can receive income support from one program (DI) and medical care from another (Medicare, but usually after two years of receiving DI). In comparing the generosity of benefits, we must proceed with caution.

29. Social Security Administration, *Annual Statistical Supplement, 2002*, table 3.C4, accessed via http://www.ssa.gov/policy/docs/statcomps/supplement/2002/index.html#preface.

30. U.S. Department of Health and Human Services (DHHS), Office of Family Assistance, *TANF Fifth Annual Report to Congress* (2003), table 2:7:a, accessed via http://www.acf.hhs.gov/programs/ofa/annualreport5/index.htm; U.S. Census Bureau, *Statistical Abstract of the United States, 2003*, table 555.

31. Unlike TANF benefits, UI benefits have no lifetime limit. Considering how many people use UI or TANF but once in their lives, it still seems to make sense to compare the potential length of the first time receiving benefits.

32. Michael J. Graetz and Jerry L. Mashaw, *True Security: Rethinking American Social Insurance* (New Haven, CT: Yale University Press, 1999), pp. 76–78.

33. U.S. Census Bureau, *Statistical Abstract of the United States, 2003*, table 600; U.S. OHHS, Office of Human Services Policy, *Indicators of Welfare Dependence: Annual Report to Congress, 2003*, table Ind 4a, accessed via http://www.aspe.hhs.gov/hsp/indicators03/ch2.htm#IND4.

34. The figures for Medicare come from U.S. Census Bureau, *Statistical Abstract of the United States, 2004–2005* (Washington, DC: Government Printing Office, 2004), tables 126 and 127.

35. U.S. Census Bureau, *Statistical Abstract of the United States, 2003*, table 146.

36. U.S. Social Security Administration, *Annual Statistical Supplement, 2003*, table 5.A1.1, available at http://www.ssa.gov/policy/docs/statcomps/supplement/2003/index.html.

37. *The 2002 Annual Report of the Board of Trustees of the Federal Old-Age and Survivors Insurance and Disability Insurance Trust Funds* (2002), table VI.E11, accessed via http://www.ssa.gov/OACT/TR/TR02/index.html; "Outcome Indicators," *Social Security Bulletin* 65, 1 (2003/2004): 70–83; Alexa A. Hendley and Natasha F. Bilimoria, "Minorities and Social Security: An Analysis of Racial and Ethnic Differences in the Current Program," *Social Security Bulletin* 62, 2 (September 1999): 59–64.

38. C. Eugene Steuerle, Adam Carasso, and Lee Cohen, "How Progressive Is Social Security When Old Age and Disability Insurance Are Treated as a Whole?" *Straight Talk on Social Security and Retirement Policy* 38 (May 2004), accessed via the Urban Institute website at http://www.urban.org/UploadedPDF/311017_Straight38.pdf. See also Jacob Hacker, Suzanne Mettler, Diane Pinderhughes, and Theda Skocpol, *Inequality and Public Policy* (Washington, DC:

American Political Science Association, 2004), accessed via http://www.apsanet.org/content_4040.cfm.

39. Colleen M. Grogan and Eric M. Patashnik, "Universalism within Targeting: Nursing Home Care, the Middle Class, and the Politics of the Medicaid Program," *Social Service Review* 77, 1 (March 2003): 51–71. About 10 percent of food stamp recipients also live above the poverty line.

40. "Outcome Indicators," *Social Security Bulletin*; Centers for Medicare & Medicaid Services, *Health Care System: Facts and Figures*, table 3.8, accessed via http://www.cms.hhs.gov/charts/healthcaresystem/.

41. U.S. DHHS, Office of Family Assistance, *TANF Fourth Annual Report to Congress* (2002), accessed via http://www.acf.dhhs.gov/programs/opre/ar2001/indexar.htm; Randy Rosso, "Characteristics of Food Stamp Households: Fiscal Year 2001" (Washington, DC: U.S. Department of Agriculture, Food and Nutrition Service, 2003), table A-23, accessed via http://www.fns.usda.gov/oane/MENU/Published/FSP/participation.htm; U.S. DHHS, *2003 CMS Statistics*, table 12, accessed via http://www.cms.hhs.gov/researchers/pubs/03cmsstats.pdf; Social Security Administration, *Annual Statistical Supplement, 2002* (2002), tables 5.A1.1, 5A.6, and 8.B4, accessed via http://www.ssa.gov/policy/docs/statcomps/. It is true that the numerical advantage women enjoy in Social Security is due largely to the survivors insurance component. But women still comprise about 50 percent of those receiving retirement benefits.

42. When President George W. Bush tried to win support for privatizing Social Security by discussing how badly blacks fared under the current program, he conveniently failed to mention either survivors insurance or disability insurance.

43. U.S. DHHS, Office of Family Assistance, *TANF Fourth Annual Report to Congress* (2002); U.S. Bureau of the Census, *Statistical Abstract of the United States, 2003*, tables 13, 571, and 572; U.S. DHHS, *2003 CMS Statistics*, table 3; Social Security Administration, *Annual Statistical Supplement, 2002* (2002), table 5.A1.

44. Robert X Browning, *Politics and Social Welfare Policy in the United States* (Knoxville, TN: University of Tennessee Press, 1986), ch. 1.

45. The growth rates for individual programs and the two tiers are based on figures from Daniel Mont et al., *Workers' Compensation: Benefits, Coverage, and Costs, 2000, New Estimates* (Washington, DC: National Academy of Social Insurance, 2002); U.S. Census Bureau, *Statistical Abstract of the United States, 1982–83* (Washington, DC: Government Printing Office, 1982), tables 517, 530, 542, 544, 548; U.S. Census Bureau, *Statistical Abstract of the United States, 2002*, table 513; U.S. Census Bureau, *Statistical Abstract of the United States, 2003*, tables 139, 141, 146, 535, 540, 544, 556, 559.

46. The figures for TANF combine cash assistance ($14.5 billion) and services ($8.3 billion), which are primarily child care.

47. U.S. Census Bureau, *Statistical Abstract of the United States, 2003*, table 540.

48. The figures for unemployment insurance are relatively low because the economy was relatively strong in 2000. But even in a weaker year like 2002, with spending of $42 billion and 10 million recipients, UI fell closer to the lower tier (U.S. Census Bureau, *Statistical Abstract of the United States, 2003*, table 555).

The size of the Earned Income Tax Credit (EITC) is actually a bit understated, for it includes only the size of tax refunds. If one adds the cost of income taxes not collected, then the total size of the EITC in 2000 was closer to $30 billion.

49. Theda Skocpol, *The Missing Middle*, ch. 2. For more detailed analysis of trust funds and payroll taxes, see Eric M. Patashnik, *Putting Trust in the US Budget: Federal Trust Funds and the Politics of Commitment* (New York, NY: Cambridge University Press, 2000).

50. Quoted in Arthur M. Schlesinger, *The Coming of the New Deal* (Boston, MA: Houghton Mifflin, 1958), pp. 308–9.

51. To reduce inequalities among the states, the national government reimburses poorer states for a larger share of their welfare spending. In 2001 the national government paid for two-thirds of the cost of TANF in Alabama and three-quarters in New Mexico. In contrast, it paid for slightly less than half the cost of welfare in Massachusetts and New Jersey. U.S. Congress, Committee on Ways and Means, *2004 Green Book*, table 7–19.

52. Paul E. Peterson, *The Price of Federalism* (Washington, DC: Brookings Institution, 1995). Technically, states paid the entire cost of AFDC and were then reimbursed for a large fraction by the national government.

53. U.S. Census Bureau, *Statistical Abstract of the United States, 2003*, table 540.

54. Graetz and Mashaw, *True Security*. One small difference is that the payroll tax is paid half by workers and half by employers in the Social Security, Medicare, and disability insurance programs, yet paid entirely by employers in unemployment insurance. Most economists argue that it matters little who pays the payroll tax, because the burden falls ultimately on workers. Employers allocate a certain amount of money for compensating their workers, so any increase in payroll taxes will come at the expense of wages or benefits.

55. As of 2001, the monthly premium for part B, also called Supplemental Medical Insurance, was $50. U.S. Census Bureau,*Statistical Abstract of the United States, 2003*, tables 141 and 559; U.S. Census Bureau, *Statistical Abstract of the United States, 2002*, tables 520 and 528, both accessed via http://www.census .gov/statab/www/.

56. Mont et al., *Workers' Compensation*.

57. U.S. Congressional Budget Office (CBO), *The Budget and Economic Outlook: Fiscal Years 2005–2014* (Washington, DC: Congressional Budget Office, 2004), p. 48.

58. U.S. CBO, *The Long-Term Budget Outlook* (Washington, DC: Congressional Budget Office, 2003); U.S. CBO, *The Budget and Economic Outlook: Fiscal Years 2005–2014*. The best-known and most effective spending limits were created by the Budget Enforcement Act of 1990. Congress allowed the Act to expire at the end of the 2002 fiscal year.

59. Before TANF replaced it in 1996, AFDC was also classified as mandatory spending.

60. Martin Gilens, *Why Americans Hate Welfare: Race, Media, and the Politics of Antipoverty Policy* (Chicago, IL: University of Chicago Press, 1999), esp. table 1.2; Steven M. Teles, *Whose Welfare? AFDC and Elite Politics* (Lawrence,

KS: University Press of Kansas, 1996); R. Kent Weaver, *Ending Welfare as We Know It* (Washington, DC: Brookings Institution, 2000), esp. ch. 7.

61. Gilens, *Why Americans Hate Welfare*, table 1.2 and pp. 42–45. See also Fay Lomax Cook and Edith J. Barrett, *Support for the American Welfare State: The Views of Congress and the Public* (New York, NY: Columbia University Press, 1992), and Ruy Teixeira and Joel Rogers, *America's Forgotten Majority: Why the White Working Class Still Matters* (New York, NY: Basic Books, 2000), ch. 2. For an explanation of why some means-tested programs fare better than others, see chapter 5.

62. *National Survey of the Public's Views about Medicaid* (Menlo Park, CA: Kaiser Family Foundation, 2005).

63. For another critique of the two-tiered model, based heavily on Medicaid, see Grogan and Patashnik, "Universalism within Targeting."

64. U.S. Congressional Budget Office, *Federal Spending on the Elderly and Children* (July 2000), available at http://www.cbo.gov/showdoc.cfm?index=2300&sequence=0.

65. Julia Lynch, "The Age-Orientation of Social Policy Regimes in OECD Countries," *Journal of Social Policy* 30, 3 (2001): 411–36. This conclusion is based on spending for retirement pensions, survivors pensions, health care, unemployment insurance, family allowances, family services, workers' compensation, and job training. We will return to the issue of generation gaps in chapter 7.

66. See, e.g., the contributors to Peter Flora and Arnold J. Heidenheimer (eds.), *The Development of Welfare States in Europe and America* (New Brunswick, NJ: Transaction, 1981).

67. U.S. Census Bureau, *Statistical Abstract of the United States, 2002*, table 199; Lynch, "The Age-Orientation of Social Policy Regimes in OECD Countries."

The inclusion of education raises another possibility. Aggregate spending totals might conceal important differences among levels of government. One of the peculiar features of the American welfare state may be that different levels of government take care of different groups of needy citizens. The elderly depend on the national government while children rely on state and local governments. This arrangement might generate serious friction across the generations if one generation was a net winner (i.e., received more in benefits than it paid in taxes) at one level of government and a net loser at another level. We might find families with children resenting how much Social Security and Medicare cost and the elderly resenting how much local schools cost. Future efforts to generalize about advantaged and disadvantaged groups in the American welfare state may need to specify whether all levels of government exhibit the same kind of bias.

68. U.S. Congress, Joint Committee on Taxation, *Estimates of Federal Tax Expenditures for Fiscal Years 2005–2009* (Washington, DC: Government Printing Office, 2005).

69. Ibid.

70. Francis G. Castles, "The Really Big Trade-Off: Home Ownership and the Welfare State in the New World and Old," *Acta Politica* 33, 1 (1998): 5–19.

71. For a political history of the home mortgage interest deduction, see Christopher Howard, *The Hidden Welfare State: Tax Expenditures and Social Policy in the United States* (Princeton, NJ: Princeton University Press, 1997), esp. ch. 5.

72. These are trends, not absolute laws. There are grants for the elderly (SSI) and social insurance for workers (unemployment benefits). These exceptions appear to be relatively small.

CHAPTER 3
TWICE IN A LIFETIME

1. Christopher Leman, "Patterns of Policy Development: Social Security in the United States and Canada," *Public Policy* 25 (Spring 1977): 261–91; Jill Quadagno, "Creating a Capital Investment Welfare State: The New American Exceptionalism," *American Sociological Review* 64, 1 (February 1999): 1–11; Margaret Weir, Ann Shola Orloff, and Theda Skocpol (eds.), *The Politics of Social Policy in the United States* (Princeton, NJ: Princeton University Press, 1988).

2. Robert T. Kudrle and Theodore R. Marmor, "The Development of Welfare States in North America," in Peter Flora and Arnold J. Heidenheimer (eds.), *The Development of Welfare States in Europe and America* (New Brunswick, NJ: Transaction, 1981), pp. 81–121.

3. Benjamin I. Page and James R. Simmons, *What Government Can Do: Dealing with Poverty and Inequality* (Chicago, IL: University of Chicago Press, 2000), esp. pp. 107–8.

4. To put these figures in context, Democrats lost "only" 54 House seats in the historic 1994 midterm election.

5. The election data come from Norman J. Ornstein, Thomas E. Mann, and Michael J. Malbin, *Vital Statistics on Congress, 1997–1998* (Washington, DC: American Enterprise Institute, 1998), and Harold W. Stanley and Richard G. Niemi, *Vital Statistics on American Politics, 1999–2000* (Washington, DC: CQ Press, 2000). For bargaining between Roosevelt and Southern Democrats, see Robert C. Lieberman, *Shifting the Color Line: Race and the American Welfare State* (Cambridge, MA: Harvard University Press, 1998); Suzanne Mettler, *Dividing Citizens: Gender and Federalism in New Deal Public Policy* (Ithaca, NY: Cornell University Press, 1998); and Charles Noble, *Welfare as We Knew It: A Political History of the American Welfare State* (New York, NY: Oxford University Press, 1997).

6. In the Senate, Democratic support for the final Medicare bill was much larger (57 in favor, 7 opposed) than was Republican support (13 in favor, 17 opposed). The same was true in the House: 237 Democrats voted in favor and 47 opposed, compared to 70 Republicans in favor and 69 opposed. In both houses of Congress, some members abstained from the final vote. Tallies available via http://www.ssa.gov/history/tally65.html.

7. For example, the Manpower Development and Training Act, the first of the modern job-training programs, passed in 1962.

8. These comments can be found on the Social Security Administration website, http://www.ssa.gov/history/fdrstmts.html#signing.

9. Alfred M. Landon, "I Will Not Promise the Moon," in Donald T. Critchlow and Ellis W. Hawley (eds.), *Poverty and Public Policy in Modern America* (Chicago, IL: Dorsey Press, 1989), pp. 156, 160.

10. Johnson made these comments during the signing ceremony on July 30, 1965, available at http://www.ssa.gov/history/lbjstmts.html#medicare.

11. "Medicare Report Filed in House," *Congressional Quarterly Weekly Report* 23, 2 (April 2, 1965): 590.

12. "House OKs Overhaul of Welfare: Biggest Change in Decades Would Shift Much Power to the States," *Tampa Tribune* (March 25, 1995), p. 1. Accessed via Lexis-Nexis.

13. Andrew Mollison, "Bitter Welfare Debate Begins, Leaders Hint at Compromise," *Pittsburgh Post-Gazette* (March 22, 1995), p. A8. Accessed via Lexis-Nexis.

14. It is tempting to attribute the late start of the American welfare state to the absence of a significant labor or socialist party. After all, left-wing parties are supposed to be one of the main engines of the welfare state; see, e.g., Gosta Esping-Andersen, *Politics against Markets: The Social Democratic Road to Power* (Princeton, NJ: Princeton University Press, 1985); Evelyn Huber and John D. Stephens, *Development and Crises of the Welfare State: Parties and Policies in Global Markets* (Chicago, IL: University of Chicago Press, 2001); Michael Shalev, "The Social Democratic Model and Beyond: Two Generations of Comparative Research on the Welfare State," *Comparative Social Research* 3 (1983): 315–51. Nevertheless, in several European countries, conservative and centrist party leaders played a major role in creating the first social programs. Germany under Bismarck is the classic example, and to that list one can add Britain, Denmark, and even Sweden; Peter Baldwin, *The Politics of Social Solidarity: Class Bases of the European Welfare State, 1875–1975* (New York, NY: Cambridge University Press, 1990); Ann Shola Orloff and Theda Skocpol, "Why Not Equal Protection? Explaining the Politics of Public Social Spending in Britain, 1900–1911, and the United States, 1880s–1920," *American Sociological Review* 49, 6 (December 1984): 726–750.

15. See chapter 1.

16. For examples of how this other history might appear, see Edwin Amenta, *Bold Relief: Institutional Politics and the Origins of Modern American Social Policy* (Princeton, NJ: Princeton University Press, 1998), and Theda Skocpol, *Protecting Soldiers and Mothers: The Political Origins of Social Policy in the United States* (Cambridge, MA: The Belknap Press of Harvard University Press, 1992).

17. Some readers may argue with the exact starting and ending dates for each era. My periodization relies heavily on decades for ease of presentation.

18. See the FHA website at http://www.hud.gov/offices/hsg/hsgabout.cfm.

19. The old Guaranteed Student Loan program is now known as the Federal Family Education loan program.

20. Skocpol, *Protecting Soldiers and Mothers*.

21. At the time, these were known as workmen's compensation laws. Most states also passed mothers' pension laws during the 1910s and 1920s. Mothers' pensions were cash payments to poor single-mother families and served as the foundation of Aid to Dependent Children. A smaller number of states created pensions for the poor elderly, which were incorporated in the old age assistance program created in 1935.

22. The main exceptions are workers' compensation programs for government workers and the Black Lung program for coal miners.

23. The home mortgage interest deduction was part of a general deduction for indebtedness.

24. Theda Skocpol (*Protecting Soldiers and Mothers*) argues that Civil War pensions ought to be counted as social policy, pushing the origins of the American welfare state back even earlier in time.

25. Cathie Jo Martin, "Stuck in Neutral: Big Business and the Politics of National Health Reform," *Journal of Health Politics, Policy and Law* 20 (May 1995): 435.

26. Paul Pierson, "The New Politics of the Welfare State," *World Politics* 48, 2 (1996): 143–79. These examples are also consistent with Pierson's claim that more inclusive middle-class programs usually resist retrenchment better than means-tested programs for the poor.

27. One exception is the significant expansion of Medicaid in the 1980s and 1990s, which will be analyzed in chapter 5.

28. Some readers may notice a distinctively American approach to family policy. Lacking European-style family allowances, the United States relies instead on tax expenditures such as the Earned Income Tax Credit and the Child Tax Credit.

29. For similar results based on a shorter time span but a wider set of policies, see David R. Mayhew, *Divided We Govern: Party Control, Lawmaking, and Investigations, 1946–1990* (New Haven, CT: Yale University Press, 1991).

30. The recent prescription drug benefit for Medicare is a notable exception. I will say more about this in chapter 7.

31. The ideological gap may have diminished in recent years as European labor and social democratic parties have moved to the right; see e.g., Seymour Martin Lipset, "The Americanization of the European Left," *Journal of Democracy* 12, 2 (April 2001): 74–87. For most of the twentieth century, however, it is fair to place the Democrats closer to the middle of political parties in Europe rather than on the left.

CHAPTER 4
OGRES, ONIONS, AND LAYERS

1. Norman J. Ornstein, Thomas E. Mann, and Michael J. Malbin, *Vital Statistics on Congress, 1997–1998* (Washington, DC: Congressional Quarterly, 1998), table 1–5; Harold W. Stanley and Richard G. Niemi, *Vital Statistics on American Politics, 1999–2000* (Washington, DC: CQ Press, 2000), tables 5–8, 5–10, and 5–11.

2. These scores are available online thanks to Keith Poole at http://voteview .com/dwnl.htm.

3. For evidence that polarization produces gridlock, see Nolan McCarty, "The Policy Effects of Political Polarization," in Paul Pierson and Theda Skocpol (eds.), "The Transformation of American Politics: Activist Government and the Rise of Conservatism" (manuscript, 2005). R. Kent Weaver discusses "zones of accept-

able outcomes" in the context of the 1996 welfare reform act: *Ending Welfare as We Know It* (Washington, DC: Brookings Institution, 2000), ch. 14.

4. A partial exception is Jacob S. Hacker, *The Divided Welfare State: The Battle over Public and Private Social Benefits* (New York, NY: Cambridge University Press, 2002).

5. "Outcome Indicators," *Social Security Bulletin* 65, 1 (2003/2004): 70–83; Social Security Administration, *Income of the Aged Chartbook, 2001* (Washington, DC, 2003), accessed via http://www.ssa.gov/policy/docs/chartbooks/income_aged/2001/iac01.pdf.

6. "When a firm terminates a pension plan that has assets insufficient to cover its liabilities, the federal pension insurer becomes the plan's trustee, takes over plan assets, and pays the pension to plan participants." Ron J. Feldman, "Government Insurance," in Lester M. Salamon (ed.), *The Tools of Government: A Guide to the New Governance* (New York, NY: Oxford University Press, 2002), p. 194. The national government's other major insurance programs back up the nation's banks, thrifts, and credit unions.

7. Social Security Administration, *Income of the Aged Chartbook, 2001*; U.S. Census Bureau, *Statistical Abstract of the United States, 2003* (Washington, DC: Government Printing Office, 2004), table 549.

8. Pension Benefit Guaranty Corporation, *2003 Annual Report* and *2004 Annual Report*, available at http://www.pbgc.gov/publications/annrpt/default.htm; Albert B. Crenshaw, "Big Pension Plans Fall Further Behind," *Washington Post* (June 7, 2005), p. A3.

9. The most comprehensive account of the enactment of ERISA is James A. Wooten, *The Employee Retirement Income Security Act of 1974: A Political History* (Berkeley, CA: University of California Press, 2004). Other sources consulted include Michael S. Gordon, "Overview: Why Was ERISA Enacted?" in U.S. Senate, Special Committee on Aging, *The Employee Retirement Income Security Act of 1974: The First Decade* (Washington, DC: Government Printing Office, 1984), pp. 1–25; Hacker, *The Divided Welfare State*; Christopher Howard, *The Hidden Welfare State: Tax Expenditures and Social Policy in the United States* (Princeton, NJ: Princeton University Press, 1997); Jacob K. Javits with Rafael Steinberg, *Javits: Autobiography of a Public Man* (Boston, MA: Houghton Mifflin, 1981); Craig MacKown and Arnold Bortz, "Jacob K. Javits," in Ralph Nader Congress Project (ed.), *Citizens Look at Congress* (Washington, DC: Grossman, 1972); and Steven A. Sass, *The Promise of Private Pensions: The First Hundred Years* (Cambridge, MA: Harvard University Press, 1997).

10. Quoted in "Two Pension Reform Bills Move to Senate Floor," *Congressional Quarterly Weekly Report* 33, 35 (September 1, 1973): 2380.

11. Teresa Tritch and John Manners, "He Fought the Good Fight for Your Pension Rights," *Money* 21, 10 (October 1992): 142.

12. Howard, *The Hidden Welfare State*, p. 127. For example, Javits told the story of Robert Pratt of Hudson, New York, who worked at the same company for forty-seven years. When he turned sixty-five he applied for pension benefits, only to be told that the company's plan had been terminated three months earlier. Javits claimed in 1973 that his office received up to five thousand phone calls, letters, and telegrams each month from individuals with pension problems. "Pen-

sion Reform," *Congressional Quarterly Weekly Report* 31, 47 (November 24, 1973): 3091.

13. My account of the ADA is based primarily on Edward D. Berkowitz, "A Historical Preface to the Americans with Disabilities Act," *Journal of Policy History* 6, 1 (1994): 96–119; Thomas F. Burke, *Lawyers, Lawsuits, and Legal Rights: The Battle over Litigation in American Society* (Berkeley, CA: University of California Press, 2002), esp. ch. 2; Thomas F. Burke, "On the Rights Track: the Americans with Disabilities Act," in Pietro Nivola (ed.), *Comparative Disadvantages? Social Regulations and the Global Economy* (Washington, DC: Brookings Institution, 1997), pp. 247–72; and Jonathan M. Young, *Equality of Opportunity: The Making of the Americans with Disabilities Act* (Washington, DC: National Council on Disability, 1997), available at http://www.ncd.gov/newsroom/publications/equality.html.

14. Cited in Berkowitz, "A Historical Preface to the Americans with Disabilities Act," p. 108.

15. U.S. Census Bureau, *Statistical Abstract of the United States, 1984* (Washington, DC: Government Printing Office, 1983).

16. Burke, *Lawyers, Lawsuits, and Legal Rights*, p. 73. To compound the irony, the Disability Rights Center had historic connections to Ralph Nader, noted more as a consumer advocate than a GOP stalwart.

17. Martha Derthick, *Agency under Stress: The Social Security Administration in American Government* (Washington, DC: Brookings Institution, 1990).

18. Cited in Berkowitz, "A Historical Preface to the Americans with Disabilities Act," p. 110.

19. Cited in Burke, *Lawyers, Lawsuits, and Legal Rights*, p. 78.

20. Named after Rep. Jim Chapman (D-TX).

21. Bush's full statement is included as appendix G in Young, *Equality of Opportunity.*

22. During the debates, several groups put forward their own estimates of the costs of compliance. The American Hospital Association, for example, put the tab at $20 billion for its members. Burke, "On the Rights Track," p. 284. Given such high costs, readers might wonder why business interests were unable to stop the ADA from passing. Burke (*Lawyers, Lawsuits, and Legal Rights*) notes that many companies could have reasonably viewed themselves as already in compliance with the new law. Moreover, it was politically difficult for any group to oppose a policy designed to help the handicapped.

23. The ADA thus relies on a combination of social regulation and tort law. Readers interested to know more about the implementation of the ADA might read the Winter 2001 issue of the *Policy Studies Journal*, which includes several relevant articles.

24. Burke, "On the Rights Track."

25. The Child Tax Credit is currently worth $1,000 for each child under the age of seventeen. For certain individuals the tax credit is refundable, meaning that if the credit exceeds their income tax liability, they receive the difference back as a tax refund.

26. For 2000 data, see Joint Committee on Taxation, *Estimates of Federal Tax Expenditures for Fiscal Years 2001–2005* (Washington, DC: Government Printing

Office, 2001), available at http://www.house.gov/jct/s-1-01.pdf. The other budget numbers can be accessed via the website of the Office of Management and Budget (http://www.whitehouse.gov/omb/).

27. Senator Jesse Helms of North Carolina, one of the most conservative Republicans of the twentieth century, attacked existing tax benefits for families in these terms: "Tax fairness for families was a major impetus for President Reagan's tax reforms during the last decade. However, when it came time to make a real difference, the big spenders in the Congress balked. . . . The child care tax credit is a prime example. Many called that tax credit 'pro-family.' But that tax credit will do nothing for those who need it most. For example, the credit can be claimed by two wage earners—but not by parents who choose to stay at home. In other words, more than one-half of America's families pay higher taxes because one parent spends more of the time at home. Those citizens subsidize the Government's march toward socialized child care." *Congressional Record*, 101st Congress, 2nd session (March 21, 1990), S2916.

28. This platform was accessed via http://www.presidency.ucsb.edu/site/docs/platforms.php.

29. Daniel P. Gitterman, Christopher Howard, and Kendra Davenport Cotton, *Tax Credits for Working Families: The New American Social Policy*, discussion paper prepared for the Brookings Institution Center on Urban and Metropolitan Policy(August 2003); Howard, *The Hidden Welfare State*, esp. pp. 152–56; Louis Uchitelle, "Rival Views on Economy: To Nurture, or to Prune," *New York Times* (November 3, 1988), p. A1. The specific GOP bills were located using the Lexis-Nexis congressional database. Coats's and Dole's NOMINATE scores were obtained via http://voteview.com/dwnl.htm.

30. Gitterman, Howard, and Cotton, *Tax Credits for Working Families*; Howard, *The Hidden Welfare State*.

31. The National Commission on Children, which Rockefeller chaired, strongly recommended a refundable tax credit for families with children as part of its final report, *Beyond Rhetoric* (1991).

32. John Harris and Eric Pianin, "Clinton Offers, Seeks Concessions on Tax Cuts," *Washington Post* (July 1, 1997), p. A1; Ben Wildavsky, "Kids' Tax Credit Splits Conservatives," *National Journal* 29, 23 (June 7, 1997): 1133–36; Ben Wildavsky and Kirk Victor, "Fighting over Taxes," *National Journal* 29, 25 (June 21, 1997): 1283–86. As we will see in the next chapter, expanding the Earned Income Tax Credit also gained support from those who wanted to make tax bills more progressive or less regressive.

33. These organizations came to support the Child Tax Credit several years after Republican officials started proposing it.

34. The growth in social spending during the former administrations was greater than the growth in the rest of their budgets as well.

35. Robert X Browning, *Politics and Social Policy in the United States* (Knoxville, TN: University of Tennessee Press, 1986), chs. 5–6. The figures for payments to individuals exclude veterans' benefits.

36. R. Kent Weaver, *Automatic Government: The Politics of Indexation* (Washington, DC: Brookings Institution, 1988), ch. 4.

37. Javits with Steinberg, *Javits*, pp. 385–86.

38. Jacob S. Hacker, "Privatizing Risk without Privatizing the Welfare State: The Hidden Politics of Social Policy Retrenchment in the United States," *American Political Science Review* 98, 2 (May 2004): 243–60. See also Karen Orren and Stephen Skowronek, *The Search for American Political Development* (New York, NY: Cambridge University Press, 2004), and Eric Schickler, *Disjointed Pluralism: Institutional Innovation and the Development of the U.S. Congress* (Princeton, NJ: Princeton University Press, 2001).

39. Michelle Rose Marks, "Party Politics and Family Policy: The Case of the Family and Medical Leave Act," *Journal of Family Issues* 18, 1 (January 1997): 55–70; Anne L. Radigan, *Concept & Compromise: The Evolution of Family Leave Legislation in the U.S. Congress* (Washington, DC: Women's Research & Education Institute, 1988).

40. Kenneth J. Cooper and Helen Dewar, "Bush Vetoes Family Leave Bill, Draws Strong Democratic Criticism," *Washington Post* (September 23, 1992), p. A14.

41. Steven A. Holmes, "House Backs Bush Veto of Family Leave Bill," *New York Times* (July 26, 1990), p. A16.

CHAPTER 5
PROGRAMS FOR THE POOR ARE NOT ALWAYS POOR PROGRAMS

1. Appendix C in John L. Palmer and Isabel Sawhill (eds.), *The Reagan Record* (Washington, DC: Urban Institute, 1984); D. Lee Bawden and John L. Palmer, "Social Policy: Challenging the Welfare State," in Palmer and Sawhill (eds.), *The Reagan Record*, pp. 177–215; Harrison Donnelly, "Millions of Poor Face Losses Oct. 1 as Reconciliation Bill Spending Cuts Go into Effect," *Congressional Quarterly Weekly Report* 39 (September 26, 1981): 1833–40.

2. Judith Feder, John Holahan, Randall R. Bovbjorg, and Jack Hadley, "Health," in John L. Palmer and Isabel Sawhill (eds.), *The Reagan Experiment* (Washington, DC: Urban Institute, 1982), pp. 271–305; James R. Storey, "Income Security," in Palmer and Sawhill (eds.), *The Reagan Experiment*, pp. 361–92.

3. Andrea Louise Campbell, *How Policies Make Citizens: Senior Political Activism and the American Welfare State* (Princeton, NJ: Princeton University Press, 2003), esp. ch. 5; Fay Lomax Cook and Edith J. Barrett, *Support for the American Welfare State: The Views of Congress and the Public* (New York, NY: Columbia University Press, 1992), pp. 27–29; Christopher Howard, *The Hidden Welfare State: Tax Expenditures and Social Policy in the United States* (Princeton, NJ: Princeton University Press, 1997), pp.145–49; Paul Pierson, *Dismantling the Welfare State? Reagan, Thatcher, and the Politics of Retrenchment* (New York, NY: Cambridge University Press, 1994), ch. 3. We will look more closely at the power of the elderly in chapter 7.

4. This phrase is usually attributed to Richard Titmuss, a British social welfare scholar.

5. Hugh Heclo, "The Political Foundations of Antipoverty Policy," in Sheldon H. Danziger and Daniel H. Weinberg (eds.), *Fighting Poverty: What Works and What Doesn't* (Cambridge, MA: Harvard University Press, 1986), pp. 337–38.

6. Theda Skocpol, "Targeting within Universalism: Politically Viable Policies to Combat Poverty in the United States," in Christopher Jencks and Paul E. Peterson (eds.), *The Urban Underclass* (Washington, DC: Brookings Institution, 1991), p. 428.

7. Jill Quadagno, *The Color of Welfare: How Racism Undermined the War on Poverty* (New York, NY: Oxford University Press, 1994), p. 155.

8. The most comprehensive political analysis of the 1996 welfare reforms is R. Kent Weaver, *Ending Welfare as We Know It* (Washington, DC: Brookings Institution, 2000). Figures for welfare caseloads came from the website of the U.S. Department of Health and Human Services, Administration for Children & Families (http://www.acf.hhs.gov/news/stats/newstat2.shtml).

9. Some of the cuts to benefits for immigrants were later restored.

10. Sally S. Cohen and Alice Sardell, "Policymaking for Children's Issues," *Policy Currents* 12, 1 (Spring 2003): 1–9; Howard, *The Hidden Welfare State*, ch. 7; Sara Rosenbaum and Colleen A. Sonosky, "Medicaid Reforms and SCHIP: Health Care Coverage and the Changing Policy Environment," in Carol J. De Vita and Rachel Mosher-Williams (eds.), *Who Speaks for America's Children? The Role of Child Advocates in Public Policy* (Washington, DC: Urban Institute, 2001), pp. 81–104; Alice Sardell, "Child Health Policy in the U.S.: The Paradox of Consensus," *Journal of Health Politics, Policy and Law* 15, 2 (Summer 1990): 271–304; Alice Sardell and Kay Johnson, "The Politics of EPSDT Policy in the 1990s: Policy Entrepreneurs, Political Streams, and Children's Health Benefits," *Milbank Quarterly* 76, 2 (1998): 175–205.

11. Medicaid also serves the elderly and the handicapped, two groups that usually rate high in deservingness. The expansion discussed in this chapter, however, primarily affected children.

12. Parts of this argument are similar to the analysis in Robert Greenstein, "Universal and Targeted Approaches to Relieving Poverty: An Alternative View," in Christopher Jencks and Paul E. Peterson (eds.), *The Urban Underclass* (Washington, DC: Brookings Institution, 1991), pp. 437–59.

13. U.S. Census Bureau, *Statistical Abstract of the United States, 1982–83* (Washington, DC: Government Printing Office, 1982), table 517; U.S. Census Bureau, *Statistical Abstract of the United States, 2003* (Washington, DC: Government Printing Office, 2003), table 540.

14. Readers interested to know more about these various sources of growth might start with Teresa A. Coughlin, Leighton Ku, and John Holahan, *Medicaid since 1980: Costs, Coverage, and the Shifting Alliance between the Federal Government and the States* (Washington, DC: Urban Institute, 1994), and Diane Rowland, Judith Feder, and Alina Salganicoff (eds.), *Medicaid Financing Crisis: Balancing Responsibilities, Priorities, and Dollars* (Washington, DC: AAAS, 1993).

15. This chapter focuses exclusively on the legislative arena. For evidence that courts can also help expand means-tested programs and protect them from cutbacks, see Martha Derthick, *Agency under Stress: The Social Security Administration in American Government* (Washington, DC: Brookings Institution, 1990), esp. ch. 7; Jennifer L. Erkulwater, "The Forgotten Safety Net: The Expansion of Supplemental Security Income" (Ph.D. dissertation, Boston College, 2001); and

R. Shep Melnick, *Between the Lines: Interpreting Welfare Rights* (Washington, DC: Brookings Institution, 1994).

16. Details about Medicaid expansion can be found in Colleen Grogan and Eric Patashnik, "Medicaid at the Crossroads," in James A. Morone and Lawrence R. Jacobs (eds.), *Healthy, Wealthy, and Fair: Health Care and the Good Society* (New York, NY: Oxford University Press, 2005), pp. 267–95; Julie Kosterlitz, "Concern about Children," *National Journal* 18, 38 (September 20, 1986): 2255–58: Sara Rosenbaum, "Medicaid Expansions and Access to Health Care," in Rowland, Feder, and Salganicoff (eds.), *Medicaid Financing Crisis*, pp. 45–81; Rosenbaum and Sonosky, "Medicaid Reforms and SCHIP"; Sardell, "Child Health Policy in the U.S."; Sardell and Johnson, "The Politics of EPSDT Policy in the 1990s," esp. table 2; Andy Schneider with Risa Elias, Rachel Garfield, David Rousseau, and Victoria Wachino, *The Medicaid Resource Book* (Washington, DC: The Kaiser Commission on Medicaid and the Uninsured, 2002), esp. appendix 1; and U.S. House of Representatives, Committee on Ways and Means, *Overview of Entitlement Programs: 1990 Green Book* (Washington, DC: Government Printing Office, 1990), pp. 1276–88.

17. Quoted in Robert Pear, "Expanded Right to Medicaid Shatters the Link to Welfare," *New York Times* (March 6, 1988), p. 1. Ironically, decoupling Medicaid from AFDC in the 1980s and early 1990s may have made welfare reform in 1996 more acceptable. Policy makers knew that even if millions of children would no longer receive income support, they would continue to be eligible for medical care.

18. U.S. House of Representatives, Committee on Ways and Means, *Overview of Entitlement Programs: 1990 Green Book*, pp. 558–60, 1021.

19. Sandra J. Tanenbaum, "Medicaid Eligibility Policy in the 1980s: Medical Utilitarianism and the 'Deserving' Poor," *Journal of Health Politics, Policy and Law* 20, 4 (Winter 1995): 939; U.S. House of Representatives, Committee on Ways and Means, *2004 Green Book: Background Material and Data on the Programs within the Jurisdiction of the Committee on Ways and Means* (Washington, DC: Government Printing Office, 2004), table 15–12.

20. Mark A. Peterson, "The Politics of Health Care Policy: Overreaching in an Age of Polarization," in Margaret Weir (ed.), *The Social Divide: Political Parties and the Future of Activist Government* (Washington, DC: Brookings Institution, 1998), pp.181–229; Sardell and Johnson, "The Politics of EPSDT Policy in the 1990s"; Weaver, *Ending Welfare as We Know It.*

21. Howard, *The Hidden Welfare State*, ch. 7 and sources cited therein; U.S. House of Representatives, Committee on Ways and Means, *2004 Green Book*, section 13.

22. There is an early payment option whereby the EITC is factored into each paycheck during the year, but very few recipients either know about or choose this option.

23. U.S. House of Representatives, Committee on Ways and Means, *2004 Green Book*, tables 13–12 and 13–14.

24. With respect to family size, the EITC distinguishes only between families with one child and with two or more children. Some of the growth in the number of EITC families resulted from the economic recession of the early 1990s.

25. Christopher Howard, "The New Politics of the Working Poor," in Martin A. Levin, Marc K. Landy, and Martin Shapiro (eds.), *Seeking the Center: Politics and Policymaking at the New Century* (Washington, DC: Georgetown University Press, 2001), pp. 239–63; the quotation from Bush appears on page 255. The small expansion in 2001 is described in U.S. House of Representatives, Committee on Ways and Means, *2004 Green Book*, section 13, p. 35.

26. E.g., Sar A. Levitan, Garth L. Mangum, and Stephen L. Mangum, *Programs in Aid of the Poor*, 7th ed. (Baltimore, MD: Johns Hopkins University Press, 1998), esp. ch. 3.

27. E.g., Helene Slessarev, "Racial Tensions and Institutional Support: Social Programs during a Period of Retrenchment," in Margaret Weir, Ann Shola Orloff, and Theda Skocpol (eds.), *The Politics of Social Policy in the United States* (Princeton, NJ: Princeton University Press, 1988), pp. 357–79.

28. Grogan and Patashnik, "Medicaid at the Crossroads"; Howard, *The Hidden Welfare State*, ch. 7.

29. Jeffrey H. Birnbaum and Alan S. Murray, *Showdown at Gucci Gulch* (New York, NY: Vintage, 1987); Richard Himelfarb, *Catastrophic Politics: The Rise and Fall of the Medicare Catastrophic Coverage Act of 1988* (University Park, PA: Pennsylvania State University Press, 1995); Howard, *The Hidden Welfare State*, ch. 7.

30. This term was used by John Cogan, associate director of the Office of Management and Budget under Reagan. Dan Morgan, "Medicaid Costs Balloon into Fiscal 'Time Bomb,'" *Washington Post* (January 30, 1994), p. A1.

31. Howard, *The Hidden Welfare State*, ch. 7.

32. This observation suggests that earlier comments about the effects of divided government may need to be qualified. By itself, divided government does not help us understand the difference between expansion and retrenchment of means-tested programs. But the interaction of divided government and concern over the deficit might. When such concern is high, Republicans have an incentive to reach out to Democrats to enact taxing and spending bills, which enhances the prospects that means-tested programs can be expanded. Such was the case between 1984 and 1993. When concern for the deficit was low, as was true in 1981 and 1996, Republicans lost that incentive.

33. Quoted in Pear, "Expanded Right to Medicaid Shatters the Link to Welfare."

34. Both quotes are from Morgan, "Medicaid Costs Balloon into Fiscal 'Time Bomb.'" Other details about Waxman and Medicaid are taken from Julie Kosterlitz, "Watch Out for Waxman," *National Journal* 21, 10 (March 11, 1989): 577–81.

35. Morgan, "Medicaid Costs Balloon into Fiscal 'Time Bomb.'" One analysis found that twenty-four Medicaid provisions enacted between 1984 and 1990 had a total first-year cost of $888 million. In the fifth year of each provision, their total cost was $5.4 billion.

36. Howard, *The Hidden Welfare State*, ch. 7.

37. Sardell, "Child Health Policy in the U.S.," p. 282.

38. Ibid., p. 281. This discussion of Medicaid and infant health is based on Sardell and on Kosterlitz, "Concern about Children"; Julie Rovner, "Drop in U.S.

Infant Mortality Goal of New Legislation," *Congressional Quarterly Weekly Report* 47 (April 8, 1989): 759–60; and Tanenbaum, "Medicaid Eligibility Policy in the 1980s."

39. By the end of the decade, the National Governors Association was opposing further expansion because of the stress placed on state budgets. Julie Rovner, "Governors' Medicaid Protests Likely to Be Swept Aside," *Congressional Quarterly Weekly Report* 47 (August 12, 1989): 2121–23.

40. Quoted in Robert Pear, "Deficit or No Deficit, Unlikely Allies Bring About Medicaid Expansion," *New York Times* (November 4, 1990), p. 24. This line of thinking allowed some individuals and groups to support Medicaid at the same time that they pushed for cuts in welfare.

41. This may be one reason why Medicaid expansion has not been extended to more of the poor. Women were covered primarily to cover their unborn children.

42. Quoted in Pear, "Deficit or No Deficit, Unlikely Allies Bring About Medicaid Expansion," p. 24.

43. This section is based on Howard, *The Hidden Welfare State*, chs. 3 and 7; Howard, "The New Politics of the Working Poor"; and Weaver, *Ending Welfare as We Know It*, esp. chs. 3 and 4.

44. Howard, *The Hidden Welfare State*, p. 143.

45. Some of these same Democrats were attracted to Medicaid expansion in order to show voters that Democrats would target scarce resources where they would have the greatest economic benefit. Liberal Democrats and antipoverty groups usually rejected the "either/or" nature of the debate. They wanted to increase the minimum wage and the EITC.

46. These episodes will be discussed more in chapter 7.

47. Leighton Ku and Matthew Broaddus, *Out-of-Pocket Medical Expenses for Medicaid Beneficiaries Are Substantial and Growing* (Washington, D.C.: Center on Budget and Policy Priorities, 2005); Robert Pear, "States Proposing Sweeping Changes to Trim Medicaid," *New York Times* (May 9, 2005), p. A1; Robert Pear, "U.S. Gives Florida Sweeping Right to Curb Medicaid," *New York Times* (October 20, 2005), p. A1.

48. Howard, *The Hidden Welfare State*, ch. 7.

49. The impact of race undoubtedly deserves more attention than I have given it in this chapter. One advantage of the Earned Income Tax Credit, for example, might be that the racial profile of recipients is unknown. Tax forms don't ask for racial identification. Likewise, the large number of elderly white women using Medicaid to pay for their nursing-home care may make that program more politically acceptable than welfare.

CHAPTER 6
SHAQ IS STILL PRETTY TALL

1. Anthony King, "Ideas, Institutions and the Policies of Governments: A Comparative Analysis," *British Journal of Political Science* 3 (1973): 418.

2. Seymour Martin Lipset, *American Exceptionalism: A Double-Edged Sword* (New York, NY: W. W. Norton, 1996), p. 74.

3. Theda Skocpol, *Boomerang: Health Care Reform and the Turn against Government* (New York, NY: W. W. Norton, 1996); R. Kent Weaver, *Ending Welfare as We Know It* (Washington, DC: Brookings Institution, 2000).

4. Michael X. Delli Carpini and Scott Keeter, *What Americans Know about Politics and Why It Matters* (New Haven, CT: Yale University Press, 1996).

5. Paul Burstein, "The Impact of Public Opinion on Public Policy: A Review and an Agenda," *Political Research Quarterly* 56, 1 (March 2003): 29–40; Robert S. Erikson, Michael B. MacKuen, and James A. Stimson, *The Macro Polity* (New York, NY: Cambridge University Press, 2002); Robert S. Erikson, Gerald C. Wright, and John P. McIver, *Statehouse Democracy: Public Opinion and Policy in the American States* (New York, NY: Cambridge University Press, 1993); Benjamin I. Page and Robert Y. Shapiro, "Effects of Public Opinion on Policy," *American Political Science Review* 77, 1 (March 1983): 175–90.

6. Tom W. Smith, "The Polls: The Welfare State in Cross-National Perspective," *Public Opinion Quarterly* 51 (1987): 404–21.

7. Robert Y. Shapiro and John T. Young, "Public Opinion and the Welfare State: The United States in Comparative Perspective," *Political Science Quarterly* 104 (1989): 69.

8. Everett Carll Ladd, *The American Ideology: An Exploration of the Origins, Meaning, and Role of American Political Ideas* (Storrs, CT: Roper Center for Public Opinion Research, 1994), pp. 40–41.

9. See, e.g., Louis Hartz, *The Liberal Tradition in America* (New York, NY: Harcourt Brace, 1955); Samuel Huntington, *American Politics: The Promise of Disharmony* (Cambridge, MA: Harvard University Press, 1981); John W. Kingdon, *America the Unusual* (New York, NY: St. Martin's/Worth, 1999); John Mickelthwait and Adrian Wooldridge, *The Right Nation: Conservative Power in America* (New York, NY: Penguin, 2004). Many of these themes were also noted by Alexis de Tocqeville in his classic two-volume study, *Democracy in America* (1835). Not everyone, of course, agrees with this reading of American values and U.S. history.

10. A classic analysis of the influence of values on welfare states is Gaston V. Rimlinger, *Welfare Policy and Industrialization in Europe, America, and Russia* (New York, NY: John Wiley, 1971).

11. Richard M. Coughlin, *Ideology, Public Opinion, and Welfare Policy: Attitudes toward Taxing and Spending in Industrialized Societies* (Berkeley, CA: Institute of International Studies, 1980); Lawrence R. Jacobs, *The Health of Nations: Public Opinion and the Making of American and British Health Policy* (Ithaca, NY: Cornell University Press, 1993); Shapiro and Young, "Public Opinion and the Welfare State"; Smith, "The Polls: The Welfare State in Cross-National Perspective."

12. The ISSP stores its data at the Zentralarchiv für Empirische Sozialforschung in Germany, and its website can be accessed at http://www.issp.org.

13. Although the trend in recent decades has been to limit comparisons to affluent Western democracies, some earlier studies included a larger number and wider range of nations. See, e.g., Phillips Cutright, "Political Structure, Economic Development, and National Social Security Programs," *American Journal of Sociology* 70 (1965): 537–50.

14. Gosta Esping-Andersen, *The Three Worlds of Welfare Capitalism* (Princeton, NJ: Princeton University Press, 1990). The quotation is from p. 26.

15. The combination of being conservative in the abstract but liberal on specific issues has been noted by a number of analysts. See, e.g., Lloyd A. Free and Hadley Cantril, *The Political Beliefs of Americans* (New York, NY: Simon and Schuster, 1968).

16. This question was not asked in the other four countries featured in table 6.1.

17. Some readers may notice that public opinion does not always fit Esping-Andersen's typology. In some cases, most notably education, Americans expressed more support than Norwegians or Swedes. Britain is supposed to be closer to the United States than Scandinavia is when it comes to social policy, and yet on several questions British respondents offered more support than either Swedes or Norwegians. The answers given by German and Italian respondents to many of the questions in table 6.1 are indistinguishable from those given by Scandinavians. Likewise, there is not much difference across the European countries with respect to government support of declining industries to save jobs; the need for less government regulation of business; and private versus public ownership of banks.

18. Coughlin, *Ideology, Public Opinion, and Welfare Policy*; Benjamin I. Page and Robert Y. Shapiro, *The Rational Public: Fifty Years of Trends in Americans' Policy Preferences* (Chicago, IL: University of Chicago Press, 1992).

19. R. Douglas Arnold, *The Logic of Congressional Action* (New Haven, CT: Yale University Press, 1990), esp. ch. 4.

20. In the context of this survey, "rich" means incomes above $100,000 and "voters" are people who voted in the 1996 elections.

21. Spending more on retirement pensions won support from 51 percent of all respondents, 25 percent of college graduates, 45 percent of voters, and 47 percent of the rich.

22. Naturally, support varied depending on party affiliation. Nevertheless, most Republicans had come to embrace important parts of the American welfare state by 1996. Only about 15 percent of self-identified Republicans wanted government to spend less on Social Security, and only 11 percent wanted less spending on health.

23. Pew Research Center for the People and the Press, *The 2004 Political Landscape: Evenly Divided and Increasingly Polarized* (November 2003), accessed via http://people-press.org/reports/pdf/196.pdf.

24. The Kaiser Family Foundation, *National Survey of the Public's Views about Medicaid* (June 2005), accessed via http://www.kff.org/medicaid/pomr062905pkg.cfm.

25. For a good summary, see Tom W. Smith, *Trends in National Spending Priorities, 1973–2000* (Chicago, IL: National Opinion Research Center, 2001), accessed via http://www.norc.uchicago.edu/online/spnd0.htm. The GSS and ISSP surveys do not word their questions identically. The preface to the GSS spending questions, for example, reminds respondents that problems cannot be solved "easily or inexpensively." The ISSP warns respondents that much more spending may require a tax increase. The GSS asks whether "we" are spending too much, too little, or about the right amount on a given policy. The ISSP asks whether people

want more or less "government spending." These differences help explain why answers to the two surveys might differ in the same year. In 1986, for example, 57 percent of Americans agreed that we were spending too little on Social Security (GSS), but only 44 percent wanted government to spend more (ISSP). In charting trends, I stick with one set of questions or the other and do not mix them.

26. Results from the 2002 GSS were obtained from the Survey Documentation & Analysis (SDA) website at the University of California–Berkeley (http://sda.berkeley.edu:7502/). Note that net support for assistance to the poor has once again surpassed support for Social Security.

27. Pew Research Center for the People and the Press, *Deconstructing Distrust: How Americans View Government* (1998), available at http://people-press.org/reports/display.php3?ReportID=95.

28. For evidence that Democrats and Republicans disagree about the causes of poverty and government's role in reducing poverty, see Pew Research Center for the People and the Press, *The 2004 Political Landscape*.

29. To understand how Republican officials could be more conservative than Republican voters, and the rest of the nation, see Jacob S. Hacker and Paul Pierson, *Off Center: The Republican Revolution and the Erosion of American Democracy* (New Haven, CT: Yale University Press, 2005).

30. If Republican officials wanted to expand their party by appealing to independents and weak Democrats, they would have pursued this same set of policies.

31. Jacob S. Hacker, "Privatizing Risk without Privatizing the Welfare State: The Hidden Politics of Social Policy Retrenchment in the United States," *American Political Science Review* 98, 2 (May 2004): 243–60; Steven M. Teles, "Conservative Mobilization against Entrenched Liberalism," in Paul Pierson and Theda Skocpol (eds.), "The Transformation of American Politics: Activist Government and the Rise of Conservatism" (manuscript, 2005).

32. Explaining changes in public attitudes toward the welfare state is beyond the scope of this chapter, but quite important. For evidence of how Social Security affected the political behavior of the elderly, see Andrea Louise Campbell, *How Policies Make Citizens: Senior Political Activism and the American Welfare State* (Princeton, NJ: Princeton University Press, 2003).

33. The trust data come from table 5A of the National Election Studies website at http://www.umich.edu/~nes/nesguide/nesguide.htm.

34. Most of the evidence in this chapter is taken from the 1980s and 1990s. For evidence that Americans had similar views in the 1960s and 1970s, see Page and Shapiro, *The Rational Public*, ch. 4; Robert Y. Shapiro and Tom W. Smith, "The Polls: Social Security," *Public Opinion Quarterly* 49, 4 (Winter 1985): 561–72; and Robert Y. Shapiro and John T. Young, "The Polls: Medical Care in the United States," *Public Opinion Quarterly* 50, 3 (August 1986): 418–28.

35. This episode is discussed further in the next chapter.

36. For a more fully developed argument about the effects of trust on policy, see Marc J. Hetherington, *Why Trust Matters: Declining Political Trust and the Demise of American Liberalism* (Princeton, NJ: Princeton University Press, 2005). As the title suggests, Hetherington argues that greater trust in government moves policy in a liberal direction while lower trust moves policy in a conservative direction. He also argues that the decline in trust is more responsible for

the move toward conservative policies than is any growing conservatism among ordinary citizens.

37. Skocpol, *Boomerang*.

38. "The Uninsured," *Kaiser Public Opinion Update* (April 2000), available at http://www.kff.org/uninsured/3006-index.cfm; "Americans' Views on Disability," *Kaiser Health Poll Report* (May/June 2004), available at http://www.kff.org/healthpollreport/archive_June2004/6.cfm. The survey about long-term care is referenced in the 2004 Kaiser report but was originally conducted by the Robert Wood Johnson Foundation in 2000.

39. The administration's very public efforts to "reinvent government" could not have helped the cause of health reform. Clinton officials routinely pointed out how inefficient and ineffective government was at the same time they asked Americans to accept a major expansion of the government's role in health care.

CHAPTER 7
THE WORLD ACCORDING TO AARP

1. Larger deficits under the current Bush administration ensure that interest on the debt will also remain a major budget outlay for the foreseeable future.

2. U.S. Census Bureau, *Statistical Abstract of the United States, 2003*, tables 152 and 697, accessed via http://www.census.gov/prod/www/statistical-abstract-03.html; Mark Nord, Margaret Andrews, and Steven Carlson, *Household Food Security in the United States, 2001* (Washington, DC: U.S. Department of Agriculture, 2002), table 2, accessed via http://www.ers.usda.gov/publications/fanrr29/; Andrea Louise Campbell, *How Policies Make Citizens: Senior Political Activism and the American Welfare State* (Princeton, NJ: Princeton University Press, 2003), ch. 2. Fewer than 1 percent of the elderly lack health insurance.

3. Quoted in Steven Pearlstein, "Older and Out to Spend: A Reason for Declining Savings?" *Washington Post* (October 2, 1996), p. C1. See also Steve Chapman, "America's Greedy Geezers," *Pittsburgh Post-Gazette* (January 25, 2004), p. E1.

4. Peter G. Peterson, *Running on Empty: How the Democratic and Republican Parties Are Bankrupting Our Future and What Americans Can Do about It* (New York, NY: Farrar, Straus and Giroux, 2004); "Fed Chief: Medicare, Social Security Pose Threats" (March 2, 2005), accessed via http://www.msnbc.msn.com/id/7066201/.

5. Lawrence J. Kotlikoff and Scott Burns, *The Coming Generational Storm: What You Need to Know about America's Economic Future* (Cambridge, MA: MIT Press, 2004); Susan A. MacManus, *Young v. Old: Generational Combat in the 21st Century* (Boulder, CO: Westview Press, 1996); see also Richard D. Thau and Jay S. Heflin, *Generations Apart: Xers vs. Boomers vs. the Elderly* (Amherst, NY: Prometheus Books, 1997).

6. Samuel H. Preston, "Children and the Elderly: Divergent Paths for America's Dependents," *Demography* 21, 4 (November 1984): 445–46.

7. AARP was ranked #1 in 1997 and 1999 and #2 in 2001.

8. Thomas Rosenstiel, "Buying Off the Elderly," *Newsweek* (October 2, 1995), p. 40; David Dahl, "AARP at the Center of Struggle for Power, Money," *St. Peters-*

burg Times (October 9, 1994), p. 1A; Vanessa O'Connell and Ellen Stark, "Taking a Hard Look at AARP's Deals," *Money* (July 1995), p. 116; Sheryl Gay Stolberg, "An 800-Pound Gorilla Changes Partners over Medicare," *New York Times* (November 23, 2003), section 4, p. 5.

9. Jeffrey H. Birnbaum, "Washington's Second Most Powerful Man," *Fortune* (May 12, 1997), pp. 122–26.

10. Eric Schurenberg and Lani Luciano, "The Empire Called AARP," *Money* (October 1988), p. 128, accessed via InfoTrac.

11. "At 50, There's Nothing Left but The Letter," *Milwaukee Journal Sentinel* (September 28, 1998), accessed via Lexis-Nexis.

12. These figures come from AARP's 2003 annual report, available at http://www.aarp.org/aboutaarp/Articles/a2003–06–24-annualreport-03.html.

13. In 2002, AARP had revenues of $636 million. The National Organization of Women (NOW), a well-known advocacy group, had revenues of less than $5 million. Tami Luhby, "AARP's Delicate Balance," *Newsday* (February 28, 2004), p. B6. If education is included as social policy, then the National Education Association would count as a major interest group.

14. Martha Derthick, *Policymaking for Social Security* (Washington, DC: Brookings Institution, 1979).

15. AARP headquarters moved to Washington around 1967. For more information about the organization's early years, see Henry J. Pratt, *The Gray Lobby* (Chicago, IL: University of Chicago Press, 1976).

16. Theda Skocpol, *The Missing Middle: Working Families and the Future of American Social Policy* (New York, NY: W. W. Norton, 2000), p. 87.

17. Some critics charged that AARP did not support Medicare because it would take health insurance business away from the organization. Christine L. Day, *What Older Americans Think: Interest Groups and Aging Policy* (Princeton, NJ: Princeton University Press, 1990), pp. 25–26.

18. Skocpol, *The Missing Middle*; Pratt, *The Gray Lobby*. Though huge now, AARP had far fewer members in the 1960s, an estimated one million.

19. Jonathan Oberlander, *The Political Life of Medicare* (Chicago, IL: University of Chicago Press, 2003), p. 40.

20. Richard Himelfarb, *Catastrophic Politics: The Rise and Fall of the Medicare Catastrophic Coverage Act of 1988* (University Park, PA: Pennsylvania State University Press, 1995), p. 54. My discussion of the rise and fall of the MCCA relies on this book and Oberlander, *The Political Life of Medicare*.

21. A related problem with the MCCA was that benefits were phased in over time, such that the average cost to the elderly would exceed the average benefit for the first five years of the program.

22. Theda Skocpol, *Boomerang: Clinton's Health Security Effort and the Turn against Government in U.S. Politics* (New York, NY: W. W. Norton, 1996), pp. 92–95.

23. See, e.g., *The Policy Book: AARP Public Policies, 2003*, available at http://www.aarp.org/legipoly.html.

24. Thomas McCluskey and Jared B. Adams, *The Budgetary Impact of AARP's Legislative Agenda* (Alexandria, VA: National Taxpayers Union Founda-

tion, 1999), accessed at http://www.ntu.org/taxpayer_issues/ntuf_policy_papers/pp_ntuf_112.php3.

25. Lawrence D. Brown and Michael S. Sparer, "Poor Program's Progress: The Unanticipated Politics of Medicaid Policy," *Health Affairs* 22, 1 (2002): 31–44.

26. Congress did, however, increase the cap on earnings subject to the Medicare payroll tax in 1990 and eliminated the cap in 1993, which effectively raised taxes on more affluent workers.

27. Oberlander, *The Political Life of Medicare*, p. 45. Ultimately, lower reimbursement rates did have an effect on the elderly; many doctors around the country now refuse to accept new Medicare patients because Medicare pays doctors too little for their services. Robert Pear, "Many Doctors Shun Patients with Medicare," *New York Times* (March 17, 2002), p. 1, accessed via Lexis-Nexis.

28. Campbell, *How Policies Make Citizens*, ch. 5; Day, *What Older Americans Think*, p. 80; Charles R. Morris, *The AARP: America's Most Powerful Lobby and the Clash of Generations* (New York, NY: Times Books, 1996), pp. 53–57.

29. Morris, *The AARP*, p. 115; see also Paul Light, *Artful Work: The Politics of Social Security Reform* (New York, NY: Random House, 1985), pp. 74–78.

30. Oberlander, *The Political Life of Medicare*; Mark A. Peterson, "The Politics of Health Care Policy: Overreaching in an Age of Polarization," in Margaret Weir (ed.), *The Social Divide* (Washington, DC: Brookings Institution, 1998), pp. 181–229.

31. For similar judgments, see Oberlander, *The Political Life of Medicare* and Skocpol, *The Missing Middle*.

32. Campbell, *How Policies Make Citizens*; Skocpol, *The Missing Middle*.

33. For information about this organization, go to www.senior.org.

34. Morris, *The AARP*, p. 64.

35. Quoted in Light, *Artful Work*, p. 77.

36. Quoted in Morris, *The AARP*, pp. 112–13.

37. Simpson quoted in Dahl, "AARP at Center of Struggle for Power, Money," p. 1A.

38. These figures come from AARP's 2003 annual report, available at http://www.aarp.org/aboutaarp/Articles/a2003–06–24-annualreport-03.html.

39. Light, *Artful Work*, p. 76; Birnbaum, "Washington's Second Most Powerful Man," p. 126.

40. Bob Baker, "AARP's Revamped Magazine Attempts Hip without the Replacement," *Los Angeles Times* (April 4, 2004), p. E1.

41. Day, *What Older Americans Think*, p. 69; see also Campbell, *How Policies Make Citizens*, pp. 100–101.

42. See, e.g., Skocpol, *Boomerang*.

43. For a more sophisticated discussion of this process, see the work of Paul Pierson, particularly *Dismantling the Welfare State? Reagan, Thatcher, and the Politics of Retrenchment* (New York, NY: Cambridge University Press, 1994) and "The New Politics of the Welfare State," *World Politics* 48, 2 (1996): 143–79.

44. U.S. Census Bureau, *Statistical Abstract of the United States, 2003*, table 419. Although the reported turnout figures are higher than the actual turnout numbers, there is no reason to suspect any major difference in misreporting among the age groups.

45. See tables 6B.5, 6D.5, and 6D.6 in *The NES Guide to Public Opinion and Electoral Behavior,* available at http://www.umich.edu/~nes/nesguide/gd-index.htm#6.

46. Campbell, *How Policies Make Citizens.*

47. For the NES data, see tables 2A.2 and 3.1 at http://www.umich.edu/~nes/nesguide/nesguide.htm. The 2000 exit poll data were obtained at http://www.cnn.com/ELECTION/2000/results/index.epolls.html. For previous elections, see Campbell, *How Policies Make Citizens,* esp. ch. 4; Harold W. Stanley and Richard G. Niemi, *Vital Statistics on American Politics, 1999–2000* (Washington, DC: CQ Press, 2000), table 3–5.

48. U.S. Census Bureau, *Statistical Abstract of the United States, 2003,* table 419; Stanley and Niemi, *Vital Statistics on American Politics, 1999–2000,* table 3–5.

49. Kaiser Family Foundation, *A Generational Look at the Public: Politics and Policy* (October 2002), accessed via http://www.kff.org/kaiserpolls/.

50. In the 1996 Role of Government survey, there was greater support among the young than the old for spending on retirement pensions in the United States and Canada. The pattern was reversed, however, in Sweden and the United Kingdom, indicating that generational differences are not universal in modern welfare states.

51. Results from this poll (#431) are available at http://www.latimes.com/news/custom/timespoll/la-statsheetindex.htmlstory.

52. "Young Americans and Social Security," a public opinion study conducted for the 2030 Center by Peter D. Hart Research Associates (July 1999), available at http://www.2030.org/pdf/report1.pdf.

53. These numbers shed some doubt on Andrea Campbell's claim that "government policy seems to have shifted seniors' self-interests away from supporting the education of younger people upon whom they were once directly dependent, toward defending the government benefits upon which their livelihoods now depend" (*How Policies Make Citizens,* p. 10). For further evidence that older Americans support education more now than in the past, see Eric Plutzer and Michael Berkman, "The Graying of America and Support for Funding the Nation's Schools," *Public Opinion Quarterly* 69, 1 (Spring 2005): 66–86.

54. In the pooled GSS data for 1980–2002, 43 percent of respondents age sixty-five and over lacked a high school degree, compared to 18 percent of the middle-age group and 14 percent of young adults.

55. These questions came from the General Social Survey.

56. Campbell, *How Policies Make Citizens,* pp. 22–25.

57. Sidney Verba, Kay Lehman Schlozman, and Henry E. Brady, *Voice and Equality: Civic Voluntarism in American Politics* (Cambridge, MA: Harvard University Press, 1995), esp. fig. 7.12.

58. The NewsHour with Jim Lehrer/Kaiser Family Foundation/Harvard School of Public Health, *National Survey on Prescription Drugs* (September 2000), available at http://www.kff.org/rxdrugs/3065-index.cfm.

59. Kaiser Family Foundation/Harvard School of Public Health, *Medicare Prescription Drug Survey* (September 2003), available at http://www.kff.org/medicare/3374toplines.cfm.

60. These polls can be found at http://www.pollingreport.com/health2.htm.

61. Novelli quoted in Sheryl Gay Stolberg and Milt Freudenheim, "A Final Push in Congress: The Endorsement," *New York Times* (November 26, 2003), p. A1; see also Baker, "AARP's Revamped Magazine Attempts Hip without the Replacement."

62. Barbara T. Dreyfuss, "The Seduction," *American Prospect* 15, 6 (June 2004): 18–23; Stolberg, "An 800-Pound Gorilla Changes Partners over Medicare."

63. Deborah Barfield Berry, "Trying to Restore Trust at AARP," *Newsday* (March 6, 2004), p. B6; Stephen J. Glain, "AARP Backing of Drug Bill Takes Toll on Reputation," *Boston Globe* (December 8, 2003), p. A1; Susan Jaffe, "AARP Tries to Win Back Angry Ex-Members," *Cleveland Plain-Dealer* (July 12, 2004), p. A1; Tami Luhby, "AARP's Delicate Balance," *Newsday* (February 28, 2004), p. B6; Stolberg and Freudenheim, "A Final Push in Congress."

64. Dreyfuss, "The Seduction."

65. Stolberg and Freudenheim, "A Final Push in Congress."

66. Campbell, *How Policies Make Citizens*; Derthick, *Policymaking for Social Security*; Julian E. Zelizer, *Taxing America: Wilbur D. Mills, Congress, and the State, 1945–1975* (New York, NY: Cambridge University Press, 1998).

67. See the Associated Press/Ipsos and CNN/USA Today/Gallup polls from February to August 2005 at http://www.pollingreport.com/social.htm.

68. Robert L. Borosage and Roger Hickey (eds.), *The Next Agenda: Blueprint for a New Progressive Movement* (Boulder, CO: Westview Press, 2001); Skocpol, *The Missing Middle*.

CHAPTER 8
THE AMERICAN STATES

1. John D. Donahue, *Hazardous Crosscurrents: Confronting Inequality in an Era of Devolution* (New York, NY: Century Foundation Press, 1999); Robert C. Lieberman, *Shifting the Color Line: Race and the American Welfare State* (Cambridge, MA: Harvard University Press, 1998); Suzanne Mettler, *Dividing Citizens: Gender and Federalism in New Deal Public Policy* (Ithaca, NY: Cornell University Press, 1998); Paul E. Peterson, *The Price of Federalism* (Washington, DC: Brookings Institution, 1995); Jill Quadagno, "From Old-Age Assistance to Supplemental Security Income: The Political Economy of Relief in the South, 1935–1972," in Margaret Weir, Ann Shola Orloff, and Theda Skocpol (eds.), *The Politics of Social Policy in the United States* (Princeton, NJ: Princeton University Press, 1988), pp. 235–63; David Brian Robertson and Dennis R. Judd, *The Development of American Public Policy: The Structure of Policy Restraint* (Glenview, IL: Scott, Foresman, 1989).

2. John Yoo, "What Became of Federalism?" *Los Angeles Times* (June 21, 2005), p. B13.

3. According to Justice Brandeis, "To stay experimentation in things social and economic is a grave responsibility. Denial of the right to experiment may be fraught with serious consequences to the nation. It is one of the happy incidents

of the federal system that a single courageous state may, if its citizens choose, serve as a laboratory; and try novel social and economic experiments without risk to the rest of the country" (*New State Ice Co. v. Liebmann*, 1932). For more recent formulations of this argument, see Sarah M. Morehouse and Malcolm E. Jewell, "States as Laboratories: A Reprise," *Annual Review of Political Science* 7 (2004): 177–203; David Osborne, *Laboratories of Democracy* (Cambridge, MA: Harvard Business School Press, 1988); Charles M. Tiebout, "A Pure Theory of Local Expenditures," *Journal of Political Economy* 64 (October 1956): 416–24. Lawrence M. Mead offers reasons why some states may be better suited than others to solve problems in *Government Matters: Welfare Reform in Wisconsin* (Princeton, NJ: Princeton University Press, 2004).

4. Samantha Artiga and Stephanie Mann, *Coverage Gains under Recent Section 1115 Waivers: A Data Update* (August 2005), accessed via http:// www.kff.org/medicaid/7374.cfm; Stephen M. Teles, *Whose Welfare? AFDC and Elite Politics* (Lawrence, KS: University Press of Kansas, 1996); U.S. House of Representatives, Committee on Ways and Means, *2004 Green Book: Background Material and Data on the Programs Within the Jurisdiction of the Committee on Ways and Means* (Washington, DC: Government Printing Office, 2004); R. Kent Weaver, *Ending Welfare as We Know It* (Washington, DC: Brookings Institution, 2000).

5. Barbara J. Nelson, "The Gender, Race, and Class Origins of Early Welfare Policy and the Welfare State: A Comparison of Workmen's Compensation and Mothers' Aid," in Louise A. Tilly and Patricia Gurin (eds.), *Women, Politics, and Change* (New York, NY: Russell Sage Foundation, 1990), pp. 413–35.

6. Daniel Mont, John F. Burton, Jr., and Virginia Reno, *Workers' Compensation: Benefits, Coverage, and Costs, 1996 New Estimates* (Washington, DC: National Academy of Social Insurance, 1999), p. 3.

7. U.S. Bureau of the Census, *Statistical Abstract of the United States, 2004– 2005* (Washington, DC: Government Printing Office, 2004), tables 541, 569, 631, 632.

8. The U.S. Department of Labor is a good place to find information about state workers' compensation laws (http://www.dol.gov/esa/regs/statutes/owcp/ stwclaw/stwclaw.htm).

9. Peter S. Barth, "Compensating Workers for Permanent Partial Disabilities," *Social Security Bulletin* 65, 4 (2003/2004): 17.

10. Michael J. Graetz and Jerry L. Mashaw, *True Security: Rethinking American Social Insurance* (New Haven, CT: Yale University Press, 1999), pp. 82–87; Cecili Thompson Williams, Virginia P. Reno, and John F. Burton, Jr., *Workers' Compensation: Benefits, Coverage, and Costs, 2002* (Washington, DC: National Academy of Social Insurance, 2004).

11. H. Allan Hunt, "Benefit Adequacy in State Workers' Compensation Programs," *Social Security Bulletin* 65, 4 (2003/2004): 24–30.

12. Only the United States, Canada, and Australia have multiple workers' compensation programs in operation. C. Arthur Williams, Jr., *An International Comparison of Workers' Compensation* (Boston, MA: Kluwer Academic, 1991); U.S. Social Security Administration, *Social Security Programs throughout the World* (1999), accessed via www.ssa.gov/statistics/ssptw/index.html.

13. Paul Pierson and Stephan Leibfried, "Multitiered Institutions and the Making of Social Policy," in Leibfried and Pierson (eds.), *European Social Policy: Between Fragmentation and Integration* (Washington, DC: Brookings Institution, 1995), p. 22.

14. Important elements of my argument are not new. Years ago the historian Edward Berkowitz summarized the program's history concisely and, I think, accurately: "The fact that lawyers, insurance companies, trade unions, and state industrial commissions all acquired an interest in workers' compensation has made reform of the program exceedingly difficult. . . . the program's basic structure, a product of the Progressive Era, remains unchanged. . . . Workers' compensation, then, must be explained in terms of the historical circumstances surrounding its origins. Modern policy problems can be traced directly from the program's origins in the Progressive Era." *Disabled Policy: America's Programs for the Handicapped* (Cambridge, MA: Cambridge University Press, 1987), pp. 15–16.

Berkowitz does not, in my view, back up this judgment with compelling evidence; his book devotes far more attention to disability insurance and vocational rehabilitation than to workers' compensation. The best-developed argument appeared a few years earlier: Edward Berkowitz and Monroe Berkowitz, "The Survival of Workers' Compensation," *Social Service Review* 58 (1984): 259–80. Nevertheless, that article failed to highlight the distinctive political economy of workers' compensation and said very little about key points in the program's development, such as the decision to omit workers' comp from the 1935 Social Security Act. Like a justice writing a concurring opinion, I intend to show that Berkowitz was right while offering a more compelling set of arguments to justify his verdict.

15. Berkowitz, *Disabled Policy*; Berkowitz and Berkowitz, "The Survival of Workers' Compensation"; Walter F. Dodd, *Administration of Workmen's Compensation* (New York, NY: Commonwealth Fund, 1936); Price V. Fishback and Shawn Everett Kantor, *A Prelude to the Welfare State: The Origins of Workers' Compensation* (Chicago, IL: University of Chicago Press, 2000); Roy Lubove, *The Struggle for Social Security, 1900–1935*, 2nd ed. (Pittsburgh, PA: University of Pittsburgh Press, 1986 [1968]); Theda Skocpol, *Protecting Soldiers and Mothers: The Political Origins of Social Policy in the United States* (Cambridge, MA: The Belknap Press of Harvard University Press, 1992); Herman Miles Somers and Anne Ramsay Somers, *Workmen's Compensation* (New York, NY: John Wiley & Sons, 1954); Harry Weiss, "Employers' Liability and Workmen's Compensation" in Elizabeth Brandeis (ed.), *History of Labor in the United States, 1896–1932, vol. IV, Labor Legislation* (New York, NY: Macmillan, 1935), pp. 564–610.

16. Somers and Somers, *Workmen's Compensation*, p. 25.

17. Edward Berkowitz recounts the case of an immigrant worker who lost his leg on the job in 1909. A court returned a verdict in his favor in 1910 and ordered payment of $1,000 in damages. The ruling was appealed by the employer, but upheld in 1911. The money was finally paid in the middle of 1912. After paying lawyers' fees, doctors' fees, expert witnesses, and an interpreter, the worker was left with less than $100—three years after the injury (*Disabled Policy*, pp. 18–19).

18. Monroe Berkowitz and John F. Burton, Jr., *Permanent Disability Benefits in Workers' Compensation* (Kalamazoo, MI: W. E. Upjohn Institute for Employment Research, 1987), p. 17.

19. As the majority wrote in the landmark *Ives* case (New York, 1911): "In its final and simple analysis [compulsory worker's compensation insurance] is taking the property of A and giving it to B, and that cannot be done under our constitutions." Cited in David Brian Robertson, "The Bias of American Federalism: The Limits of Welfare-State Development in the Progressive Era," *Journal of Policy History* 1 (1989): 278.

20. It is worth noting that the first workmen's compensation law for federal employees passed in 1908, before the first state laws.

21. Arkansas adopted workmen's compensation in 1939 and Mississippi in 1948.

22. For a careful analysis of the ways in which Civil War pensions triggered charges of corruption and cronyism in the early 20th century, see Skocpol, *Protecting Soldiers and Mothers*.

23. Cited in Lubove, *The Struggle for Social Security*, p. 62.

24. In states with public funds, unions were usually stronger politically than insurers, and a strong reform movement, led by Progressives or Non-Partisans, existed. Price V. Fishback and Shawn Everett Kantor, "The Durable Experiment: State Insurance of Workers' Compensation Risk in the Early Twentieth Century," *Journal of Economic History* 56 (1996): 809–36.

25. Michalina M. Libman, "Workmen's Compensation Benefits in the United States, 1939 and 1940," *Social Security Bulletin* 5 (1942): 6–14. These crucial decisions about public versus private insurance are absent from Berkowitz and Berkowitz, "The Survival of Workers' Compensation."

26. Cecili Thompson Williams, Virginia P. Reno, and John F. Burton, Jr., *Workers' Compensation: Benefits, Coverage, and Costs, 2001* (Washington, DC: National Academy of Social Insurance, 2003).

27. Fishback and Kantor, "The Durable Experiment"; Arthur H. Reede, *Adequacy of Workmen's Compensation* (Cambridge, MA: Harvard University Press, 1947); I. M. Rubinow, *The Quest for Security* (New York, NY: Henry Holt and Company, 1934), ch. 8.

28. William Graebner, "Federalism in the Progressive Era: A Structural Interpretation of Reform," *Journal of American History* 64, 2 (September 1977): 331–57.

29. Quoted in Edwin E. Witte, *The Development of the Social Security Act* (Madison, WI: University of Wisconsin Press, 1962), p. 21, with italics added.

30. S. Kjaer, *Workmen's Compensation* (Washington, DC: Committee on Economic Security, 1934). I thank Larry DeWitt of the Social Security Administration's Historian's Office for making a copy of this report available to me.

31. Skocpol, *Protecting Soldiers and Mothers*, pp. 295–96; Theda Skocpol and John G. Ikenberry, "The Political Formation of the American Welfare State in Historical and Comparative Perspective," *Comparative Social Research* 6 (1983): 108–9.

32. Committee on Economic Security, *Report to the President of the Committee on Economic Security* (Washington, DC: Committee on Economic Security, 1935), accessed via www.ssa.gov/history/reports/ces/ces.html.

33. Arthur Altmeyer, *The Industrial Commission of Wisconsin: A Case Study in Labor Law Administration*, University of Wisconsin Studies in the Social Sciences and History, no. 17 (Madison, WI: University of Wisconsin, 1932).

34. Edward D. Berkowitz and Kim McQuaid (eds.), *Creating the Welfare State: The Political Economy of 20th-Century Reform*, rev. ed. (Lawrence, KS: University Press of Kansas, 1992), p. 107.

35. Quoted in Marshall Dawson, "Adequacy of Benefit Payments under Workmen's Compensation," *Monthly Labor Review* 47 (1938): 471.

36. Edwin Witte, "Workmen's Compensation Insurance during the Depression," in *Papers of Edwin E. Witte, 1905–1967*, Box 252 (Madison, WI: State Historical Society of Wisconsin Archives); Altmeyer, *The Industrial Commission of Wisconsin*. It seems reasonable to infer that because the science of predicting industrial accidents was in its infancy in the 1920s, the most "successful" insurers were those who gained customers by offering low rates based on faulty actuarial assumptions, rates that later proved too low to cover claims by injured workers.

37. Skocpol and Ikenberry, "The Political Formation of the American Welfare State."

38. Altmeyer, *The Industrial Commission of Wisconsin*; Theron F. Schlabach, *Edwin E. Witte: Cautious Reformer* (Madison, WI: State Historical Society of Wisconsin, 1969).

39. Anthony Bale, "Medicine in the Industrial Battle: Early Workers' Compensation," *Social Science and Medicine* 28 (1989): 1113–20. The quotation is from p. 1116.

40. Committee on Economic Security, *Social Security in America* (Washington, DC: Government Printing Office, 1937).

41. Eveline Mabel Richardson Burns, *The American Social Security System* (Boston, MA: Houghton Mifflin, 1949), p. 187; U.S. Census Bureau, *Historical Statistics of the United States: Colonial Times to 1970* (Washington, DC: Government Printing Office, 1975), p. 126.

42. For reasons why mothers' pensions, which also spread quickly to most states in the 1910s, were nevertheless included in the Social Security Act, see Christopher Howard, "Workers' Compensation, Federalism, and the Heavy Hand of History," *Studies in American Political Development* 16, 1 (Spring 2002): 28–47.

43. W. F. Roeber, "Memorandum re Workmen's Compensation Rate Situation (1931)," in *National Council on Compensation Insurance Records, 1930–1943*, Box 4 (Madison, WI: State Historical Society of Wisconsin Archives).

44. Martha Derthick, *Policymaking for Social Security* (Washington, DC: Brookings Institution, 1979).

45. Edward Berkowitz and Monroe Berkowitz, "Challenges to Workers' Compensation: An Historical Analysis," in John D. Worrall and David Appel (eds.), *Workers' Compensation Benefits: Adequacy, Equity, and Efficiency* (Ithaca, NY: ILR Press), pp. 158–79.

46. Altmeyer, *The Formative Years of Social Security* (Madison, WI: University of Wisconsin Press, 1966), p. 95.

47. The Board was renamed the Social Security Administration in 1946.

48. Arthur Altmeyer, *The Formative Years of Social Security*; Derthick, *Policymaking for Social Security*.

49. Berkowitz and Berkowitz, "Survival of Workers' Compensation," pp. 266–67.

50. U.S. Congress, House, Committee on Ways and Means, "The Development of the Disability Program under Old-Age Survivors' Insurance, 1935–74" (1974), accessed via www.ssa.gov/history/pdf/dibreport.pdf.

51. Altmeyer, *The Formative Years of Social Security*, pp. 185–86; Derthick, *Policymaking for Social Security*, ch. 15. This opposition was a switch for both organizations: the AMA had endorsed disability insurance as recently as 1947, and the Chamber of Commerce as recently as 1944.

52. Edward D. Berkowitz, "The American Disability System in Historical Perspective," in Berkowitz (ed.), *Disabled Policies and Government Programs* (New York, NY: Praeger, 1979), p. 41.

53. Berkowitz, *Disabled Policy*, p. 34.

54. Berkowitz, *Disabled Policy*; Derthick, *Policymaking for Social Security*; Martha Derthick, *Agency under Stress: The Social Security Administration in American Government* (Washington, DC: Brookings Institution, 1990).

55. The following discussion of the Black Lung program is based primarily on Peter S. Barth, *The Tragedy of Black Lung: Federal Compensation for Occupational Disease* (Kalamazoo, MI: W. E. Upjohn Institute for Employment Research, 1987); "Labor Legislation," *Congress and the Nation, vol. III, 1969–1972* (Washington, DC: Congressional Quarterly, 1973), pp. 707–26; and U.S. Congress, House, Committee on Ways and Means, *Overview of Entitlement Programs* (Washington, DC: Government Printing Office, 1990), pp. 1339–44.

56. Peter M. Lencsis, *Workers Compensation: A Reference and Guide* (Westport, CT: Quorum Books, 1998); Willis J. Nordlund, *A History of the Federal Employees' Compensation Program* (Washington, DC: U.S. Department of Labor, 1992).

57. Previous efforts to regulate mine safety in 1941 and 1952 were also precipitated by mining disasters. Michael Lewis-Beck and John R. Alford, "Can Government Regulate Safety? The Coal Mine Example," *American Political Science Review* 74 (1980): 745–56.

58. Some readers may note that this case has several parallels to Downs's discussion of the life cycle of public problems. Anthony Downs, "Up and Down with Ecology: The Issue Attention Cycle," *Public Interest* 28 (1972): 38–50.

59. Quoted in Lewis-Beck and Alford, "Can Government Regulate Safety?" pp. 746–47.

60. Both quotations are from Barth, *The Tragedy of Black Lung*, p. 22.

61. Legislators later made the Black Lung program permanent after states failed to make expected changes in their compensation laws.

62. Evidence for this section is taken from Berkowitz and Berkowitz, "Survival of Workers' Compensation"; "Labor Legislation" (1973); and especially Charles

Noble, *Liberalism at Work: The Rise and Fall of OSHA* (Philadelphia, PA: Temple University Press, 1986).

63. Johnson's decision not to seek reelection came in 1968, well after he had made occupational health and safety a top priority.

64. Noble, *Liberalism at Work*, pp. 88–89.

65. The Bipartisan Commission on Entitlements and Tax Reform, created in the mid-1990s, failed in part because it was asked to do too much.

66. National Commission on State Workmen's Compensation Laws, *The Report of the National Commission on State Workmen's Compensation Laws* (Washington, DC: National Commission on State Workmen's Compensation Laws, 1972). Other sources consulted for this part of the chapter include Berkowitz, *Disabled Policy*; John F. Burton, Jr., "Introduction," in Burton (ed.), *New Perspectives in Workers' Compensation* (Ithaca, NY: ILR Press, 1988), pp. 1–20; John F. Burton, Jr., and Alan B. Krueger, "Interstate Variations in the Employers' Costs of Workers Compensation, with Particular Reference to Connecticut, New Jersey, and New York," in James R. Chelius (eds.), *Current Issues in Workers' Compensation* (Kalamazoo, MI: W. E. Upjohn Institute for Employment Research, 1986), ch. 7; and Glenn Merrill Shor, "The Evolution of Workers' Compensation in California, 1911–1990" (Ph.D. dissertation, University of California–Berkeley, 1990).

67. National Commission on State Workmen's Compensation Laws, *The Report*, p. 126.

68. Ibid., p. 127.

69. Paul Pierson, "Increasing Returns, Path Dependence, and the Study of Politics," *American Political Science Review* 94, 2 (2000): 251–67.

70. U.S. House of Representatives, Committee on Ways and Means, *2004 Green Book*, section 15.

71. I have said little in this chapter about the politics of workers' compensation within and across the states, a good topic for future research.

72. For a skeptical view of states as laboratories for health reform, see Michael S. Sparer and Lawrence D. Brown, "States and the Health Care Crisis: The Limits and Lessons of Laboratory Federalism," in Robert F. Rich and William D. White (eds.), *Health Policy, Federalism, and the American States* (Washington, DC: Urban Institute, 1996), pp. 181–202.

73. Peter Bachrach and Morton S. Baratz, "The Two Faces of Power," *American Political Science Review* 56, 4 (1962): 947–52; Frank R. Baumgartner and Bryan D. Jones, *Agendas and Instability in American Politics* (Chicago, IL: University of Chicago Press, 1993); Matthew A. Crenson, *The Un-Politics of Air Pollution: A Study of Non-decisionmaking in the Cities* (Baltimore, MD: Johns Hopkins University Press, 1971); John W. Kingdon, *Agendas, Alternatives, and Public Policies* (Boston, MA: Little, Brown, 1984); David A. Rochefort and Roger W. Cobb (eds.), *The Politics of Problem Definition: Shaping the Policy Agenda* (Lawrence, KS: University Press of Kansas, 1994).

74. Bachrach and Baratz, "The Two Faces of Power."

75. For a good review of the literature, see Pierson, "Increasing Returns, Path Dependence, and the Study of Politics."

CHAPTER 9
RACE STILL MATTERS

1. For the optimistic view, see Stephan Thernstrom and Abigail Thernstrom, *America in Black and White: One Nation, Indivisible* (New York, NY: Simon and Schuster, 1997), and the essays in Abigail M. Thernstrom and Stephan Thernstrom (eds.), *Beyond the Color Line: New Perspectives on Race and Ethnicity in America* (Stanford, CA: Hoover Institution Press, 2002).

2. Orlando Patterson, "Race Over," *New Republic* (January 10, 2000): 6.

3. Robert C. Lieberman, *Shifting the Color Line: Race and the American Welfare State* (Cambridge, MA: Harvard University Press, 1998). See also Theda Skocpol, "The Limits of the New Deal System and the Roots of Contemporary Welfare Dilemmas," in Margaret Weir, Ann Shola Orloff, and Theda Skocpol (eds.), *The Politics of Social Policy in the United States* (Princeton, NJ: Princeton University Press, 1988), pp. 293–311. For an opposing view, see Gareth Davies and Martha Derthick, "Race and Social Welfare Policy: The Social Security Act of 1935," *Political Science Quarterly* 112, 2 (Summer 1997): 217–35.

4. Martin Gilens, *Why Americans Hate Welfare: Race, Media, and the Politics of Antipoverty Policy* (Chicago, IL: University of Chicago Press, 1999); Sanford F. Schram, Joe Soss, and Richard C. Fording (eds.), *Race and the Politics of Welfare Reform* (Ann Arbor, MI: University of Michigan Press, 2003); Gerald C. Wright, Jr., "Racism and Welfare Policy in America," *Social Science Quarterly* 57 (March 1977): 718–30.

5. Sarah M. Morehouse and Malcolm E. Jewell, "States as Laboratories: A Reprise," *Annual Review of Political Science* 7 (2004): 177–203.

6. Robert S. Erikson, Gerald C. Wright, and John P. McIver, *Statehouse Democracy: Public Opinion and Policy in the American States* (New York, NY: Cambridge University Press, 1993); Rodney E. Hero, *Faces of Inequality: Social Diversity in American Politics* (New York, NY: Oxford University Press, 1998).

7. Data for TANF come from the U.S. Congress, Committee on Ways and Means, *Overview of Entitlement Programs, 2000 Green Book* and *2004 Green Book*, available at http://waysandmeans.house.gov/documents.asp. The population figures are taken from the U.S. Census Bureau, *Statistical Abstract of the United States, 2002*, table 22, available at http://www.census.gov/prod/www/statistical-abstract-2001_2005.html.

8. See chapter 2 for more evidence of these differences.

9. The Medicaid figures come from table 108 of the 2001 Medicare and Medicaid Statistical Supplement to the *Health Care Financing Review*, available at http://www.cmms.gov/Review/Supp/.

10. SCHIP figures come from the U.S. Census Bureau, *Statistical Abstract of the United States, 2003*, table 148. The percent of children in poverty by state can be found in U.S. Census Bureau, Current Population Survey, "Detailed Poverty (P60 Package)," table 25, available at http://ferret.bls.census.gov/macro/032001/pov/toc.htm.

11. Unemployment benefits by state can be found at U.S. Census Bureau, *Statistical Abstract of the United States, 2002*, tables 528 and 600. The workers' com-

pensation data came from "Workers' Compensation Comparisons, 2001," available from the AFL-CIO website (http://www.aflcio.org).

12. Lieberman, *Shifting the Color Line*, ch. 5. For my earlier attempt to relate race to unemployment benefits at the state level, see Christopher Howard, "The American Welfare State or States?" *Political Research Quarterly* 52, 2 (June 1999): 421–42.

13. Hero, *Faces of Inequality*; Joe Soss, Sanford F. Schram, Thomas P. Vartanian, and Erin O'Brien, "The Hard Line and the Color Line: Race, Welfare, and the Roots of Get-Tough Reform," in Schram, Soss, and Fording (eds.), *Race and the Politics of Welfare Reform*, pp. 225–53.

14. Hispanic population by state can be found in the U.S. Census Bureau, *Statistical Abstract of the United States, 2002*, table 23.

15. Erikson, Wright, and McIver, *Statehouse Democracy*, esp. ch. 4; Hero, *Faces of Inequality*, esp. ch. 5. My education variable refers to the percentage of adults age twenty-five and over with a college degree in each state. It and the income and poverty variables are based on U.S. Census Bureau, *Statistical Abstract of the United States, 2003*, tables 231, 671, and 705. Data for the urban variable come from the U.S. Census Bureau, *Statistical Abstract of the United States, 2001*, table 30. See http://www.census.gov/prod/www/statistical-abstract-2001_2005.html.

16. I am assuming that workers' comp follows the same pattern as disability insurance in which claims go up when unemployment goes up. Some people with disabilities who were employed when the economy was strong, but find themselves out of work when the economy weakens, then decide to apply for disability benefits. Michael J. Graetz and Jerry L. Mashaw, *True Security: Rethinking American Social Insurance* (New Haven, CT: Yale University Press, 1999), pp. 72–73.

17. The figures for this index come from U.S. Census Bureau, *Statistical Abstract of the United States, 2000*, table 468, available at http://www.census.gov/prod/www/statistical-abstract-1995_2000.html, and U.S. Census Bureau, *Statistical Abstract of the United States, 2001*, tables 394 and 395. Because Nebraska's state legislature is nonpartisan, it was dropped from the analysis. That is why some of the models have 49 cases (N) and not 50.

18. See, e.g., Benjamin I. Page and Robert Y. Shapiro, *The Rational Public: Fifty Years of Trends in Americans' Policy Preferences* (Chicago, IL: University of Chicago Press, 1992); Gilens, *Why Americans Hate Welfare*; Erikson, Wright, and McIver, *Statehouse Democracy*.

19. Paul Brace, Kellie Sims-Butler, Kevin Arceneaux, and Martin Johnson, "Public Opinion in the American States: New Perspectives Using National Survey Data," *American Journal of Political Science* 46, 1 (January 2002): 173–89.

20. Rufus P. Browning, Dale Rogers Marshall, and David H. Tabb, *Protest Is Not Enough: The Struggle of Blacks and Hispanics for Equality in Urban Politics* (Berkeley, CA: University of California Press, 1984); David T. Canon, *Race, Redistricting, and Representation* (Chicago, IL: University of Chicago Press, 1999); Kerry L. Haynie, *African American Legislators in the American States* (New York, NY: Columbia University Press, 2001); Raphael J. Sonenshein, *Politics in Black and White: Race and Power in Los Angeles* (Princeton, NJ: Princeton University Press, 1993).

21. David A. Bositis, *Black Elected Officials: A Statistical Summary,* 2000 (Washington, DC: Joint Center for Political and Economic Studies, 2002); U.S. Census Bureau, *Statistical Abstract of the United States, 2001,* table 400. In several states, the Census Bureau could not identify any Hispanic public officials. While it might be tempting to mark these states down for a 0, they include states like Arizona that must have some. Consequently, I chose to omit these states. For voter turnout by race, see U.S. Census Bureau, Current Population Survey, "Voting and Registration in the Election of November 2000," table 4a, available at http://www.census.gov/population/www/socdemo/voting.html.

22. When I substituted percent Hispanic for percent black, the race variable lost its statistical significance.

23. Interestingly, race appears to have a stronger impact on Medicaid spending for the elderly than for children. Similar regression equations with spending per child as the dependent variable showed that neither population measure was even close to statistical significance. The racial attitude measure was significant at the .10 level.

24. For evidence that racial differences influence a wide range of opinions, including those without obvious racial content, see Donald R. Kinder and Lynn M. Sanders, *Divided by Color: Racial Politics and Democratic Ideals* (Chicago, IL: University of Chicago Press, 1996), and Donald R. Kinder and Nicholas Winter, "Exploring the Racial Divide: Blacks, Whites, and Opinion on National Policy," *American Journal of Political Science* 45, 2 (April 2001): 439–53.

25. See, e.g., Haynie, *African American Legislators in the American States.*

CHAPTER 10
CHANGE VERSUS PROGRESS

1. Paul Krugman, *The Great Unraveling: Losing Our Way in the New Century* (New York, NY: Free Press, 2004); Robert H. Frank and Philip J. Cook, *The Winner-Take-All-Society* (New York, NY: Free Press, 1995); Gary Burtless and Timothy Smeeding, "America's Tide: Lifting the Yachts, Swamping the Rowboats," *Washington Post* (June 25, 1995), p. C3; Sheldon Danziger and Peter Gottschalk, *America Unequal* (New York, NY, and Cambridge, MA: Russell Sage Foundation and Harvard University Press, 1995).

2. Lately, liberals have been angered by the Bush tax cuts, which benefit primarily the rich and the near rich. Rep. Rahm Emanuel, "Middle Class Squeeze," *Congressional Record* 150, 101 (July 20, 2004): H5985; David R. Francis, "Partisan Lines Harden in Debate over Tax Cuts," *Christian Science Monitor* (March 31, 2003), p. 21; Robert Kuttner, "The Hidden Issue of Class," *Boston Globe* (July 21, 2004), p. A15.

3. E.g., Robert B. Reich, foreword to Joshua Cohen and Joel Rogers (eds.), *The New Inequality: Creating Solutions for Poor America* (Boston, MA: Beacon Press, 1999).

4. Lawrence Mishel, Jared Bernstein, and Sylvia Allegretto, *The State of Working America, 2004/2005* (Ithaca, NY: Cornell University Press, 2005);

Kathryn M. Neckerman (ed.), *Social Inequality* (New York, NY: Russell Sage Foundation, 2004).

5. Edward N. Wolff, "Changes in Household Wealth in the 1980s and 1990s in the U.S.," Working Paper no. 407 (Annandale-on-Hudson, NY: Levy Economics Institute, 2004).

6. Although historical data on inequality are fragmentary, it seems safe to conclude that the Gini index is higher now than at any time since World War II. See Robert D. Plotnick, Eugene Smolensky, Eirik Evenhouse, and Siobhan Reilly, "The Twentieth Century Record of Poverty and Inequality in the United States," Institute for Research on Poverty Discussion Paper no. 1166–98 (1998), accessed via http://www.irp.wisc.edu/publications/dps/dplist1998.htm. See also Carmen DeNavas-Walt, Bernadette D. Proctor, and Cheryl Hill Lee, *Income, Poverty, and Health Insurance Coverage in the United States, 2004* (Washington, DC: Government Printing Office, 2005), table A-3.

7. Danziger and Gottschalk, *America Unequal*; DeNavas-Walt, Proctor, and Lee, *Income, Poverty, and Health Insurance Coverage in the United States, 2004*; Luxembourg Income Study (LIS), "Income Inequality Measures," available at http://www.lisproject.org/keyfigures/ineqtable.htm.

In 2005 Chinese officials publicly expressed concern than inequality in that country was a threat to social order. The poorest quintile had 4.7 percent of total income while the richest quintile controlled half of the total, which is quite close to the distribution of income in the United States. MSNBC, "China's Income Gap Provokes Alarm, Report Says" (September 21, 2005), accessed via http://www.msnbc.msn.com/id/9424936/.

8. DeNavas-Walt, Proctor, and Lee, *Income, Poverty, and Health Insurance Coverage in the United States, 2004*; Jacob Hacker, Suzanne Mettler, Diane Pinderhughes, and Theda Skocpol, *Inequality and Public Policy* (Washington, DC: American Political Science Association, 2004), accessed via http://www.apsanet.org/content_4040.cfm; Luxembourg Income Study, "Relative Poverty Rates for the Total Population, Children and the Elderly," available at http://www.lisproject.org/keyfigures/povertytable.htm.

9. See, e.g., Danziger and Gottschalk, *America Unequal*; James K. Galbraith, *Created Unequal: The Crisis in American Pay* (New York, NY: Free Press, 1998); Christopher Jencks, "Does Inequality Matter?" *Daedalus* 131, 1 (Winter 2002): 49–65; Frank Levy, *The New Dollars and Dreams: American Incomes and Economic Change* (New York, NY: Russell Sage Foundation, 1999); Mishel, Bernstein, and Allegretto, *The State of Working America, 2004/2005*; Benjamin I. Page and James R. Simmons, *What Government Can Do: Dealing with Poverty and Inequality* (Chicago IL: University of Chicago Press, 2000).

10. For inequality and poverty, see Vincent A. Mahler and David K. Jesuit, "Fiscal Redistribution in the Developed Countries: New Insights from the Luxembourg Income Study," Working Paper no. 392 (updated September 2005), available via http://www.lisproject.org/publications/liswps/392.pdf. For evidence that U.S. public policies did less to reduce inequality in 2000 than in 1979, see Lane Kenworthy and Jonas Pontusson, "Rising Inequality and the Politics of Redistribution in Affluent Countries," *Perspectives on Politics* 3, 3 (September 2005): 449–71. For poverty, see Timothy Smeeding, Lee Rainwater, and Gary Burtless,

"U.S. Poverty in Cross-National Context," in Sheldon Danziger and Robert Haveman (eds.), *Understanding Poverty* (New York, NY, and Cambridge, MA: Russell Sage Foundation and Harvard University Press, 2001), pp. 162–89.

11. Hacker et al., *Inequality and Public Policy*; Sidney Verba, Kay Lehman Schlozman, and Henry E. Brady, "Political Equality: What Do We Know about It?" in Neckerman (ed.), *Social Inequality*, p. 658; Lawrence R. Jacobs, "Health Disparities in the Land of Equality," in James A. Morone and Lawrence R. Jacobs (eds.), *Healthy, Wealthy, and Fair: Health Care and the Good Society* (New York, NY: Oxford University Press, 2005), p. 53. See also Thomas Byrne Edsall, *The New Politics of Inequality* (New York, NY: W. W. Norton, 1984), and Page and Simmons, *What Government Can Do*.

12. For 1980 I recoded the GSS family income variable as follows: less than $8,000 (lower income); $8,000–15,000 (lower middle); $15,000–25,000 (middle); $25,000–50,000 (upper middle); and over $50,000 (upper). For 2000 I recoded the income categories as less than $22,500, $22,500–35,000, $35,000–60,000, $60,000–90,000, and over $90,000.

13. Either way, the figures are lower than those from the 1996 Role of Government survey (48%), which gave people a choice of only four answers and no option of saying that they neither agreed nor disagreed. The figures in table 10.1 make me suspect that the numbers from 1996 are too high. The true level of support in other nations might also be lower, but there is no good reason to expect that the relative placement of nations is any different.

14. Support also varies by race, with more blacks than whites favoring redistribution from rich to poor. Nevertheless, only about 40 percent of African-Americans strongly supported redistribution in 2000, meaning they answered "1" or "2" on the 7-point scale.

15. One possible reason why the less affluent in the United States express little support for redistribution is that they believe strongly in social mobility. See Alberto Alesina and Edward L. Glaeser, *Fighting Poverty in the US and Europe: A World of Difference* (New York, NY: Oxford University Press, 2004), esp. ch. 7.

16. Again, because so few people called themselves lower class, not much should be made of the apparent jump in their support for redistribution between 1980 and 2000. Other surveys yield similar results. In 1993 over half of those who called themselves working class agreed that "people should be allowed to accumulate as much wealth as they can even if some make millions while others live in poverty" (GSS 1972–2002 cumulative data file, 1993 topical module: culture, accessed via http://sda.berkeley.edu:7502/archive.htm). For evidence that the less affluent did not embrace redistribution in the 1970s, see Jennifer Hochschild, *What's Fair? American Beliefs about Distributive Justice* (Cambridge, MA: Harvard University Press, 1981).

17. Lars Osberg and Timothy Smeeding, "'Fair' Inequality? An International Comparison of Attitudes to Pay Differentials" (June 2005), manuscript accessed via http://www-cpr.maxwell.syr.edu/faculty/smeeding/.

18. The ISSP continues to report separate results for East and West Germany in order to facilitate comparisons before and after unification, and the numbers cited in this chapter refer to West Germany.

19. Explaining why these attitudes have changed is beyond the scope of this chapter.

20. DeNavas-Walt, Proctor, and Lee, *Income, Poverty, and Health Insurance Coverage in the United States, 2004.*

21. U.S. Census Bureau, *Statistical Abstract of the United States, 2003* (Washington, DC: Government Printing Office, 2003), table 647.

22. Congressional Budget Office, *Utilization of Tax Incentives for Retirement Saving* (Washington, DC: Congressional Budget Office, 2003), esp. table 2. The data in this study are from 1997.

23. U.S. Congress, Joint Committee on Taxation, *Estimates of Federal Tax Expenditures for Fiscal Years 2005–2009* (Washington, DC, Government Printing Office, 2005).

24. Richard V. Burkhauser and Mary C. Daly, "The Potential Impact on the Employment of People with Disabilities," in Jane West (ed.), *Implementing the Americans with Disabilities Act* (Cambridge, MA: Blackwell, 1996), p. 155.

25. Jane Waldfogel, "Family Leave Coverage in the 1990s," *Monthly Labor Review* 122, 10 (October 1999): 13–21.

26. Jane Waldfogel, "Family and Medical Leave: Evidence from the 2000 Surveys," *Monthly Labor Review* 124, 9 (September 2001): 17–23; Brian Headd, "The Characteristics of Small-Business Employees," *Monthly Labor Review* 123, 4 (April 2000): 13–18. Moreover, a survey taken in 2000 found that 40 percent of employees had not heard of the Family and Medical Leave Act, and 50 percent did not know if they were covered by the law.

27. "Table 1.12, Maternity, Paternity, and Parental Leaves in the OECD Countries, 1998–2002," The Clearinghouse on International Developments in Child, Youth, and Family Policies, Columbia University, accessed via http://www.childpolicyintl.org/.

28. Ibid.

29. U.S. Congress, Joint Committee on Taxation, *Estimates of Federal Tax Expenditures for Fiscal Years 2005–2009*; U.S. Census Bureau, *Statistical Abstract of the United States, 2003.*

30. U.S. Census Bureau, *Statistical Abstract of the United States, 2004/2005* (Washington, DC: Government Printing Office, 2005), table 524, accessed via http://www.census.gov/prod/www/statistical-abstract-2001_2005.html.; U.S. Congress, Joint Committee on Taxation, *Estimates of Federal Tax Expenditures for Fiscal Years, 2002–2006* (Washington, DC: Government Printing Office, 2002).

31. Mahler and Jesuit, "Fiscal Redistribution in the Developed Countries."

32. Michael J. Graetz and Jerry L. Mashaw, *True Security: Rethinking American Social Insurance* (New Haven, CT: Yale University Press, 1999); Jacob Hacker, "Privatizing Risk without Privatizing the Welfare State: The Hidden Politics of Social Policy Retrenchment in the United States," *American Political Science Review* 98, 2 (May 2004): 243–60.

33. Mahler and Jesuit, "Fiscal Redistribution in the Developed Countries."

34. This pattern resembles the creation of new bureaucracies described in James A. Morone, *The Democratic Wish: Popular Participation and the Limits of American Government* (New York, NY: Basic Books, 1990).

35. E.g., Gosta Esping-Andersen, *The Three Worlds of Welfare Capitalism* (Princeton, NJ: Princeton University Press, 1990); Peter Flora and Arnold J. Heidenheimer, "The Historical Core and Changing Boundaries of the Welfare State," in Flora and Heidenheimer (eds.), *The Development of Welfare States in Europe and America* (New Brunswick, NJ: Transaction, 1981), pp. 17–34; Norman Furniss and Timothy Tilton, *The Case for the Welfare State: From Social Security to Social Equality* (Bloomington, IN: Indiana University Press, 1977).

Index